The Untold Story of the Battle of Imphal

Salam Irene is a retired Professor and former Head of the Department of History, Manipur University. She began her academic career in the Post Graduate Centre of JNU in Imphal. When the centre was converted in 1980 to Manipur University, she continued her teaching in the latter as she is married to a Manipuri and resides in Imphal. After four decades of teaching, she retired from Manipur University in 2016. She, however, continued teaching civil service aspirants and mentoring research scholars, giving occasional lectures in different institutions. She has travelled extensively and presented several papers in different countries and universities. Her most recent paper published was her presentation at the 24th National and International Humanities and Social Sciences Conference at Naresuan University, Thailand in July 2021. During the lockdown she decided to write a book on the Battle of Imphal as when she delivered a lecture at Kobe University, Japan on this battle not only were the Japanese audience very attentive, she received a request to assist a senior Japanese citizen to help locate the bones of her granduncle who died in Manipur during this Battle of Imphal. She is also assisting Rayburn College Churachandpur, Manipur as a Visiting Professor.

THE UNTOLD STORY OF THE BATTLE OF IMPHAL

Salam Irene

AKANSHA PUBLISHING HOUSE

4649-B/21, Ansari Road, Darya Ganj, New Delhi-110 002 (India)

AKANSHA PUBLISHING HOUSE
4649-B/21, Ansari Road,
Darya Ganj, New Delhi-110 002
Phones : 011-23263193, 09435116718
E-mail : ektabooks@yahoo.com
visit us : www.akanshapublishinghouse.com

The Untold Story of the Battle of Imphal

First Published : 2022

ISBN 978-81-8370-624-7

PRINTED IN INDIA

Published by Akansha Publishing House, New Delhi - 110002.

Dedicated to my parents

Sir Peter

&

Lady Florence De Noronha

Contents

Preface

It was only recently, in the second decade of this Century, that a sudden awakening occurred about a missing Chapter in Manipur's History, i.e., the Battle of Imphal, 1944. A number of military histories had been written by the British and others, but in Manipur the history of this Battle and its impact did not form part of the syllabus of history in schools, colleges and universities. Yet this Battle had a particular significance for Manipur and its people. It has also been described as Britain's Greatest Battle of World War II. This aroused consciousness of the Battle, but among a small group of people in Manipur.

But in 2014, the Manipur Tourism Forum and the 2nd. World War Imphal Campaign Foundation jointly organized a Commemoration of the 70th Anniversary of the Battle of Imphal (WW II) from March to June, in association with the Government of Manipur. A number of dignitaries from Manipur were closely associated with all activities relating to the Commemoration and a small number of Britishers and others also attended. Simultaneously, a researcher in Manipur introduced War Tourism to the state, and provided Battle of Imphal Tours, sharing the various battle sites and providing a detailed history of the battles that took place in Manipur.

These tours aroused the interest of tourists and

families of' veteran combatants of the war, both British and the Japanese, and Indians from outside of North East India. Every year, the Anniversary of the Battle was commemorated in Imphal, and gradually the number of people visiting Manipur because of their interest in the Battle of Imphal increased.

A Japanese Professor, keenly interested in the subject, send a request to me, to present a lecture in the History Department of Manipur University. His avid interest and knowledge of Manipur, made me realise that there were many more Japanese who wanted to come to Manipur to see where their ancestors had breathed their last, and initially it was the Japanese who carried out excavations in Manipur to find the remains of the dead soldiers. Soon they were assisted by the team of the 2nd. World War Imphal Campaign Foundation.

Many British veterans' families also started coming annually to Manipur for the same reason, and they too received help from the Imphal Campaign Foundation.

But what made me decide to write on the Battle of Imphal were first- a request made to me by a Japanese national who met me in Japan and requested my assistance in finding the remains of her granduncle who had taken part in the Battle of Imphal. Secondly, I attended a Peace and Reconciliation Meet organised by the Imphal Campaign Foundation between Britain and Japan at Imphal in 2019. The Manipuris present at that Meet stated that there was no literature on the Impact of the Battle, especially on the Manipuris. But it was only during India's Total Lockdown in 2020, that I started my actual research. Having taught History for four decades, I knew that a mere narration of the history of the

Battle would not appeal to popular imagination. So, I have used the methodology of 'Oral Testimony' in this book, producing verbatim what the Manipuris, the Japanese and the British had to say about the Battle. Chapters Two, Three and Four are a narrative of People's Voices, what they felt, what they witnessed and what they experienced, during the Battle and its aftermath, and the stories told to them by family members who witnessed and participated in the war. It is a story of human interest which I hope will bring closure to families who lost someone in the Battle; especially those who have not been able to find the remains of their loved ones who died in Manipur in 1944. It will also facilitate a better understanding between nations that fought in the Battle because the testimonies sent to me are personal stories, which provide a better insight into how people felt in 1944 and how their descendants feel today, and Manipur can be a lodestar for better relations not only between India and Britain, India and Japan, but between Britain and Japan.

Salam Irene

Acknowledgements

I express my sincere gratitude to all who have shared so generously their stories, recollections and war memories of the Battle of Imphal. These are people of three countries: the Manipuris, Nagas, Kukis, Meitei Pangal and Meiteis of Manipur, India, the Japanese from Japan and others living in India and elsewhere, and the British from the UK. Many of the Britishers and the Japanese had to relive painful memories while telling me their stories. I really appreciate the sharing because many of the Japanese and British are not known to me personally. Yet they spent time and energy patiently answering all my queries. This book would not have been possible without their valuable insights. I am extremely grateful to all the individuals named here in:

1. *Dr. Yoshihiro Kaburagi*, a retired Lecturer of the Osaka University of Commerce, Japan. He spent many days writing his account as he is very knowledgeable on the subject of the Battle and has been visiting Manipur for many years. He also very kindly offered to read a Japanese book on War Memories and to translate into English the main findings of this book.
2. *Tomio Isogai San*. He was the friend who put me in touch with a lot of Japanese who were interested

in sharing their views on the Battle of Imphal. Mr. Tomio Isogai is a Freelance Advisor in Indo-Japanese Relations and resides in Pune, India.

3. *Ms. Sonoko Sawai*, the intrepid Japanese lady who is still seeking closure by being engaged for several years in a quest to find her granduncle's remains in Manipur. She is a jewelry designer residing in Kyoto, Japan.

4. *Dr. Haruhisa Asada*, Associate Professor, Nara Women's University, Japan. He is a frequent visitor to North East India.

5. *Tomio Mizokami San*, Professor Emeritus, Osaka Japan. He is the President of Kansai-Japan-India Culture Society, Kobe, Japan. He is a recipient of many awards in India. 1. Hindi Ratna at New Delhi, May 2001, 2. George Grierson Prize from President of India, Dr. Abdul Kalam at Rashtrapati Bhavan, October 2002, 3. Vishwa Hindi Samman, Sixth World Hindi Convention, London, September, 1999, 4. Prashasti Patra, Hindi Academy, Delhi from Chief Minister of Delhi, Ms. Sheela Dikshit, August 2006, 5. Bharat Bhasha Bhushan from Governor of M.P. Dr. Balram Jakhar at Bhopal August, 2006, 6. Jai Jaivanti Samman, Jai Jaivanti Second Vashikutsav, August 2009, New Delhi, 7. Friends of LiberationWar Honor, from Prime Minister, Bangladesh, Ms. Sheikh Hasina, Dhaka, March 2018.

6. *Kaz Nakajima San*, he is a well-known popular Volunteer Tour Guide of Nara Sightseeing Goodwill Guide Club for overseas visitors in Nara. He is well versed in the History and Culture of Nara where he also resides.

7. *Atsufumi Mikami*, Professor Emeritus (Economics), Osaka Gakuin University. He is Vice-President Kansai Japan-India Cultural Association and resides in Kashwara City, Osaka Japan. He has provided valuable insights of the Battle.

8. *Chihiro Koiso*, Professor, Asia University, Tokyo, Japan, has travelled extensively in Manipur and Nagaland.

9. *Manabu Koiso*, Professor, School of Contemporary Society, Department of Tourism, Kansai University of International Studies, Kobe, Japan. The Professor has done and published research on Nagaland.

10. *Shinichi Iriyama* is a Professional businessperson of Japan interested in the Battle of Imphal.

11. *Hidehito Jay Arami* a well-known and recognized Japanese businessman residing in Delhi NCR. He holds many positions—Managing Director, Casa Blanka Consultative Pvt. Ltd., Director, Japan Business, Udyon Jain and Associates, Official Co-ordinator for Jetro's SME Overseas Expansion Platform, Acting Director, JTEKT India Ltd., Mindarika Pvt. Ltd., Rex Industries Pvt. Ltd., Sekisui Chemical India Pvt. Ltd.

12. *Noriko Yoshida,* an accountant with a keen interest in this Battle, resident of Settu City, Osaka, Japan.

13. *Hiroko Ozaki*, a Japanese language education consultant working in the field of Japanese language education as a teacher's trainer and advisor since 1984, in various countries, seconded by the Japan Foundation. She has a great liking for the people of Manipur.

14. *Toru Tak*, Assistant Professor, Studies in Language and Society, Graduate School of Language and Culture, Osaka University, Japan. He very kindly introduced me to a new publication in Japan on War Memories "Senso-Keiken" no Sengoshi, 2020 by Ryuichi Narita, Zouho.
15. *Hiroyuki Ishida*, he is a Director of a Company and is currently based in Bangalore, India.
16. *Taibe Kiyoshi San*, is working as an investor in Singapore.
17. *Maki Hisada* works from and resides in Bangalore, India.
18. *Manami Mogari* is a Bharatnatyam Dancer and Instructor and resides in Nishinomiya-shi, Hyogo Prefecture, Japan. She connected me to the Professor Emeritus.
19. *Mary Cole*, a retired registered nurse with 42 years of work experience. She has shared her family story related to Battle of Imphal and also introduced me to two of her friends who also very graciously shared their personal stories. Mary resides in Somerset, UK.
20. *Paula McGuigam*, a retired licensee a friend of Mary Cole who resides in Sheffield South Yorshire, UK.
21. *Matt Stanyard*, a retired engineer from Leicester, UK. Manage and RUN Battle of Burma and Far East Website, also Burma SEAC Veterans Data Base.
22. *Mike Balmer*, a retired teacher of Maths and ICT a resident of West Yorkshire, UK, has also shared his family story of the Battle of Imphal.

23. *Khumi Tonsing Burton*, Former Justice of the Peace (Magistrate) in Manchester, Team Attache for Turks and Caicos during the Commonwealth Games held in Manchester. Invited as 'A Pioneer of the Nation' in 2003 by Buckingham Palace. Appointed Deputy Lieutenant of Great Manchester, representative of Her Majesty, The Queen, in the country, the first South East Asian Woman at that time in the country-until she reaches the age of 75. She is a member of The Royal British Legion, Involved with the Poppy Appeal—all voluntary services. She resides in Wilmslow, Cheshire UK but she is originally from Manipur.

24. *Ram Muivah* (Retd) Indian Administrative Service, Government of India. He has generously shared with me the recollections of the war in the Tangkhul Hills of Manipur.

25. *Home Raikhan* (Retd) Indian Revenue Service, Government of India. He has provided a lot of information for the first of the WWII battles fought in Manipur.

26. *Dr. Michael L. Haokip*, Assistant Proffesor Ambedkar University, New Delhi. He has given a graphic account of his grandfather who took part in the Battle of Imphal.

27 *ArambamAngamba Singh*, one of the Co-Founders of the 2nd World War Imphal Campaign Foundation and its Vice President. He is a self-taught war historian extremely Knowledgeable about the Battle of Imphal and has been very helpful. He resides in Imphal, Manipur.

28. *Salma Anhaa*, Ph.D. Scholar, Manipur.
29. *Dr. Nengneivah Eva Haokip*, Assistant Professor Churachandpur College, Manipur. She helped me in typing the manuscript.
30. *Dr. Haobam Bidyarani Devi*, Assistant Professor Kumbi College, Manipur, who also assisted in typing the manuscript.
31. *Dr. Susma Sharma Gurumayum*, Assistant Professor Tamenglong College, Manipur, who also assisted in the typing the manuscript.
32. *Phazang*, Entrepreneur who has done the final assembling and corrections.

Salam Irene

1
Introduction

Why Imphal? A place largely unknown in 1944, and remote from both the U.K. and Japan. And yet, the most fierce battle of World War II (WW II) was fought in Imphal. 'Manipur was the place most affected by the Second WW in India.[1] Even more surprising, because Manipur had remained an independent kingdom until 1891 A.D., and yet 53 years later a war in which Manipur had no stake, was fought on its soil. An Indian Defence Personnel reflecting on why any people or country need to reach the point of war, questioned whether any war actually achieves the goal it had set out to achieve.

India is a huge densely populated sub-continent, where most Indians outside of what today is known as the Eight States of North East India, had no knowledge of Manipur, its location, its history, its people, its centuries- old culture. They were unaware till very recently, that Manipur is strategically poised to be a gateway to South-East Asia, and Manipur shares a common border with Myanmar which is fairly porous in nature.

The Battle of Imphal in local parlance, is often referred to as 'Japan Lan' or 'Japan Gal'. The Japanese invaded Manipur, but after the event of the Indian War of

Independence in 1857, India was ruled by Her Majesty's Government in Britain. Manipur, however was not a part of India in I857, and even a hundred years after the Battle of Plassey (1757), the British East India Company had made no inroads into North East India. In the Anglo-Manipur War of 1891, Manipur was defeated, and the British Political Agent was stationed in Manipur, directed the affairs of the State, despite the fact that Manipur was a Princely State. "The war of 1891 marked .... the beginning of a new era in the history of Manipur .... British rule in Manipur commenced, the Government of India declared that the state of Manipur had become forfeit to the Crown, but the Queen Empress of India had become graciously pleased to forego her undoubted right and to permit re-establishment of native rule under a minor Raja. Churachand was selected as the future ruler of Manipur. The decision to re-establish native rule and the setting up of a Regency administration during the minority of the young Raja apparently under the overall control of British Officers largely suited the convenience of the Government.[2] When the Japanese attacked Manipur; the British would naturally retaliate. The Japanese perspective on 'Japan Lan' could perhaps be ascribed to the fact that because the Japanese claimed that by defeating Britain in the battle, Japan would be helping to liberate India from British rule. Historically, however Manipur only became a part of India when it merged into the Indian Union on the 15th of October 1949. Yet the Battle of Imphal, whose impact still resonates, was fought in Manipur, where the native population were not very clear about its reasons, as it was a battle that involved the British Fourteenth Army and the Japanese Fifteenth Army.

In the introduction of his book: 'The Battlefields of

Imphal', Hemant Katoch has stated: Manipur and Imphal are not names that the world at large is familiar with nor ones that many fellow Indians can locate on a map.' And he wrote this in 2016.

When fighting commenced, and bombing became commonplace, many Manipuris, especially those residing in and around Imphal, the capital of Manipur had to leave their homes and possessions, and find refuge in villages, with relatives, friends and even strangers. They experienced emotional turbulence, and trauma of great intensity, uprooted and displaced because of a war fought by the British and Japanese in their land. And after the war was over, their trauma did not end, as they had to contend with many difficulties when returning to their original homes; homes destroyed completely or partially, rice stocks hidden or buried in their homes or around it, rotten and spoiled.[3] Distraught and anxious, the returnees were compelled to start life anew: rebuilding a house no matter how difficult, is far easier than rebuilding a life. Compensation for the destruction was provided by the Government, but that did not assuage the grief and sorrow within their hearts. And many families who fled their homes, had to out of necessity, leave behind aged, sick and even pregnant women, who were unable to walk on foot to a place of shelter. Some pregnant mothers did make the journey and even gave birth on the way. Other young mothers made the agonising journey carrying babies, young children on their backs. The people suddenly found themselves confronted with mayhem- life became uncertain. Yet they clung to the hope that even if tomorrow was not a better day, there would be a tomorrow—they believed this as they possessed the quality of resilience. A native who as a child also had to flee his home stated: World War II brought a hive of energy to Meitei society, accompanied by spiritual laxity among the youth: We began to eat chicken curry prepared in the Kabui village in the evenings, and full-boiled duck's egg sold by Kabui women.[4] (The Meiteis had for the most part converted to Vaishnavism in the eighteenth century, and followed a vegetarian diet, which included fish). In tribal areas especially those populated by the Tangkhuls, the Japanese forces appropriated large number of domestic livestock and stocks of rice, as their supplies were either exhausted or running low. This adversely affected the people; the Japanese did pay for their supplies in Japanese currency, which though novel was regarded as worthless by the natives, as they could not use it for any market or financial transactions.

It has been stated that nowhere else was the war as keenly felt and directly experienced as by this then princely state on the India-Burma frontier. And perhaps, no other place was transformed by it.Indeed, by the time the war ended, Manipur had changed forever socially-economically, infrastructure-wise, as well as politically.[5] In like vein, Yaiphaba Meetei Kangjam has written that the Japan Laan was in a way, 'the Golden Era' of Manipur. These statements are true, they also present a dichotomy. No doubt, the statement often repeated by historians in Manipur, that 'Christianity' catapulted the tribals from their old ways to new ways, is also applicable to the transformation effected by the Allied Forces and the Japanese during the course of the war in Imphal. The world-view of the Manipuris was transformed, they too were now catapulted into a new world, inhabited by new ideas, new ways of thinking and living, new technology, different dietary habits, different clothing, different means of transport and communication, etc., because of their exposure to people of different nationalities possessing different cultures and ways of living. The native people adopted many changes, most of them permanent in nature, in their style of dress, diet, house and road construction and so on, which hastened the process of change and modernity, which had been ushered into Manipur from the last decade of the nineteenth century, when the Christian missionaries, resident in Manipur, became synonymous with the spread of education. Profound and long lasting changes were effected in Manipur in the aftermath of the Battle of Imphal, especially in polity, because when India gained Independence in 1947, so also did Manipur gain Independence. In 1948, before the drafting of the Indian Constitution, the Manipur State Constitution Act of I947 ensured that Manipur had its own elected Constituent Assembly. There were various other factors that influenced political thinking and action, but the Battle of Imphal also accelerated the process of change.

The infrastructure of roads, bridges, airfields, and construction of various kinds undertaken by the Allied Force was left for the Manipuris to use in whatever manner they felt, even to improve upon and expand. But changes that occurred whether in society, polity, economy, diet, dress, manner of living etc., can not be ascribed just to the Battle of Imphal. Many historic and significant changes had occurred prior to 1944, the most important and permanent in many ways, was the great change that occurred in Meitei society, when King Garibniwaz (1709-1748) converted to Vaishnavism, gave up the primordial religion—Sanamahism. During one generation, the social cultural and even the racial identity of the Meiteis was radically Sanskritised. The King and all the Meiteis had become a single caste society. Eating of meat by the people was forbidden. Rearing of pigs and keeping of poultry were banned in the capital area. The Meitei Puyas were burnt and burning of the dead was introduced in 1725.[6] These were definitely much greater changes than that effected after the Battle of Imphal. The Meitei began to regard the tribals as 'impure' which created a schism in Manipuri's pluralistic society. (Mangba-sengba-pure-impure).[7]

Another equally historic and significant change in Manipur occurred as a result of the 'Divide and Rule' policy of the British in Manipur, the British Political Agent instructed all Christian missionaries commencing with Rev. William Pettigrew to confine their evangelising activities to the hills of Manipur. The majority of the tribals who dwelled in the Hills converted to Christianity before the Battle of Imphal. Because of the modern education imparted by the foreign Christian missionaries, a new class came into existence in Tribal Society – a modern educated middle class.

The impact of the Battle of Imphal was to facilitate and accelerate the pace of modernity. Angamba Singh remarked: 'Manipur society in general was already in the move towards what was considered "Modernity", since the conversion to Vaishnavism; so, it would be right to say that the movement gained significant momentum again after the war.' (The Battle of Imphal).[8]

Most important, this battle was fought in Imphal, so the chief stakeholder was Manipur, but the Manipuris were not taken into confidence with regard to the conduct of the war.

However, Maharaja Churachand 'placed the resources of his State at the King Emperor's disposal for the prosecution of the war.'[9] And some of the local populations were employed by the British to assist in building essential infrastructure such as buildings, roads, airfields, bridges, so necessary to ensure success to the Allies in the war. A few Manipuris, especially some Tangkhuls joined the British Indian Army, where the officers were British, and the ordinary soldiers (sepoys) were Indian.[10] The Maharajas of Manipur and their administration firmly supported the Allies, throughout the period.

Another form of local support for the British came in the form of the V Force, a few thousand men in the hills of Manipur and the most prominent being Major. Ralengnao (Bob) Khathing.[11]

It was not that the Manipuris had no contact with foreigners prior to the Battle of Imphal. They have a long tradition of military history. In addition, the Silk Route facilitated trade, with neighbouring kingdoms of South East Asia, especially that of Pong and Ava. In the early centuries, traders moved freely between the kingdoms of Manipur and Burma. As early as the 4th century A.D., during the reign of Khui Ningomba, Pengsiba and Naokhamba, Manipuri traders, travelled on horseback to upper Burma and China.[12] Manipur was also brought under Burmese rule for seven years 1819-1827, known in the history of' Manipur as 'Chahi Taret Khuntakpa' or 'Seven Years Devastation'.[13] The devastation wrought by the Battle of Imphal and that caused by the Chahi Taret Khuntakpa vary greatly. During the latter event, the population of Imphal Valley was reduced to about 10,000 or about 2000 households.[14] A little over a century later Imphal was again devastated. According to figures of the Census Year 1941, the population of Manipur was as follows:

2,49,183 Males, 2,62,866 Females

Total Population: 5,12,069

In 1951, there were 2,83,685 Males and 2,93,950 Females

Total Population: 5,77,635.

There was a sizeable increase in the total population- approximately 65,000 in 1951. This would mean that despite the Battle of Imphal occurring in 1944, there was no decrease in population; the bulk of the dead after the Battle, were soldiers belonging to both the Allied and Japanese forces. But with reference to the urban population of Manipur in 1941, it was as follows:

Males: 47, 44 8

Females: 52,268

Total Population: 99,716

A total population of 99,716, not even a fifth of the total population for 1941.

The Rural Population was:

Males: 2,01,735

Females: 2, 10,618

Total Population: 4,12,353.

A decade later in 1951, the numbers changed dramatically; urban males were only 1753 and urban females 1109, a total of 2,862. The Battle of Imphal had forced many people from the town to seek shelter in the rural areas; the statistics speaks for themselves:

Rural Males: 2,81,932

Rural Females: 2,92,841

Total: 5,74,773.

In 1951, villages inhabited were 1601, and the same one town existed.[15] Till the Census of 1961, Manipur had only one Municipal town.[16] A comparative analysis of villages inhabited is not possible but obviously the bulk of the land mass of Manipur was comprised of villages. The 1941 Census states that 19.47% of the total population was urbanised. But the 1951 Census shows a steep decline- only 0.50% was urbanised.[17]

The sex ratio of the population of Imphal in 1951 was as follows:

Male.: 1753

Female: 1109

Sex Ratio: 632.[18]

Two explanations are relevant. In the 1951 Census, an area of only two sq. miles covering Imphal Bazar, the Office and Residential portions, looked after by the then Imphal Town Fund, was considered as Imphal Town, but in previous Censuses, the area of Imphal Municipality was taken as Imphal town. Secondly, maybe, some original residents of Imphal remained in the rural countryside after the Battle of Imphal, temporarily. 'In 1961, when population had been increased to 67,717' and the 'population density increased from 552.50 in 1951 to 3873.97 in 1961.'[19]

It is possible that the Manipuris encountered the Japanese people for the first time at the time of the Battle of Imphal. Manipur is however, one of the routes between South Asia and South East Asia and Central Asia. Various ethnic groups belonging to the Southern Mongoloid group, the Tibeto-Burmans the Indo-Aryans, and a sizeable section of 'Tai (Shans) came to Manipur from pre-historic times down to the present day. The present ethnic groups of Manipur,viz. the Meiteis, Naga tribes, the Kuki-Chin tribes and other ethnic communities, are the descendants of those migrating people. They are pre-dominantly Mongoloid, and speak the Tibeto-Burman language.[20]

There are many different theories on the origin of the Meiteis. In the absence of any universally accepted theory of origin, it has been propounded that in the course of time, the Meiteis came to the Imphal Valley, from where again they once again dispersed in groups, to finally reach China. But being subjected to severe hard labor, involved in the construction of the Great Wall of China, they migrated from there, traveled across South East Asia, and then returned to Manipur. The region now known as Manipur, situated at the cross-roads of South Asia and South-East Asia, must have evidently retained a section or those early immediate Mon Mon Khemer speakers, Australoid-Mongoloid population of South China/ South-East Asia origin on the way to their westward migration.[21]

Generally believed to have migrated from China during the reign of the Chinese Emperor Chinglung or Chienlung around 200 B.C, the ancestor of the Kukis according to a Mizo historian Zawla, must have come out of the Great Wall in or about 225 BC.[22] According to B.B. Ghosh, Nagas belong to the Mongoloid stock of human races. It is believed that the Mongoloid people originated in the upper reaches of the Hwangho River in Sinkiang Province of China, and then migrated in 2000 B.C. According to the folklore of the

'Hao' (Naga) communities, ancestors of the Nagas migrated from China in search of a safer place for settlement.[23]

'India is a root of Japanese culture. Both regions arc located within Monsoon Asia, Maritime Asia, and Forest of Shinny Leaves: North-East India and Japan share the common cultural tradition under Forest Belt of Shinny Leaves, North East India is located in the centre of 'East Asian Half Moon Arc' creating the same human way of life, under slash and burn cultivation, in clothing, fashion, food cooking, housing and utensils, like reeling of silk of cocoons, dyeing teeth in black, fermented soyabeans, wooden hut with high leveled floor and thatched roof and bamboo work. Praying to Supreme Existence in Nature, was the beginning of religious notion, maintained as the basic layer of people's faith. Shinto, literally God's way, has succeeded to nature worship. People have worshipped hundreds of nature gods, such as big rock, stone circle, tree and waterfall. They revered holy mountains, where souls of the dead return. Water purification is a popular and basic practice. Yamato Dynasty, beginning Japanese nation, has continued a line of Tenno unbroken for ages eternal, as manifested deity, direct descendant of Sun-Goddess Amaterasu and mediator of Kami worship in Shinto.[24]

Yamato is the original place, located in the Nara Prefecture, where the nation of Japan was founded by Tenno 2,680 years ago, according to the estimation based on 'Kojiki' (Records of Ancient Matters). Then, Japanese people, originated from Yamato, proudly called themselves Yamato race who stands to revere Ten'no, as the descendants of Kami or the God Alive. Under such a sense of the superior and chosen people as above, Imperial

Japan promoted the propaganda - the emancipation of Asia by the dogma of Great Asia-ism, against the Whites, or Americans, and Europeans. In fact, Imperial Japan annexed Korea in 1910, and prepared to found Manchuria Empire in 1932, advocating the Five Races under One Union, viz. Japanese, Korean, Manchurian, Mongolian and Chinese (Han). Kojiki, the ancient chronicle edited in AD 712, the most important text of Shintoism, mentions that the Heavenly God and Goddess, created the Japanese archipelago by themselves.[25]

In India Goddess Lakshmi is worshipped as the Goddess of Fortune, Prosperity and Beauty, depicted with gold coins in her hand, and either sitting or standing on Lotus Flower: Goddess Benzaitan is represented with a musical instrument 'Biwa' in her hand, whereas Goddess Saraswati is represented with the musical instrument 'Veena' in her hand. Lord Ganesha is just one of the deities worshipped in Japan, derived from India. Saraswati is known as Ben-Zai-Ten, Ganesha as Kan-Gi-Ten, and Kubera as Ta-Mon-Ten.[26]

The Meiteis believe in nature worship as did the tribals before their conversion to Christianity. The *Puyas* (Sacred Scripture of the Meities) reveal that ancestor worship lay at the base of all religious beliefs. The Immortal Lord of the Universe is known as 'Taibang Mapu Sidaba. All the families trace their roots from this Immortal Father. The ancestral spirits, both divine and human are designated as 'Umanglais'. One can perhaps draw a parallel between the Meitei Umanglais and the Japanese 'Kami'. Ono defines 'Kami ' as: Fundamentally the term 'Kami' is an honorific for noble virtues and authority. All beings have such spirits, so in a sense, all beings can be called 'Kami'. The similarity also consists in both being ubiquitous, powerful and sacred.[27] Meiteis even after conversion to Hinduism, still believe in the Supreme Lord Sanamahi (son of Guru Sidaba).[28]

These statements reveal a close affinity between the Japanese and the Manipuris. Aishwarya Sugandhi stated that the 'Japanese could be one of the most religious people's.[29] North East India shares some similarities with Japan in terms of culture, food habits and traditional practiccs.[30]' The Japanese physical appearance was just like ours. The Japanese were not rude to us. They were good and helpful people- gave us medicines.'[31] There were many reasons which consciously or unconsciously attracted the Manipuris towards the Japanese, even though the latter were the aggressors in the Battle of Imphal.

The Kukis of Manipur welcomed the arrival of the Japanese and the INA troops. Their attitude is reflected in an immensely popular song LAKOl-PA, which came into vogue in 1942.

Theilou koljang toni let pbanna

Ging dengdeng 'e Japan lenna huilen Kon

Pegol hemlhei , saigin bang

Mao ding deng' e van tham jola Japan lenna

Amao deng deng' e Japan lenna mong mo

Vailoukon sunsol selung hem fante

Atwi theikhong tabang ging deng deng

Gin deng deng'e Japan lenna huilen Kongjin

English Translation

From the horizon of Burma plain,

Like the sweet note of the bamboo flute

Japanese planes hums in the sky above.

When the Japanese plane floats its sweet note

The depressed farmer forgets his sadness

Like. The sweet melody of the water mill

The Japanese plane floats its sweet note.

This song is particularly revealing. Japanese lighter planes symbolized the Japanese power; its thundering sound was delightful as the sweet notes of popular Kuki flutes and water mills. To the Kukis, the Japanese planes and the Japanese themselves, came to liberate the depressed Kukis from their state of sadness under the colonial regime.[32] This song was so popular among the Kukis that almost all of them, irrespective of age or sex used to sing it, particularly the youths, who used to spend their days humming this sweet song. The song got so deep rooted in their psyche that threats of bitter punishment or intimidation by the Britishers, to those who sang the song failed to produce any effect.[33]

One of the most important functions of folklore or folktale is that it becomes a vehicle of social protest. Such elements of folklore though frequently relating to minor events, often have references to matter of highest national importance.[34] The Thadou-Kukis as also the Japanese, used a 'origin myth', for propaganda purposes. Zamkithanga, a second clerk in the SDO, Tamenglong office stirred up the Thadou-Kuki people secretly saying: The relationship with the Japanese is that our clan originated from two brothers—(1). Sawngthu, (Chongthu).(2). Saungja (Chonaja). The Thadou clans are descendant from Saungthu and the Japanese from Saungja. So, we are very closely related and cannot but help them (Japanese).[35] The Japanese Force

(JIA) also tried to appeal to the emotion of the Kukis, claiming that they descended from Chongji brother of Chongthu, from whom the Kukis claimed their descent. There was yet another form of propaganda. A widely known prophesy 'Nongpokthong hangani (Eastern gate will be opened) had been convincingly interpreted by the Japanese, and claimed that they represented the Eastern power.' [36]

Anthropologically, the direct ancestor of Japan was Proto-Mongoloid, who originated from the South part of East Asia in the late Palaeolithic Age. On the other hand, North-East India has been inhabited mostly by Australoid and Southern Mongoloid, followed by Indo-Aryan. Due to far long distance between India and Japan, they had very few occasions of human interchanges, particularly until the end of the nineteenth century, as only two Indian priests were recorded of their visits to Japan in ancient times. However, in 1944, Japan's first and direct encounter with North East India, viz., 60,000 soldiers of the Japanese Imperial Army crossed the Chindwin River marching towards Imphal. [37]

The Origin Myth used by both the Kukis and to a much lesser extent the Japanese is not cited in most academic works dealing with the origin of the Kukis. The Kukis as also other tribals of Manipur, depend on 'Oral History' to reconstruct their history. Oral History is the first kind of history, and especially important for communities whose history was not committed to the written form for centuries. But the Myth of Origin from Two Brothers was used very successfully during the World War II Battle in Manipur. This is obvious from the statement of Nungkhogin, Chief of Suangsang, who welcomed the Japanese to his house. 'Our generation started from two Brothers, and we are closely related. We are very glad you come to us:[38]. Lambert also mentioned that the Kukis also considered the Japanese as their half-brothers.[39] One Nungkhothang of Lungba village said: 'We are closely related to the Japanese, being generation of two brothers...their enemy is our enemy. He was one of the greatest agents of the Japanese.[40] The truth of the story is open to question·, but the point to be noted is that the creator of the story, skillfully interwoven myth with the then prevailing situation of that time, to find authority to legitimize Kuki co-operation with the Japanese. The legendary tale served the purpose.[41]

Haozathang Haokip, an INA veteran commented: The Kuki is yearning for freedom was so high in their hearts, that's why, the sounds of the Japanese planes, sounds so sweet to them, and the very sound is the 'sound of freedom' to them.[42]

The Japanese planes appear to have made an indelible impression upon the Kukis .

Agam thimthu jing nan Jong

Huilen Kong chunga lunghem Jangvan ahung lenge;

Lunghem ja a na hung lenleh;

Tolkum tado lunglha gol tongkai sah na ding;

Japan Mangpa tolso in tol son in;

Vankikhup noi Mantin cha lonlhi longlou umponte.

English Translation:

In the darkness of the land;

The Japanese planes come like charming bird (Jangva)

If you come because of my sorrow;

To the ground to console your disgraced friend;

Mighty Japan! to the ground! to the ground.

All nations will be over joyed with tears. [43]

The song certainly resonates both with hope in and adulation for the Japanese but most Kuki tribes claim that they came out of the bowel of the earth, or a cave- Chinlung, believed to be somewhere in China.[44] But since the movie—'Bose, the Forgotten Hero,' was given Japanese sub-titles, it would seem that the Japanese too still have adulation for Netaji, whose INA Force was linked to the Japanese army during the World War II Battle; and they also have great warmth and consideration towards the people of Manipur.

A Free Thinker wrote: INA with the Japanese army played havoc in the East: The Great.

British Empire was shaken, the spirit of INA and Netaji could infiltrate the Great British- Indian Army.[45] The close bond between the JIA (Japanese Imperial Army) and Netaji and the INA is another reason for the cordial relations between the Japanese and the Manipuris. This is illustrated by a short excerpt from narration of the historic events that took place in Moirang during the Second World War. 'The Indo-Japanese forces advanced very fast...the 17th British Division could not resist the advancing forces.... The people of Moirang and the surrounding villages were jubilant at the sight of the Indo-Japanese forces. Thus, the withdrawal of the British 17th Division was completed on April 13, 1944... Some leaders of Moirang led by M. Koireng Singh, L. Sanaba Singh, K. Kanglen, Meinam Mani Singh and others went to Tronglaobi village and had discussions with the Indo-Japanese forces on the 14th of April 1944. About 5 p.m., Col. Soukat Ali Malik planted the tricolour with springing Tiger as the emblem of the historic Moirang Kangla. Many Japanese officers and soldiers were also assembled. Col. Malik's address was translated by M. Koireng Singh. The assembled crowd welcomed Col. Malik's message, and felt elated that they were the first liberated people of India, although many of their family members were evacuated from Moirang, and took shelter on the Eastern hillocks situated at Loktak lake.

Local people gladly donated rice, dry fish and vegetables to the Indo-Japanese forces. 13 members of the Nikhil Manipuri Mahasabha, namely, Th. Angou Singh, P. Tomal Singh, S. Ibohal Singh, L. Bijoy Singh, L. Kanhai Singh, M. Jatra Singh, W. Gyaneshwor Singh, M. Amuba Singh, L. Irabot Singh, Kh. Jugeswor Singh, Keinya Devi, and M. Randhoni Devi reached Moirang secretly from Imphal and other places.

They joined with the members of Moirang and worked together in carrying out espionage activities. All the surrounding villages upto Ningthoukhong were liberated from the British forces. The building of the INA quarters at Moirang for three months in 1944, belonged to H. Nilamani Singh an INA freedom fighter. Manipur freedom fighters like K. Gopal Singh, L.Sanaba Singh, M. Koireng Singh and H. Nilamani Singh were declared traitors by the British Political Agent and 'Shoot on Sight order' was passed on them. All the 17 members of the Mahasabha, (13 from Imphal and 4 from Moirang) were blacklisted. The Scorched Earth Policy was extended from Torbung to Ningthoukhong. The area was highly bombarded and many civilians were killed and injured. In Moirang alone, more than one thousand homes were set ablaze with the exception of five or six figures like Hemam Nilamani Singh and M. Koireng Singh feature in the State's folklore, even today. Both of them went on to play crucial roles in shaping Manipur's graph after Independence. The idea that INA meant contributing to the society lives on in the great work they did in their times as colossal political figures in the state, post-Independence.[46]

It would appear that a good number of people of Manipur supported the Japanese when they came to Manipur. In accounts written by native scholars and other interested and informed persons in Manipur, there is a definite tendency to eulogize the Japanese. The Co-Convener of the Organizing Committee, 70th Anniversary of the Battle of Imphal wrote: 'The tenacity and the valor of an ordinary Japanese soldier is far beyond one can imagine. Its determination and the resolute character is not a recent one.'[47] General Slim himself commented about the Japanese: whatever one may think of thus pursuing a hopeless object, there can be no question of the supreme courage and hardihood of the Japanese soldiers, who made the attempts. I know of no army that could have equalled them.' Yet, 'The Japanese soldiers was always depicted as a little bloke wearing long puttees and running around shouting "Banzai."[48] However a poignant documentary film Imphal 1944 (UK and Japan, 2014) was made in Manipur by Junichi Kajioka and when it was screened at a Reconciliation Meet by the 2nd World War Imphal Campaign Foundation in April 2019 at Imphal, it moved the entire audience, comprising of interested people of Manipur, Japan and the UK.

"The Second World War brought people from many parts of the country and the world to Manipur. There were the Indians, who made up the British 14th Army, as well as those in the INA. The British, Americans and Canadians were here, as were the Japanese, and even soldiers from East Africa. And then of course, were the people of Manipur themselves, who got caught up in some of the bitterest fighting the world had ever seen. The period of the war was a momentous one in Manipur's history, and had a deep impact on the state and its people. Many had to evacuate, their homes and seek shelter elsewhere in 1944, villages were bombed and houses destroyed. And these were just the physical costs. Psychologically, besides being exposed to people from other parts of India and the world in large numbers during the entire period of the war, Manipur's population was subjected to intense propaganda, both in favour of the Allied war effort, and to a more limited extent, the INA and the Japanese. But the latter were often greeted by shouting out "Banzai". While some sections of the people did side with the latter, others led by Maharaja Bodhachandra extended their support to the British".[49] Arambam Angamba Singh with reference to some sections of the Manipuri people siding with the Japanese and INA stated: The, sense of freedom has always been something that we (the Manipuris) have always been proud of. And joining the INA, contributing to India's struggle for freedom was quite natural.[50]

What motivated the Indians in particular during the Battle? 'Morale is a state of mind. It is that intangible force which will move a whole group of men, to give their last ounce to achieve something, without counting the cost to themselves that makes them feel they are part of something greater than themselves. If they are to feel that, their morale must— if it is to endure and the essence of morale is that it should endure- have certain foundations. These foundations are spiritual, intellectual and material and that is the order of their importance. Spiritual first, because only spiritual foundations can stand real strain, next, intellectual, because men are swayed by reason, as well as feeling. Material last-important because the very highest kinds of morale are often met when material conditions are lowest.[51]

Manipur took a role in support of the INA's movement. News of approaching INA under the leadership of Netaji, had already created a stir in the Valley. A sense of extreme pride, mixed with euphoric nationalism, resonated with many locals. Many would join the Bahudar group led by Col. S. A. Mallick, which was responsible for gathering intelligence, and conducting covert operations. And many more in the front lines, bearing the brunt of bloody encounters. In spite of the ever-present repercussion, many families openly supported the INA movement, donating their meagre sayings, and secretly stocked grains. However, few of the active volunteers had to retreat back to Burma with the Japanese army. Many were later apprehended and jailed in Rangoon. They were later shipped back to Calcutta, and released under terms and conditions of a general amnesty.[52] As a result of the retreat to Burma, patriotic Manipuris suffered great trauma in the Rangoon jail. (The Azad Hind force has a list of Meiteis of the INA, who were missing after the battle. Whether they died, or were jailed, or went back to Japan, remains a question mark. This would amount to their families receiving no closure, as they had no information on the family members found missing).

The Japanese and the INA personnel had to depend more and more on the ration and livestock of the local people. An eye-witness account maintains that all the male folk and young women in the occupied villages were engaged in pounding rice day and night to feed the soldiers. At other times, the male folk also served as coolies and porters carrying ration and ammunition to different camps. Zathuoi, who was a volunteer, also testified that he and his two friends one day carried a wounded Japanese soldier whose leg was completely torn asunder just below his knee, from the Saidan peak to the Saikawt camp. Deeply impressed by his forbearance, Zathuoi further stated that not even once did the soldier groan.[53]'

So the fiercest Battle of World War II was fought in Imphal, the Manipuris had no stake in the Battle- the Japanese were the aggressors, yet a close affinity developed between the native people and the Japanese.

References

1. Hemant Katoch in Preface of Yaiphaba Meetei Kangjam: *Forgotten Voices of Japan Laan*: *The Battle of Imphal and the Second World War in Manipur.*
2. Lal Dena, History of Modern Manipur 1762-1949, pp.49,73-74.
3. Rice is the staple diet of the native population.
4. Mohendra Irengbam: My Memories of Imphal from 1941, part 6, *The Sangai Express*, Wednesday 4th November, 2020.
5. Hemant Singh Katoch, *op. cit.*
6. Gangmumei Kabui, *History of Manipur*, Volume I, Pre-Colonial Period, pp. 253- 254
7. Salam Irene, *The Politics of Identity in Manipur*, p.3, Seminar Paper, Calcutta University.
8. Interview with Arambam Angamba Singh, Imphal, 10th September 2020
9. Lydall: Administration Report for the Manipur State for the Year 1943 -44, p.7
10. Interview with an Indian Defence Forces Officer, Imphal, 5th September 2020.
11. Hemant Singh Katoch: *The Battle fields of Imphal,* p. 32
12. Salam Irene: Policy Brief 2012, *The Manipur Diaspora in Myanmar*, Calcutta University.

13. Ibid, op. cit
14. Gangmumei Kabui, op. cit
15. Directorate of Economics and Statistics, Government of' Manipur, Statistical Handbook of Manipur 2017, pp.6-8, I8, 24 -2 5.
16. Kamei Gaikhonlu, *Dynamics of Urban Life in Modern Imphal* p. 115, unpublished Ph.D. thesis, Manipur University, 2011.
17. Directorate of Economics and Statistics, op. cit
18. Kamei Gaikhonlu op. cit., p.123
19. Ibid, op. cit pp.116,122
20. Gangmumei Kabui op. cit. p.12
21. Thangjam Chinky Devi, Society and Culture of the Meitei of Manipur and Tai-Shan of Burma: A Comparative Study, unpublished Ph.D. Thesis, Manipur University, 2019
22. Salam Irene: Ethnicity Across the Borders-The Kuki Chins of Manipur and Myanmar p.5 Seminar Paper, Jamia Milia lslamia, Delhi.
23. Salam Irene: Origin of the Nagas, International Relations and Diplomacy, May 2020, Vol. 8, No.5 pp.213 -219.
24. Dr. Yoshihiro Kaburagi and Kazuki Nakajima: Culture in Forest Belt of Shinny Leaves as a Common Root for India and Japan and Fusion between Buddhism and Shinto, Nature Worship, Seminar Paper, February 2018, Manipur, India.
25. Dr. Yoshihiro Kaburagi: Answer to Questionnaire, 2020
26. Respondent Information, Japan, I6 th November, 2020
27. Rena Laisram: Early Meitei History- Religion, Society and the Manipuri Puyas.pp.73-67.
28. Dr. Chihiro Koiso: Animistic Beliefs among Nagas and Meiteis in Manipur before and after Conversion, Seiryo University, Japan, Seminar Paper February 2018, Manipur, India.
29. Dr. Aishwarya Sugandhi: The Religious outlook of the Japanese, Bukkyo University, Kyoto, Japan, Seminar Paper February 2018, Manipur, India.

30. Dr. Ajit Singh Naosekparn: Japanese Technology with potential for Socio-Economic Impact in North- East India, Seminar Paper February 2018, Manipur, India.
31. Paojalhing cit.in Yaiphaba Meitei Kangjam, op. cit., p. 149 - 150
32. Sonthang Haokip: Anglo-Kuki Relations 1777-1947 A.D p. 202-203 cit P S. Haokip-Zalengam: The Kuki Nation, unpublished Ph.D. thesis, Manipur University, 2011.
33. Ibid. p. 203, cit. J.Guite: Representing Local Participation in INA, Japanese Imphal Campaign: The case of the Kukis in Manipur 1943- 45, Indian Historical Review 2010
34. lbid. p. 217 cit. M. Islam (1985), *Folklore: The Pulse of the People*, Concept Publishing House, New Delhi, p. 383.
35. Ibid. p. 218 cit.copy of Translation of Lalzuaia's report dated 17. 7.44 forwarded by SI, FIB, Aijal under his Secret Memo dated 26.7.44 10 Central Intelligence Officer, Assam File No. XLI Manipur Secretariat Library, Imphal.
36. Hemant Singh Katoch, *op.cit.*, p. 36, Singh, *Manipur during World War II* (1941-45): Socio-Economic Change and Local Responses pp. I8- 19. The above cited prophesy was also quoted on 12th April 1995, when the Moreh Tamu trade post was inaugurated by the Trade Minister of Myanmar—Lt. General Tan Kyi and Commerce Minister of India Mr. P. Chindambaram:' The Eastern Gate was open·, symbolising prosperity for Manipur, Salam Irene, Pol icy Brief op. cit.
37. Dr.Yoshihiro Kaburagi: Japan and its Relationship with North-East India, Seminar Paper, Manipur, 2018.
38. Sonthang Haokip op.cit p. 218 cit,. Copy of Lalzuaia's report op. cit
39. Ibid p.218 cit. Lambert, Notes on the Kuki Situation 3, Assam State Archives.
40. Ibid p. 219 cit.copy of Lalzuaia's Report op.cit
41. lbid.,op. cit, p. 205
42. Ibid., p.20, 5 Interview with Shri. Haozathang Haokip, 29th September, 2010, Bethel, Churachandpur.

43. Ibid p. 200 J.Guite op. cit. 'Jangva is the common name for a variety of singing birds. Literally Jang means delighted. "Va" means "Bird". The bird is a feeler and charmer in times of deep sadness

44. SalamIrene: Manipur, Land, People, Demography pg. 63 cit.T.S.Gangte 1973: Kuki Naga Ethnicity in Current Manipur Polity, Ed-Madhu Rajput-Understanding North East India.

45. The Sangai Express, January 24,2021: Was Netaji really in Manipur?

46. M.Asnikumar Singh: The idea of Netaji, Manipur and the INA cit.in the SangaiExpress, 22nd and 23rd January 2021

47. Arambam Angamba Singh: Imperial Japanese Army WW II, The Code of Bushido, p.48 Souvenir, 70th Anniversary of the Battle of lmphal (WW II) June, 2014.

48. Richard Hill: Nungshigum'? Where's that? p. 29, Souvenir 2014, op. cit

49. Hemant Singh Katoch: Battle of Imphal and Manipur's Experience of WW II, Seminar Paper, Manipur, February 2018.

50. Interview with Arambam Angamba Singh, op. cit.

51. Col. M.G. Abhyankar : The War in Burma, p. 49.

52. Azad Hind Force Imphal Front, FB, 15th September 2020.

53. Hemant Singh Katoch: The Battlefields of Imphal, p.26, Laldena: Indo-Japanese Soldiers in the Khuga Valley of Churachandpur, Hueiyen Lanpao, Imphal, 28th March, 2014.

2
Manipur: The Epicenter of the Battle

All men are more or less a product of their environment, and their literary or intellectual efforts must be understood with reference to that milieu. Today 76 years after the Battle of Imphal, there are varying perceptions about the Impact of the Battle on the people of Manipur. Literature on the Battle, primarily consists of war or military histories, and contain only incidental references to the impact of the Battle not just on the combatants but on the people who resided in the theatre where the war was staged. Military history is read by a very small section of people, even among historians. Words in parlance at the time such as 'invincible' (usually applied to the Japanese Imperial Army) and 'defeat' are viewed from a different prism today. Every Battle fought has 'victors' and the 'vanquished', but a war which goes on till the finish is never kind to either of the warring sides, who both bear the scars of Battle. It is difficult to estimate who or what people/nation were more adversely impacted, as there was no scale then to measure the atrocities and sufferings that occurred in the course of the war. Participants and those in habiting the area where the Battle occurred, experienced a gambit of emotions ranging from a focus on physical survival, to panic, fear, terror, uncertainty, hope, delusion, joy, sorrow, depression and a myriad more. Brains become addled, nerves are frayed; in the clamour and heat of the Battle, it is difficult to think clearly. Over a period of time, memories whether joyful or otherwise of the Battle grow hazy. Yet, to come to terms with loss or to receive closure, it is necessary to understand and analyze what ·combatants and bystanders felt during the duration of the war. Some earlier writers on the Battle of Imphal, have included data collected through interviews with people, who witnessed the war or their descendants. Personal Recollections - War Memories are the key to understanding the Impact of this battle on the people of Manipur. Oral testimony passed down from generation to generation is another important source for understanding the emotions of the people and their world - view. When a considerable time has elapsed between the event and the collection of data through field research, lapses of memory do occur. Nevertheless, their importance cannot be discounted, as the theatre for WW II Battle in India, was Imphal and Kohima, places which prior to the battle had remained in comparative isolation not only from the rest of India, but the rest of the world. The Battle of Imphal created an indelible memory on Manipuri consciousness.

It is not certain whether the Manipuris knew before the event, that the Japanese were going to come to Manipur to engage in a fierce battle with the British. There were some rumblings, and some of the population were told that war was imminent, and to save themselves, they needed to construct trenches in which to hide when the war operations commenced. When the first Japanese planes which were a novel sight were spotted, they did not rain down fire or brimstone. The Manipuris may have assumed that as this was not their war, the sighting of the planes were akin to 'much ado about nothing'. But when the Japanese planes swooped down a second time, they received a rude shock; before they could grasp the implications of the maneuver, bombs were falling everywhere causing death, destruction, devastation. A young boy about five years, had been given some money to purchase _milk from a shop close to his home. As he stepped out of his house, a bomb fell on his house, killed his family, destroyed his house and made him an orphan.

Manipur was an ancient kingdom, a cradle of human civilisation and creativity. 'Manipur' literally meaning 'The Land of Gems' has a recorded history commencing from 33 A.D. Proud of these traditions, even though a battle waged in Imphal, the people continued their cultural activities, which were so dear to them and which provided a semblance of normality in an abnormal time. This normality was necessary, because in the course of the war, many families in and around lmphal were compelled to evacuate and find shelter in the countryside. A few families used bullock carts to transport some necessary provisions/possessions, but the majority trekked. Those people suffered fear, uncertainty, anxiety, dread. They were compelled to set free their livestock, and most of their rice stores had to be left behind. The displaced people faced many travails; young children and babies were carried on the backs of women walking considerable distances. Aged and infirm people had to be left behind, as they were unable to make the long trek. Families were sorrowful, but there was no other option. Some pregnant mothers gave birth during the exodus in difficult unsafe conditions, some died while giving birth, and the new born was left with the dead mother. Despite the hardships, people celebrated events associated with 'The Passage of Rites'.

From personal recollections, one fact stands out. Some of the hill tribes stated that not only were the Japanese a friendly people; they resurrected an old legend/myth, that claimed that the Japanese and the Tangkhuls (A Naga tribe of Manipur) were brothers, both being of Mongoloid stock. Just as some of the civilian population of Imphal were allowed to purchase some provisions from the Allied Forces Canteens, novelties like bread, English biscuits, butter, canned food, imported yarn, buttons, etc, the Tangkhuls of Ukhrul district were happy to receive cows as a gift from the Japanese. Their craving for eating beef was satiated, as every house in a village got a portion of meat; they contrasted this Japanese gift with the attitude of the Allied Forces, who never gifted them anything. The Japanese gesture coming in the midst of the war, was akin to an unexpected birthday or Christmas gift.

But inevitably as the war progressed, Japanese provisions dwindled to nothing, and they were forced to seize paddy from the locals; not only that, the villagers were made to pound the paddy, sometimes the task could not be completed and they were forced to eat half pounded uncooked rice which they carried in their helmets. This uncooked rice adversely impacted their health. They also commanded livestock as an essential requirement of their diet. But the Japanese paid for the paddy and the livestock in Japanese currency. They also hired locals as coolies and porters to carry their rations and ammunition. These practices would be an imposition upon the Manipuris; but the Manipuris in general found the Japanese to be a very likeable people, and of their own volition offered them free foodstuffs such as boiled eggs. They also admired the forbearance of the injured Japanese who despite being in pain, never whimpered or complained.

Many Manipuris also experienced acts of kindness from British and Indian soldiers- they received gifts of food, and children received some clothes- these items were both novel and exotic and were greatly appreciated, especially tins of condensed milk, canned meat, British cigarettes, chewing gum, liquor. And the army vehicles of the Allied Forces aroused wonder and curiosity especially in young minds, who wanted to drive the very same vehicles at high speed, whenever an opportunity arose. (The opportunity came when the war ended and most of the army vehicles were left behind).

The majority of Manipur's population remained aloof from the war- they neither sided with the Allies or the Japanese. Many did not even know the reason for the Japan Lan. This chapter will focus on the lived experiences of the people of Manipur in 1944. Often, books and research articles make mention of the three dominant communities that reside in Manipur viz. the Meiteis of the Imphal Valley, the Kukis and Nagas who primarily reside in the Manipur Hills.

Maybe because the Meitei Pongal (Muslim) came to Manipur only in the seventeenth century and non-Manipuris approximately two centuries later.

The People's Stories

The Tangkhul Hills- The Story of Beautiful Sarengla

During the war, in the Tangkhul areas of Ukhrul a

story that gained wide publicity was that of the beautiful, Tangkhul woman Sarengla. There was a famous romance between a Tangkhul nurse Sarengla and a Japanese doctor (of the JIA). Sarengla was probably from a Tangkhul village near Kampong. She had studied nursing in Assam, and she happened to be home, when the Japanese Army entered Ukhrul in the early part of 1944. The Japanese doctor persuaded her to accompany him and assist him in his medical duties. During the war. The couple subsequently fell in love and married briefly, till about July 1944, when the doctor had to go back to Japan. He however promised to return, and to take her with him to Japan after the war. Sadly, she never heard from him again.[2]

There are several stories told about Sarengla. One Tangkhul lady categorically stated that Sarengla married a Japanese during the war, but not a doctor, rather an Army General. Another Tangkhul lady was of the opinion that Sarengla married a Chinese doctor, and yet another stated that Sarengla's daughter bore a Chinese surname i.e. Lucy Liu.

Though there are variances, it appears, that when Sarengla married for the first time, which was after the war, she married a Kuki doctor Dr. Gampu. But she later divorced him, and married a Chinese doctor who had come to Manipur from Calcutta, a Dr. SF Liu, a Chinese dentist from Calcutta.[3]

The story goes like this: A Japanese intelligence Officer in Ukhrul (District) got friendly with Sarengla, who was beautiful as also accomplished, and most important, able to communicate with him in English (The Intelligence Officer must have been fluent too in English). This officer, initially used Sarengla to collect information from the Tangkhrul villages about the enemy's movement. After some time, Sarengla was on intimate terms with the officer, and began to live with him. It is not certain whether she married him because war was raging, the Japanese were invaders, and it would have been almost impossible to tie the knot legally in the circumstances. What seems certain is that the couple loved one another during that brief period of the war. The Intelligence Officer, Major Masata, probably did not survive the monsoon retreat after the Japanese defeat in the war. However, his faithful German Shepherd dog called 'Abei', who left with him in retreat, returned back to his beautiful Tangkhul lover, Sarengla, a nurse from Nambisha village, in what is now Kasom -Khullen, sub-division of Ukhrul district as he said it would, if he did not make it to Mandalay (during the retreat). In a way, typical of the time and its people, the Naga villagers of Nambisha hated the dog, as it represented the Japanese soldiers, who had brought upon the village much torture, miseries and sufferings. The Village Council in its deliberation decided to do away with Abei, the dog. They killed Abei within a week of his return, and served him up for a village feast.[4]

This human story is like a beacon- a light shining in the darkness, giving hope when there was only fear, uncertainty, defeat, death- it traces the evolution of the steadfast love between Sarengla- a Tangkhul, who risked her life when she gave her love to Major Masata, who as the enemy had a large stake in the war of Manipur. During a period marked by trauma, torment and devastation love bloomed, signaling hope and perhaps reconciliation.

Killing of a dog, and sharing its cooked meat is not a barbaric or inhuman act, as dog meat has been and is still eaten and relished by the Nagas. This practice is common to people of Mongolian origin, and widely prevalent in countries of South East and East Asia. What is abhorrent is that a pet dog was killed in retaliation to the attack of the Tangkhul village by the Japanese, but as Home Raikhan has mentioned, 'it was typical of the time and its people'. The Third Japanese Army Division entered Manipur, out of which the 15th and 30th Division entered Ukhrul with over 60,000 Japanese soldiers. Only the 33rd Division covered Tiddim Road and Pallel Road -their target was Imphal, while the 15th and 30th Division' targets were Kohima and Dimapur. So, one can make out that Ukhrul was the most affected; Incidentally, the Japanese first set foot in Ukhrul, and not Moirang. By the early part of 1944, they had entered Ukhrul and Kamjong Districts, but the heaviest fighting was in Shangshak. After fierce fighting, Shangshak fell into Japanese hands-on 21st March 1944, and probably the tri-colour flag was first hoisted in Shangshak (The Japanese captured Moirang only in May 1944). After Shangshak, the Japanese occupied Ukhrul in March 1944, and they remained in Ukhrul till July 8,1944 under the Japanese Captain.

Both my father and mother told a few unforgettable things, when they (the Japanese), first entered my village Shokvao near Shangshak, they butchered fourteen pigs belonging to my father's family. (Livestock was a source of wealth in the Hill areas). They were paid in Japanese currency, which was practically worthless. By the time they entered Ukhrul or Manipur, they had run out of their provisions, and they mostly depended on locally available rice or meat, both buffaloes and pigs. During the heavy bombardment, houses were burnt, many people, both

Japanese and Tangkhuls died. Subsequently, the Tangkhuls all abandoned their villages, and took shelter in the forest, till the withdrawal of the Japanese in July 1944. My parents were eye-witness, the death toll was unimaginable: dead bodies, mostly of Japanese soldiers were piled up in the streams and rivulets.

There was continuous bombardment for days. Even many Tangkhuls lost their lives. May be thats' why in Ukhrul, they called the Second World War, "Japan War" One Mr. N. Luikham IAS (Retd), mentioned to me, that at the beginning of World War II, a shell landed in his family courtyard and exploded. Two or three people died on the spot. Miraculously, he escaped. He was very young then.[5]

I also read that thanks to World War II, lmphal-Ukhrul road was constructed in 1942, and another road from Shangshak to the international border beyond Kamjong was also constructed in 1942. Col. Finch was the road engineer, and hence the name Finch Corner. One of the road contractors was late Mr. Suisa Rungsung from Somdal Village, who went on to contest the first General Election of the Lok Sabha in 1952. One Mr. Ramung was the road construction supervisor under Col. Finch. He became a rich man and settled down in Ukhrul.[6]

After the withdrawal of the Japanese on 8th July, 1944, they left behind a large number of ammunitions, including rifles/guns, swords, helmets and other articles like tiffin boxes, water bottles, etc. My father, though a young man, had fourteen rifles, large number of Japanese swords, helmets, tiffin boxes, water bottles of both Japanese and Allied soldiers. ('Hanggo' or the multipurpose tiffin boxes- you don't part with Hanggo until you are dead, as you do with your arms. - posted on Facebook on the 5th of January 2019 by Arambam Angamba Singh). But the significant fact was, that by the late 1960's, the tiffin boxes, water bottles and helmets of the Allied soldiers, Americans, British or Australian, were mostly rusted. Surprisingly, the Japanese swords, helmets, tiffin boxes and water bottles, were in good condition. All the Japanese rifles were collected by the SDO (Sub- Divisional Officer) in Ukhrul, with the help of Lambus. (Minor intermediary officials used by the British) after the war ended. Among the Lambus, one Haokholet Haokip, managed to collect 2000 Japanese rifles, and handed them over to the SDO, Ukhrul, who was a 'White' man. The latter was so impressed with Haokholet's performance, that I am told, the SDO Ukhrul, recommended his name for promotion to Sub-inspector of Police

In conclusion, let me state that the Tangkhul people suffered a lot during World War II; villages were burnt during bombardment; many lost their lives. In certain respects, the people of Manipur and Nagaland contributed their services to the defense of the country during World War II.[7]

What is of note and interest, in the stories related by Ram Muivah's parents to him, and also by the late Mr. Yangmaso Shishak of Shangshak (the latter subsequently constructed a small Japanese War Memorial in Shangshak) is the reference to the tri-colour flag being hoisted at Shangshak- a fact often overlooked, although in contrast, there are several references to the flag hoisting at Moirang. The Battle at Shangshak was fought two months prior to the Battle at Moirang in 1944.

Secondly, the stories inform about why the Tangkhuls

did not take so kindly to the Japanese: Their perspective was very different to the Kukis especially.

The reference to butchering of pigs and livestock by the Japanese was a common practice, as the Japanese Army had long run out of provisions and needed food urgently, for purposes of survival. The appropriation of domestic animals reared by Tangkhuls for their livelihood, was no doubt a harsh measure, but what cannot be condoned in peace time can be condoned during a war. The animals appropriated were paid in Japanese currency, but as a Tangkhul lady from that area narrated: as a young girl in 1944, she requested her parents for some money (Japanese) to purchase 'Kabok'(puffed rice balls), but she was told that the Japanese money could not purchase even the least costly item, as it was of no value in Manipur, and not acceptable either in the marketplace or to a vendor.

The trauma of seeing their houses bombarded and destroyed made a lasting impression on the minds of the Tangkhuls. They were forced to seek shelter in dense jungles, and their diet was limited to wild plants and berries, until the time the JIA left Ukhrul. And the term 'Japan Lan' was appropriate, because of the many Japanese corpses left behind in the Tangkhul Hills (Mortality was high among the JIA).

The retreating Japanese Army left behind a large amounts of war equipments which not only came in handy, but was highly prized by the Tangkhuls who had a preference for them in contrast to British, American or Australian equipment, which was highly vulnerable to rust. A Tangkhul woman stated that her father, a farmer, always carried with him to the paddy fields, his Japanese water bottle, which had a unique, novel design and was resistant to rust.

Innocent Tangkhuls lost their lives although they were not specifically targeted. However, the British built a proper road which facilitated access to and from Ukhrul to Imphal and back. The Finch Corner Memorial is dedicated to the Australian engineer of Bombay Sappers and Miners and his team, who made the first motorable road till this junction in 1942.[8] The road was a Godsend, it facilitated travel from and to the plains and the hills of Manipur. The construction involved the engagement of local labour, which would have contributed to improving the quality of sustainable livelihood.

The Japanese invasion of India came during the month of March, 1944. It came through three routes- Tiddim sector, Tamu-Moreh-Kongkan Thana Sector and the Tamanthi-Layshi Sector. The Japanese 31st Division came in swiftly, and swarmed into the Southern Tangkhul country. Ukhrul was Tolloi's deeper, Southern neighbour. When Ukhrul was abandoned on 20th March, 1944 by the 4th Bn. Assam Rifles, it was immediately occupied by the Japanese Army. Further, to the South, lay the village of Shangshak. The British had to withdraw from Shangshak to Litan, then lmphal. The aim of the Japanese was to cut the Imphal-Kohima route, and to attack Kohima. The first inroads into Tolloi therefore occurred on the 26th March. My father, Arim who the Japanese addressed as 'Lamo' as they could not pronounce 'Arim' who was the Head- Master of the UP School in Tolloi, told me that about a thousand Japanese soldiers had suddenly appeared around the school complex, and had taken charge of the school building and the adjoining playground. The twin villages of Tolloi and

Phungton were then directed to provide provisions and porters.

Though the villages had good equation with the Japanese Army, their hearts and loyalties were with the British. The arrival of such a Japanese contingent into Tolloi, along with their numbers, were regularly informed to the small British platoon stationed at Mt. Tareikachui. When a company sized Japanese force of over a hundred strong entered the village, Phanitphang (late Rev. Phanitphang Vashum), took upon himself to inform the presence of the Japanese soldiers in the village. When the British enquired as to the strength of the Japanese, Phanitphang informed them that they were less than forty. Thinking that they had a good chance at success, in a surprise ambush, the British-Indian force came down to engage the Japanese. A sharp-eyed Japanese sentry chanced to see a file of men coming down from the village, an alarm was raised, and the Japanese soldiers alerted. On query, the Japanese were told by one of the interpreters, that it was probably a party of men gone out to shoot a pig for the latter's food. The reply somehow pacified the Japanese soldiers, and they began to take their rest and snooze, but not the sentry who had seen the small column, and he became more alert.

The small British Indian platoon began to take up position outside and near about the second village gate at Vashum Tang. While waiting for an opportune moment to open fire, a villager who was with the British-Indian soldiers, feeling anxious for the villagers and interpreters, who were with the Japanese, suddenly yelled out a loud warning "Kep Kichi Haira", meaning, that they were about to shoot. As the ambush was given away, the British force started firing. The Japanese soldiers, the villagers and the interpreters who were at the school compound ran for cover into the nearby thick jungles. Phanitphang, on the contrary, ran straight into the hail of bullets towards the village. Miraculously, he escaped without a scratch. In the ambush, a Japanese soldier died, and two sustained injuries.

Much before the Japanese soldiers came to their country, the Tangkhul villagers had noticed "akap vanao", meaning warplanes, roaring and thundering over their skies; Two years back the Japanese had flown in from Tamanthi, Upper Myanmar, to bomb Imphal in May,1942. In the midst of the Japanese forces, regular passage through Tolloi, the villagers had also witnessed a returning Japanese squadron of fighter bombers which had bombed Imphal, being attacked by the Allied fighters over their skies on 6th May, 1944. In the attack, a twin seater Japanese fighter bomber was shot down over the Asui paddy fields of Maliew. Tolloi villagers (including my brother Mingmayang) swarmed down towards the field and found the plane grounded, but broken, its machine guns still firing intermittently. The pilot and the gunner were found dead on their seats. They were taken out from the mangled cockpit, and buried by the villagers (a humanitarian, caring gesture). Many villagers collected souvenirs, and one brought home a part of the broken wing span, which he erected as a showpiece and another, parts of the main engine block, which he used as a stepping stone. The young boys of the village collected memoralia.

During the Japanese occupation, my father Arim, acted as an interpreter for the village along with others, and frequently interacted with the Japanese Officers who passed through Tolloi. One such officer was Maj. Ishewara Masata, who looked after counter-intelligence in the

Tangkhul country. He probably took a liking for my father, for whenever in need, Maj. Masata would only call out for him, and addressed him as 'Lamo'. When Japan lost the battle for Imphal and Kohima, and its starving armies began their disorderly retreat, Maj. Masata bade goodbye to my father and presented him with a Shin Gento Type 98 Japanese Army Officer's sword. Maj. Masata probably did not survive the monsoon retreat.

Tolloi was an important village in the old days. It lost a brilliant student who was sniped to death in 1944, on a mistaken belief that he was a Japanese soldier (racial affinity- similar physical features), and another twelve students were blown to bits by a live World War II bomb explosion in 1947 near the school compound.[9]

The general Tangkhul public had no knowledge of who the Japanese were, and what their purpose was. They came to know about the Japanese through the administration, and their propaganda of the Japanese being a cruel and vicious people, and the need to help the British administration and the Allied Forces against the Japanese Army. The Tangkhul country for the first time became aware of the harbingers of war in the form of Japanese bombers and fighters flying over their homeland towards Imphal with terrifying noise and aggression. They then began to witness how these metal birds shoot at each other, and how they dropped bombs. Ten British warplanes and one Japanese bomber were shot down over the Tangkhul country. And quite as suddenly, the Japanese Army which had steam-rolled South East Asia, came into Ukhrul sub-division in thousands, and moved towards Shangshak and Ukhrul, through the river valleys of Maklang and Tuyungbi- on foot, cattle, buffaloes, horses, elephants, carts, and later in motor vehicles, through the

Khongkan Thana route in March 1944. They were also accompanied by Mayang (non-Manipuris) soldiers (INA), but one of them was a Tangkhul officer of the INA, Lt. Ringshi Keishing. The Japanese and the INA soldiers spoke of how the time had come, to throw the White people out of the country, and how it was time to co-operate with the Japanese people and its forces (this would have been to counter the British propaganda that the Japanese were cruel and vicious). To gain goodwill among the villagers, the cattle which they had brought from Myanmar for transporting their arms and supplies, were slaughtered for providing a feast in Tangkhul fashion, in villages which they considered were important to the Japanese. The Tangkhuls were however wary, as the British Government had warned them in advance about the Japanese, and directed them in no uncertain terms not to co-operate with the Japanese.[10]

(Although providing some important Tangkhul villages with meat, which was greatly relished by the Hill-people, was for the specific purpose of winning them over, nevertheless a feast in Tangkhul fashion is a great incidence on income, and was in effect, a generous action by the Japanese to the Tangkhul villagers).

The Japanese had approached India from Myanmar through three wings. The Southern prong, in the shape of the Japanese 58th regiment, under the command of Col. Utata Fukunaka encountered strong resistance near the Tangkhul village of Shangshak. The Japanese Commander Maj. General Miyakazi came and camped at the Tangkhul village of Nungshang, in preparation for the attack on Shangshak. The Battle at Shangshak was one of the fiercest and most important battle in the North-East, Ukhrul came to be occupied by the Japanese.[11] Arambam Angamba Singh had also commented that the Bloody Battle at Shangshak was the most critical engagement during the Battle of Imphal, World War II.

After the capture of Ukhrul and Shangshak, the Japanese took the northern route to Kohima via Tolloi village. The village Chief and elders of Tolloi were summoned for provisions and porters, and the Chief was detained to ensure good and timely action, (All Naga and Kuki villages have a Chief who is held in great esteem and wields considerable power and influence). The educated leaders of Phungton Village, comprising of Marasan Zimik, Tareya Lungleng, Phanitphang Vashum, Shangreiyorn Rungsung and Arim Raikhan, mobilised themselves as interpreters for the villages of Tolloi and Phungtom. Chief Phungshin Shangcham of Tolloi, who had earlier been detained by the Japanese over the issue of porters, was released through the intervention of the interpreters and their promise of giving the Japanese, timely supply of provisions and porters till the next stoppage point, which was usually, the nearest village. So, the Japanese were authoritarian in demanding provisions and services from the Chief and villagers, whose war it never was. This policy proved a great success, as the two villages were never harassed (the Japanese honor) or mistreated, throughout the period of the Japanese occupation. The Eastern Tangkhul villages bordering Myanmar were badly mistreated and capital punishment was also inflicted. (A strong contrast in the Japanese attitude towards these villages). Pastor Yarteo of Nambisha (Sarengla's) village, who married a girl from Hundung village was beheaded in Ukhrul, and his head impaled and exhibited on the main road in Ukhrul, for his failure to provide hundred porters as promised by him. He had contacted the village authorities of Hundung, and they had agreed to do the bidding. The villagers however had taken Zum and food. and while waiting for the appointed time, they had dozed off, missing the time schedule. (This definitely connotes a deadly stain on the character of the Japanese Army, who inflicted 'capital punishment' on an innocent Pastor-a man of God, for no fault of his own. They also did not give any allowances for Custom and human frailty- the villagers falling asleep not deliberately, after consuming Zum and food).

Tolloi became an important stoppage point for the Japanese in their war effort to capture Kohima and Imphal. But in Kohima, and other areas of the war front in the Naga Hills, and in Manipur, the Japanese were now facing an entrenched enemy with much better resources, a regular supply line, and enjoying popular local support. The Japanese Army were now too far stretched in difficult terrain, and facing an unfriendly populace. Their armies, which basically relied on living off the land and had banked heavily on using the supplies and provisions to be taken from Imphal to Kohima, soon ran out of supplies and provisions, with no sign of replenishment or reinforcement. Unable to crack the defence of the British at Imphal and Kohima, and facing definite starvation and death, the Japanese began retreating.

A Japanese diplomat, Toshi Kazu, had this to say of the Japanese defeat and retreat:

> Our expeditionary force of 2,70,000 men, which had marched to the gates of Imphal, in Manipur, India, met defeat. Most of the force perished in battle, or later of starvation (a tragic loss of life). The disaster of Imphal

was perhaps the worst of its kind, yet chronicled in the annals of war... the sick and the wounded had to be abandoned by the hundreds. (What trauma they must have experienced, helpless and prostrate in a foreign land). In order to avoid capture, these men were usually forced to seek death at their own hands. Only 70,000 of the original force survived.[12] 'The sheer waste of human lives is mind -boggling, and seeking death at one's own hand is not just traumatic, but requires a steely form if courage, and a particular kind of mind-set and most of the soldiers were very, very young, even below the age of Twenty.

Stories abound in Naga villages of how the retreating Japanese soldiers, many without arms, were followed by Nagas and slaughtered, (an inhuman act) of how they reached villages, begging for food with swollen mouths and bellies, how they would hungrily eat the food left uneaten by pigs in their troughs. The bodies of dead Japanese soldiers lay strewn on roads and paths (no shroud and nobody to perform the last rites) unable to be given proper burial by their comrades or villagers.[13] These statements give rise to the question of why the retreating Japanese were followed and slaughtered, was it retaliation for their invasion into the Tangkhul country, or was it a humane consideration, a mercy killing, as the retreating Japanese would have never survived the retreat, and would have suffered greatly, mentally, emotionally, physically till death provided relief. Today we look askance and abhor seeing human beings eating the leftovers in a pig's trough. Such actions must have caused unimaginable grief to the Japanese soldiers' families their father, sons, brothers had no grave cloth nor grave.

'The suffering, was not limited to the Japanese soldiers alone. The entire Tangkhul population had also been affected by the bombings, shootings, executions, mass scale requisition for transporting supplies and provisions, food shortages, diseases etc. In the small village of Ukhrulalone, two hundred deaths occurred between July to September 1944 due to the effects of the war.'[14] The Tangkhul country comprised of villages, and experiencing a new form of warfare, which took a heavy toll of life, must have been appalled and traumatised by the events and the course of this war. Arambam Angamba Singh commented: June end 1944, the battle for the Japanese has taken a serious turn. The fight is now broken by hunger, disease and the over whelming momentum of the enemy. But this has not broken the Japanese Bushido spirit. The fight was still on, in spite of mounting casualties.[15]

Nevertheless, when the tide of the battle turned, many Japanese soldiers must have experienced Post Traumatic Stress Disorder (PTSD) whether they admitted it or not. Even today, people in general look askance at individuals visiting a psychiatrist, or clinical psychologist for treatment in Asian countries. In the 1940's, the stigma of shame attached to seeking help from such professionals would have been much greater. And it would not have been possible for defeated soldiers who returned to Japan to seek such treatment- it would be a stain on their honor. A Japanese professor stated that: Memory is an exceptionally sensitive issue today, and the memories of that old generation themselves have changed as time went by. However, the study of the transformation of war memories, have been available in Japan. The most famous monograph I know in this regard is: Ryuichi Narita Zouho "Senso- Keiken" No

Sengoshi (Katara Reta Taiken, Shogen, Kioku, Iwanami, Shoten, 2020)- Post war History of "War Experience" -Narrated Experience/ Testimony/Memory, lwanami Shoten 2020.[16]

The immediate effect of World War II on the Tangkhuls and the Nagas in general was the realization of how behind they were in the scale of human civilisation and development. The war showed beyond doubt that the modern world would not he attained, possessed or reached through their traditional aged old ways of life, polity or culture, but through modern education alone. Many, therefore, began to turn to education to make a mark, and many more who never attended schools, turned towards Christianity, as it was seen to provide a base towards education and a better way of life. (Christianity and Modern Education had come to the Tangkhul Hills in the last decade of the nineteenth century, when Rev. Pettigrew established the first Christian Mission in Manipur at Ukhrul. But the war facilitated and pushed forward the agenda of Modem Education). These changes sounded the beginning of the end of the old village polity, its culture and belief system. The hold and the power of the village Chief began to fade. The war effectively ended the importance and the primacy of the village Chiefs and the Village Council in the affairs of the village, and the Tangkhul people at large. The Village state as the centre of the Tangkhul political world slowly began to give way to modern notions of one tribe and one larger people.[17] It was actually post-Independence measures that eroded the powers of the Chief and Village Council; the 73rd and 74th Amendments as also the establishment of Autonomous District Council in the Hills.

The demands of World War II automatically brought in

the educated people to represent the villages and its people before various authorities and new elites, and leaders began to emerge from those who received education. The successful example of Maj. Bob Khathing who was the first Tangkhul to get a commission in the British Indian Army, became an example worthy of emulation. The leadership of the people soon passed into the hands of those who were educated and who were Christians. During the latter part of the middle 1940's, the Tangkhul people directed their energy into rebuilding and reconstructing their lives, homes and fragile economic base, which had been totally destroyed during the disastrous World War II fought within their homes and countryside. [18]

The main impact of Christianity was felt in the sphere of education. The spread of education was facilitated by the British Political Agent. The impact of modernisation and introduction of Western education, enabled the Tribals to take advantage of new opportunities that come with learning, and in course of time, a new class emerged in tribal society- a middleclass, comprised mainly of bureaucrats. police and army officers, teachers, doctors, nurses, lawyers, theologians, pharmacists, writers, scientists and scholars.[19]

Major Ralengnao Bob Khathing's Story

The Story, "The Life of the Unsung Hero- Major Ralengnao Bob Khathing" by his son John S.R. Khathing provides the rationale of why his father became the Local Captain of Manipur Sector V force . Unfortunately, however as John stated in his Introduction, 'no records were available to him to cover his father's early life.'(In fact all files pertaining to his father have been kept confidential by the Government).

Ralengnao was quite happy as the Headmaster of Ukhrul ME school. The day before the summer vacation in May 1941, he was called by the SDO (Sub-Divisional Officer), who placed an application form for King's Commission in the Army, which had been sent by Mr. C. Grimson, the Political Agent of Manipur. Actually, when Ralengnao heard that war had been declared with Germany on 3rd September 1939, he was prepared to join the War Service, if his people had to report their being drafted as was done during the earlier war of 1914-1919. Thus, it was on the spur of the moment, that he had, written to Mr. C. Grimson, intimating his willingness to join the Army. That was a couple of years back, and he had actually forgotten about it, until now. He went ahead and filled the form and handed it over to the SDO Mr. SJ. Duncan, for forwarding it to the Political Agent. Thereafter, on his application being accepted, he had to undergo four gruelling and tough interviews: Primary Test at Imphal, Provincial Test at Shillong, Presidential Test at Fort Williams, Calcutta, and Federal Interview at Simla. He cleared all the interviews, and was selected and appointed to the KClO (King's Commissioned Indian Officer). The hill leaders were not keen that he join the war service, as he was till then, the only Graduate among the hill people of Manipur. After training and passing out of the Officer's Training School, Mhow, he was commissioned as a Second Lieutenant at the 19th Hyderabad Regiment. One day, while Ralengnao was giving field craft exercise to the recruits, the Company Commander, Maj. Thimmaya sent for him and handed over a telegram from GHQ (General Head Quarter) Delhi, ordering him to report immediately to GR Force, Jorhat. At that time, the Japanese Army had just overrun Burma, and the Allied troops were withdrawing to India through Manipur. He therefore rushed to Jorhat, and presented himself to Col. Rawdon Wright, who was in charge of organising 'V' Force in the North-East. The 'V' force was envisioned to be a guerrilla type of force, tasked with gathering intelligence on the Japanese, as well as harass the Japanese, once they entered Indian territory. Ralengnao was instructed to recruit volunteers from the hill people, bordering Burma, to the 'V' Force, as informers, guides, etc. Even though he was fresh as an army officer, the situation was such that he was promoted as local Captain. He reported to Major E. Murray at Imphal, officer in charge of Manipur Sector 'V' force organization. At this point of time, Ralengnao was assigned to operate in border areas of Manipur and Burma, to gather intelligence on the movement of the enemy troops, to harass enemy movements, etc. For this task, Ralengnao went to Ukhrul areas to meet Village Headman, and elders /leaders, to explain his mission. He was able to convince them, and they all agreed to help in the war effort and recruitment of men for 'V' Force commenced, starting first from Bungpa area, as refugees from Burma started pouring in.[20]

'I was studying in Class II at ME (Middle English) School, Ukhrul where Bob Khathing (later Major) was the Headmaster, when Major E. William visited our school to meet us, Tangkhul boys. After that meeting, our Headmaster asked us if anyone wanted to become a soldier. Twelve students including myself, said we wanted to join. Of the twelve, only four of us finally followed Major William to Imphal. The others were stopped by their parents. Some were even kept home with their hands and feet tied to stop them from running away. (A telling statement!).

When I reached Imphal, the Sahebs told me that I was a bit young to become a soldier but above the age to become a 'boy. Luckily, there was one Subedar Mangtse who came up, with the idea of keeping me as a 'boy' for just six months. I must have been above fifteen years old then. When the Japanese bombs fell in Imphal, we ran back home, but returned very soon. The bombs were dropped at many places including our camp at Kangla. All the residents of Imphal had fled to safer areas. Our camp was shifted to Uripok for some time and further shifted to the Jail area at Lambulane.

In the early days of the war, I was under the command of Major E D. Murray. We were defending the village of Gamnom and then we moved to Shangshak, where a fierce battle took place. After we withdrew from there, we had to march all the way upto Imphal. lt was a very tough withdrawal. We walked day and night continuously, and I can't even remember now how many days it took us to finally reach Imphal. I heard many stories of the village during the war. One person named Kachaching was killed by the Japanese because he refused to give up the boot he was wearing when they asked for it (a cruel, wasteful death). I retired as a Subedar from military service in 1972.[21]

After completing recruitment of around 5000 villagers as runners, informers, home guards and guerrillas from Tangkhul area right from Chingjarai in the North to Kasom-Khullen-Nambashi in the South, he (Maj. Bob Khathing) was ordered to go to South Manipur to organize the 'V' Force. He did so, established his Base Head Quarters at Chakpikarong to organize the V force from the area, lying North of Kasom Khulen-Nambashi and Khongtal in the South, covering the whole of Kabaw Valley (now a part of Myanmar). Later, he shifted his base headquarters to Sunle in Kabaw Valley itself, for better control of the region.

When the Japanese forces overran Shangshak and Ukhrul areas, he was again ordered to leave the South, and proceed onto the Tangkhul area to guide the British Army in counter-action against the Japanese. On reaching the Tangkhul area, he at once contacted most of the Tangkhul and 'V' force leaders, and found them fully ready to extend help. He at once organized the Intelligence system in all the villages. Here, the local leaders wonderfully united and organised a good network, to pass on information on Japanese movement to the Allied Forces. The very active co-operation extended by these local leaders and people helped the Allied Forces to regain control of the places which had earlier been over-run by the Japanese, within a time-frame shorter than anticipated or envisioned.

It should be mentioned that during the 'War, the American/British fellow officers were unable to pronounce ' Ralengnao' properly so they called him 'Robert'. This was further shortened to 'Bob[22] (He was later known as Major Bob Khathing even after he resigned from the Army and joined the Interim Government of Manipur State as the Minister-in-charge of Hill Administration, October 1947, and was Ambassador of India to Burma from 1972-1975).

Another Tangkhul has also stated why he became a soldier and supported the British Force. 'I was about fifteen years old at that time of the war in 1944. We were asked by the Indian soldiers to move out of our village. We ran to the nearby jungle with a small amount of food and some clothes. It was really hard to survive in the thick jungle without proper food and water.

Sometimes we saw planes flying above us. They dropped bombs at Ukhrul and some other areas. Luckily,

Bob Khathing, who was a Tangkhul army officer, instructed our elders on how to stay safe. He told them to spread our Tangkhul traditional shawl, whenever we saw a plane flying above us. That way, the pilot would easily know that we are civilians and would not harm us. (The shawl's importance was indeed critical to survival).

There were heavy gun battles between the Japanese and the British-Indian soldiers in and around our village for about a week. Our elders constantly worried about the conditions of our homes, the rice stockpile and livestock. They were also worried at the same time about the men from our village being used as porters by the Japanese. My elder brother was also one of them.My parents cried a lot thinking about him, wondering if he would make it back. (Uncertainty, fear, trauma were the lot of the village people). Luckily, he came back after some days. V.R. Azip composed a song in memory of the Battle of Shangshak and the soldiers who fought in the battle.

English Translation

Oh Subhash Chandra Bose of India

Borrowed army from Japanese Prime Minister Tojo,

The valiant soldiers from Japan fought their way through the North-Eastern hills.

Oh, during spring time of 1944

The Japanese army invaded British India and landed at Shangshak.

Valiant Japanese army sought India's help

Oh, against the British, under the leadership of Khongsan , Mahratta, Gurkha

Para regiment fought through the war

Oh, many valiant Japanese soldiers lost their lives.

Oh, the British Army having won the war,

We Shangshak people lived with the British Army in the woods for a brief period.

Oh, the valiant Japanese Army, many lost their lives.

We cannot forget the memory of the brave Japanese soldiers

Villagers spent seven months in the wooded jungle and returned home in October 1944.

The war made the lives of the people of Shangshak most miserable.

We will never forget the memory of the brave soldiers.[23]

The poem is poignant, but it resounds with praise for the brave Japanese soldiers, most of whom were very, very young. It only alludes to the compulsory stay of the villagers in the jungle- but one can easily visualise the trauma the villagers experienced for a long seven months. L. Ngaraipam also stated that although the Japanese soldiers took most of the adult men of his village (Shirui), including his brother for use as porters, the soldiers were good and did not misbehave with the women or children. (In other words, the Japanese were honorable). There was a group of three or four villagers, who were working with the 'V' force. These men stayed low, and did not do anything when the Japanese were there (probably from fear). The Japanese soldiers came back to our village after some days. They were in a terrible shape. One of them died in our village. He might have died of injuries or starvation. I do not remember what happened to his body. They asked for food and other things. We fled to the nearby jungle until the soldiers left.

Nobody in the village knew why the Japanese came to our village and why the battle took place. I came to know the reason of the fighting, and also about the INA some years after the war. [24] This account reveals that from fear and because of the demands of the Japanese soldiers, the villagers fled their homes. But more important, they were not aware of the reasons for the WW II Battle in Manipur. Yet they were forced to find shelter in the jungle.

In some cases, such as Shangshak, the sudden outbreak of fighting in 1944, made an orderly evacuation of citizens impossible. Shankazip Varu remembers the scenes at the time: There was chaos everywhere. The Indian soldiers, 'Maratha's as we called them, told us that they would be fighting here, and asked us to leave. Our village playground was filled with vehicles. We could see from a distance that many soldiers had reached our village. Nothing was certain. Was the fighting going to take place today or tomorrow? What will we eat? Everybody was running on all sides crying. The Indian soldiers also didn't tell us when the fighting will happen exactly. They just drove us out.

But when we reached the jungle at night, we could see guns firing, sending out bright lights from a distance. It was in one-way, great fun to watch the fireworks for young children like us. But the elders were crying, assuming their houses were burnt and their granaries and livestock gone. The Indian soldiers informed us that we won't be able to go back to our village for some time, since they will be there and they are fighting with the Japanese army. So, we took shelter in the ditches.[25] Once again, the dominant emotions of the villagers were fear, anxiety, grief and uncertainty and the trauma of being forced to leave their homes. N. Luikham recalls the arrival of the Japanese in Ukhrul:

> 'I vividly remember that it was a Sunday morning on the 20th March 1944, when we saw hundreds of vehicles of Allied forces in Ukhrul, to transport the things left behind by the soldiers at the Ukhrul HQ. After a day or two, hordes of Japanese soldiers reached Ukhrul HQ without a fight, as Allied forces had left two days earlier. But before entering the Ukhrul HQ one brave Japanese soldier came without a shirt, holding a sword. But there was no enemy force to shoot him, except children and civilians looking at him with curiosity: 'Only one soldier without gun'. (A Novelty) He then sat down. Few minutes after, we saw many Japanese soldiers coming out from all sides. Occupation of Ukhrul was complete! Luikham also refers to the first Japanese as 'brave', an adjective commonly used to describe the soldiers of the JIA, and the Japanese troops entered in a manner, that was not known to the villagers, until they crowded and occupied Ukhrul-a tribute to their military strategy.

'After occupation of Ukhrul HQ, the Chief and his Council Members and all leaders met the Japanese commanders who were very friendly and said that Japanese and Tangkhul were brothers (of Mongoloid stock); not many days later the people were given many cows, free of cost for food by the Japanese. It was a great economic elation as people got to eat beef (by every house); we praised the Japanese as Allied Forces never gave us things free of cost like that, we saw the generosity of the Japanese forces in the midst of the war devastation'.[26] The villagers were attracted both by the friendly nature and the generosity of the Japanese. It was customary for villagers who gave a feast to invite all in the village to partake of the feast, and the main dish would be made from meat. (As to common ethnicity, similarities between the people of Manipur and Japan have been highlighted in the Introduction).

As the Battle of Imphal wore on, the problem of supplies for the Japanese worsened ...the Japanese turned to the civilian population to meet their needs. According to one report, as the situation became more desperate in the hills, the Japanese seized any available paddy and killed livestock; if they paid, it was said to be via Japanese Burma notes or forged Rs.10 British India notes[27]

N Lokendra Singh writes of the local coolies of the hills: The treatment of the local coolies although fine in the beginning became more torturous. Coolies were made to carry loads for long distances, and occasionally they used to be tied up at night to prevent escaping.[28]

A.S. Arthur has also given an account of his village Shangshak: The Japanese occupied the area for about four months. But they were kind people, they did not harm or torture anyone. During those days, there were only about six houses where the main village now is. The Japanese occupied that entire area. Apart from those houses, the entire area was a jungle. The 'V' force informed the British soldiers about their location. Thats' when a fighter plane crashed in the area when they were trying to the bomb the jungle. The pilot died; I don't know what happened of the other one. My father and some others buried the pilot in a trench, because the Japanese would not bury him for several days.

There were two Japanese soldiers who were trying to flee. They came and took shelter in our hut one had a knife with him. The other one was very sick and looked like he would die soon. We decided to hand them over to the

British soldiers, otherwise the sick soldier would have died. We knew the British who had just re-captured Shangshak, would not kill them, but treat them as prisoners of war. But that soldier who could barely walk, left the hut and took shelter in the field. The other soldier was waiting in the hut for us to give him some rice. He asked for a matchbox and when he was trying to light it, my cousin reached for his knife, but the soldier jumped up, grabbed his knife and ran off. [29] It is obvious that the Tangkhuls did not resent the Japanese, in fact despite the latter being invaders, it was the Tangkhuls who took the initiative to bury the dead Japanese pilot on humanitarian grounds. They also felt compassion for the sick Japanese soldier, and informed the British, as they were afraid, he would die, he was so ill, and they believed that he would be in better hands, as they could not care or treat his sickness. But some villagers like Arthur's cousin who grabbed the knife may have had some suspicion about the two Japanese soldiers who were trying to run away.

'We went to look for the other one, found him, and first brought him back to the hut to feed him...my sister who was feeding him, reached up to clean the rice from his chin, but it turned out to be maggots which had infested the lower portion of his face. We later took him to the British camp. We know they took care of him but I don't know what became of him.' One feels pity for the young sick Japanese who aroused so much compassion in the heart of those Tangkhuls villagers.

'The only time the Japanese killed someone in the village was, when a gentleman from Lungphu, his name was Yarteo, promised to give them about forty coolies, but did not keep his promise. They shot him. Apart from that one incident, there were never any trouble with the Japanese.[30] (This incident has already been explained in detail in Home Raikhan's Naga History). Some people among the Tangkhuls are said to have supported the Japanese around Ukhrul. In particular, there is a mention of a co-operation committee, divided into three departments, to provide intelligence, supplies and labour to the Japanese in the area. But for the most part, the Tangkhul Nagas did not help the Japanese-INA.[31]

The Administrative Report of 1943-44 seems to corroborate this view. (With reference to the eviction of the Japanese).

This eviction was first taken in hand in the Ukhrul area where the local hill man had throughout been a thorn in the side of the Japanese of whom a preliminary account showed that they captured 79 and killed 95. Shortly, before they left, the Japanese held meetings in the villages of Maipi and Khengoi at which a Japanese officer told headmen: We came 5,000 strong, but we had 3,000 casualties. We are withdrawing to Mawlaik and will return in December. When we came, we trusted Kukis and Nagas but they deceived us. Next time we come, we will have no mercy on the civilian population.[32] Yet from the accounts of the Tangkhul themselves, they found the Japanese both valiant and kind. Although, they themselves experienced fear and trauma and were forced to vacate their homes during the duration of the war.

A Kuki Story

The reactions of the Kukis to the Japanese was in many ways very different to that of the Tangkhuls.

Dr. Michael Lunminthang has written a poignant

account of his grand uncle, to whom he dedicated this article:

Pu Capt. Lamkhothang of INA The Hill Patriot of Japan Gal 'No Ordinary Person'.

'A few days ago, when I was reading through the diary of my late granduncle, I came across a line, which ignited my curiosity.

"I am not an ordinary man, I was a Captain for the Independence of India".

In fact, I saw the line repeated again on other pages of his old, tatty, ragged diary, where he wrote some of his reflections, and drafted his official communications. I reflected on the line, and many questions emerged: What motivated him to write that particular phrase? Was it his dominating spirit? Were those his self-motivating, silent words? Was he echoing the voices of those on the fringe')? There are many more questions that can be pondered upon, but sadly, there are no answers for all of them.

Pu (Kuki gentleman usually have 'Pu' prefixed before their names) Lamkhothang loved the word 'Patriot' to describe himself. He confessed he had the zeal to liberate his people from the bondage, since his childhood. (This bondage probably refers to the treatment meted out to the Kukis by the Colonial Authorities following the Kuki War of 1917 -1919- also referred to as the Kuki Rebellion or Kuki War of Independence). Born and brought up in a small village of Wayang, situated in the wilderness of Dingpi Ridge, surrounded by Amazon-like Forest, where the nearest town is three to four days on foot, he was determined to do something for his country. To commit to his patriotic yearning, he joined the Assam Regiment in 1939. Everything was peaceful and he got married and settled down, and like any other normal Indian Jawan, left his wife and kids at home, to serve the nation, wherever duty called.

However, the idyllic life of the new Jawan was short-lived, as the world plunged into another war. The British who controlled India at that time joined World War II, and India became a base for the Allied powers. But India was safe from destructions and bombings. Unexpectedly, the fringe areas bordering Burma felt the maximum casualty of war. The damage and bombings were so severe, many historians termed it as "Stalingrad of the East", when measuring the destruction caused by the war. The Battles of Kohima and Imphal were later voted as "Britain's Greatest Battle " during World War II. (The Battle of lmphal has been voted as Britain's Greatest Battle by the National Army Museum, UK on 20th April 2013- L. Ashok Kumar in Souvenir-70th Anniversary Battle of Imphal op.cit pg17).

The years 1942-43 were challenging times for people living in the trans-border region of India and Burma. The Japanese/INA after annexing Burma, planned their 'Forward Policy', and started recruiting the ethnic communities in their intelligence networks of Hikari Kikan (Rising Sun Organisation) and Nishi Kikan (Western Organisation). Along with the enrollment, Netaji Subhash Chandra Bose made appeals to the people to support the Japanese and the INA. Simultaneously, the British in India, did not remain silent to the developments. They also recruited the same communities in the guerilla insurgent Organisation known as 'V' Force. It was a difficult time for the people of the region, when two great campaigns, knocked on every door, for their selfish motives.

It was at this juncture, that Pu Nohhao, the Chief of Wayang village, and father of Pu Lamkhothang was tortured and arrested for attending a meeting at Chahmol village, that was summoned by the Japanese Army. This episode (of brutality) infuriated the young jawan of the Assam Regiment. He did not believe how, the same country for which he took a solemn oath of allegiance, could not protect his own family; He was full of questions, and was a disturbed man in the barracks of the 4th Battalion.

The incident became a turning point in his life. He took a short leave/holiday from his regiment, and rushed to his village. He was able to see the developments and the preparations for war more closely. His inner zeal to liberate his country became intensified. His childhood dream of patriotism was renewed. He was determined not to return (to his regiment). He went down to Burma, met the Japanese Army and the 1NA. (Manipur shares an international border with Myanmar). Believing in the promises of Bose, he was determined to rekindle his childhood dream 'to free his country and his people'. He changed his allegiance and joined the INA. The Japanese INA welcomed him wholeheartedly, and appointed him as Captain (he was earlier only a 'Jawan' of the Assam Regiment, despite being the son of a Chief). Later on, he was promoted as Civil Organizer and Facilitator. With his contribution, he was able to convince members of his community and neighbouring tribes to support the INA. At the peak of the war, he was asked to join the combat force. He led many battles of the Japanese/INA, and was lucky enough to survive the war. For his very act of patriotism, he was captured, tortured, jailed and released only after the war ended.

For the Patriots of the Hills, it is worth remembering

the words of R. Palta, the personal Intelligence officer of NSC Bose in his book: 'My Adventures with the INA', where he acknowledged the contributions. He wrote, "the local population on the borders of India on the whole, whole-heartedly welcomed and helped the INA. The Kuki people at the risk of their lives, assisted the INA whole-heartedly. The INA had nothing to pay back for such support, except 'Thank You' and 'Jai Hind'.

My memories take me back to my village Wayang in the early 1980's, where we as kids, ran after him barefoot in shorts, asking stories of his ordeal during the war...again and again. To accommodate the childhood curiosities, he would sing songs that they sang during his days in the army. Sometimes, he told us the jokes he remembered, but every time he would have a different and interesting story to share. Festivals and Celebrations were lively and merry, because he would always have something special for the occasion. But then he passed away in the hands of few villagers, whom he loved so dearly, while we the kids who ran beside him for stories, left the village for our schooling. Many years have passed by with many political changes since then. The Japanese who lost the war, deleted the whole episode from their children's curricular, the narratives of the INA are forgotten by the nation (in this, the 125th Birth Anniversary Year of Netaji, attempts are being made to highlight the achievements and contributions of Netaji and the INA to the Freedom Movement of India), and the life of NSC Bose is still a mystery. (Many of the files relating to Netaji have not been declassified by the Government). The serene village was deserted due to insurgencies and land-mines. But the War and the Heroes of Japan-Gal(war),lived through songs and stories of people who remember them.'[33]

The Story as told to me by Michael makes it very clear that first and foremost, Pu Lamkhothang was a sincere patriot, who wanted to free his country from foreign domination. It also highlights the different attitudes of the British on the one hand and the Japanese/INA forces on the other, towards the Kukis. This must have been one of the reasons why a large number of Kukis supported the Japanese and the INA both passively and actively.

Michael had stated that Japan Gal (Lan) is a localised name signifying the importance of the Japanese over the British. The Tangkhul view already stated is different. But there was a general perception that the Japanese Army was 'invincible.' Another reason cited for the Kuki inclination towards the Japanese was racial closeness. However, his grandparents' knowledge of the Governance system around the world must have been limited. In addition, there was a strong campaign that the Kukis and the Japanese were brothers from the same mother. Dolly Kikon talks about an incident where a Japanese man shed tears when he saw fermented soyabean 'akhuni' in Nagamese, during the Japan War. (Akhuni is a delicacy in North East India and in Japan). The Japanese never interfered in the politics and life of the people. My grandparents said that they respected our women, children and people. There was no rape (so common in war-time) reported during their short alliance.[34] Michael's granduncle commanded respect and was one of the highest-ranking officers among the Kukis during the duration of the war.

The Hills occupy nine-tenth of the geographical area of Manipur. As stated earlier, in 1941, the population or the state was 5,12,069. Of which some 343,000 lived in the Imphal Valley and 1,68,000 lived in the Hills.[35]

About the undying spirit of the Kukis for 'Freedom', Gangte wrote: Their (Kukis) virtue of sacrificial spirit prompted them to join the INA in hundreds. They were a gallant and a martial lot, who among the people of North East India, could challenge the invincible power of the 'British Empire'. There are about 150 Kuki INA pensioners, about 80 of them, were listed in Freedom Fighters of Manipur.[36]

The failure of the Anglo-Kuki War (1917-1919), was a severe blow not only to the powers of the Kuki-Rajahs, but also to the Kukis in general. They were now subjected to intensified colonial presence and exploitation. (The Government of India approved the arrangements which the Local Government proposed to make in connection with the deportation of the Chiefs, and their proposal for periodic examination of their cases, in order to consider the reduction of the periods of deportation if circumstances permit- Priyadarshini M. Gangte, Souvenir 2006, Anglo Kuki War 1917-1919, pg.42).

They also had to contend with other problems. In addition to the Lambus,, there was a hierarchy of colonial officials, the Sub-Divisional Officer, assisted by Lam-Subedars, Mohiris, interpreters, etc. The erstwhile old taxes were vigorously collected with certain additional ones. Besides, more Assam Rifles post were established and stationed in strategic positions.[37] The advent of World War II further exacerbated the situation. Being in the militarily operational zone, the hillman were 'impressed' for various military projects such as forced labour. The hillman were also used as porters.[38]

Besides, the influx of refugees (from Burma) and

laborers brought several new strains of malaria, dysentery, small- pox and cholera, which even infected livestock. This was exacerbated by crop failure in the hills since 1942. Many Kukis fled their homes to refugee camps set up by some generous Kuki Chiefs. The coming of the INA-Japanese forces were considered to be-'God send saviors' by the Kukis, to free themselves of colonial yoke.[39] The leaflets which were air dropped for local support were note-worthy: Now is the time for India to get her Independence. This is the Golden opportunity to drive the British out of India. The Imperial Japanese Force have full power and are very sincere in their decision to assist you fight against Britain.[40]

The Kukis were one of the first groups to contact the Indo-Japanese forces in the Chindwin valley (Burma). A Central Intelligence Officer (Assam), E.T.D. Lambert in his report noted that the Kukis first contacted the Japanese in and around the area in Chindwin belt in 1943.[41] The Kukis collaborated with them to oust the British from their ancestral land, so that their lost freedom maybe restored once again. In retaliation, the British unleashed a reign of terror on the Kuki villages which were found to be in the list of villages helping the INA Japanese forces. The INA and the Japanese personnel depended increasingly on the ration and the livestock of the local people. All the male folk and the young women in the occupied villages, were engaged in pounding rice day and night, to feed the soldiers. Male folk also served as coolies and porters. The Japanese conversed with the local people through the Gurkhali sepoys serving in the INA. The Chief of Saikot was encouraged by the Japanese to open a school, a village school at Saikot was opened by the Japanese, where the Japanese language and script were taught.[42] (That would mean that in 1944 already the Japanese were advocating learning of the Japanese language and script). It was compulsory for those attending the school to memorise the Japanese National Anthem. Some who attended the school remember the Anthem as:

Aronga Khitah

Aronga Khitah

Kokhoni Khitah

Jammani Khitah

Nanimo Khitah

The words maybe akin to, but are not a part of the Japanese National Anthem which goes:

Kimi-ga-yowa

Chiyo Ni yachi yoni

Sazare - ishi no

Iwao to Narite

Koke no musu made

English Translation

Under your beloved life,

Continue for a thousand,

eight Thousand generation's

Until the tiny pebbles

Grow into massive boulders

Lush with moss.[43]

The school soon shut because of the bombings but the Kukis co-operation was appreciated; in the words of a high-ranking INA Commander: 'I have come all the way from Rangoon. I am so thrilled, and particularly grateful to you for what you and your villagers have done for my soldiers...when India achieves her freedom, you folks will never be forgotten.[44] It is apparent that the Kukis were inclined towards and reposed faith in the Japanese-INA forces, but they were not completely swayed by the Japanese propaganda 'The Kukis" believed that there was no country like theirs, no chief greater than theirs, no religion like theirs, nothing whatsoever to match their own. They did not like any foreigners infringing upon their right of living independently. This was manifested in the hostile relationship between the Kukis and the British in their first contact. The Kukis had not at any stage of their relationship with the British, accepted British domination, and as such, despite subjugation in the 1917-1919 war, their inherent instinct for a fight to free themselves from foreign yoke never died in thcm.[45]

Japanese Propaganda ran on these lines

We have come to your country to set you free from the British bondage. They (British)seek their own good and satisfaction. Their aim is to get all for themselves...leaving the other tribes, races and nations hungry. (No doubt many Britishers did believe then that the 'sun would never set on their Empire) They regard you and we (Japanese) to be lower than dogs, swine, cats and animals... we being of the same race, we shall equally lift you up in the same level of civilisation in which we are living, we shall not rule over you, but you will rule over yourselves. We shall be brothers and friends as we are all Mongolians. We shall help one another...the help you have given and will give us, we shall never forget, you will get back all things in double after Imphal is fallen:[46]

The parallel made to animals is unfortunate, and it is difficult to accept that the British viewed the Kukis or the Japanese in this light. Ethnicity is a factor which binds people together and undoubtedly both the Kukis and the Japanese were of Mongolian origin. The propaganda was designed to appeal to the ardent desire for freedom by the Kukis. The Kukis had been smarting under the 'intensified administrative and political control of British Imperial Power' after the Anglo-Kuki War. Though the Kukis were defeated in the Anglo-Kuki War, their discontent against the British did not cow them down. In spite of their untold sufferings during and after the war, their love for freedom and the instinct to fight, never died. The historical significance of the Anglo-Kuki War of 1917-1919 lies in the fact that it established strong and valuable local tradition of resistance to the British rule.[47]

The promises made by the Japanese through their propaganda could not be translated into reality, as the Japanese forces suffered a crushing defeat at the hands of the Allied Forces. The Kukis must have felt despondent and experienced grief and despair. But their encounter and interaction with the Japanese also changed their world view. One Onkholet Haokip (Japan Pakang) retreated along with the Japanese and preferred to follow them even upto Japan, as he could not bear to stay in his own land in the face of the enemy's domination.[48]

Pu Japan Pakang composed a dirge to mark his departure for Japan:

Kathi leh, toni, pha, lkhat

Kahin leh janglei chung chon ding.

English Translation

If I die, it is destined for me,

If I live, I shall be exonerated worldwide.

The meaning behind the eulogy is that Pu Japan Pakang planned to embark upon great deeds for the Kukis after he reached Japan. To this day, Kukis refer to the World War II as 'Japan Gal' (Japanese War) not 'British Gal' (British War):[49] There is no tangible estimate of the number of Kukis who actively assisted the Indo-Japanese forces. But Grimson had remarked: 'The Kukis, particularly dislike working for other people. In fact, the very presence of large military personnel itself was disliked: the influences of so many British Indian troops of various classes, and by their habit of treating (Hill people) strangers, all men and women in the hills let alone those who know little education, all felt their differences more:[50] In the Memorandum of the Kuki INA veterans, submitted to the Chief Minister of Manipur, there were almost 6000 Kukis, who actively helped.[51] This does not mean that the entire Kuki community stood behind the INA-Japanese forces in one way or the other. However, their popular support and consciousness is embedded in their folk songs for example:

Pummei chang dang ijat in hatjongleh;

Japan Meipum chang sanga hatjo ding umlou

Hungkon uvo Japante;

Thingmang damnoi sunsot hijong leh kangah uve.

English Translation

Of all the cannons;

Japan cannons are the strongest;

Japanese! March on;

We are waiting for you in the deep forest.

They provoked and made fun of the British:

Hungwo Sapkangte;

Nalaito ding Japan galhat meltheisa;

Tulai Sorkar mangkang in tho non;

Lungdei gol angkoi ponte

English Translation

March on Britishers

Japanese soldiers are here to kill you:

Japanese bravery is known to all;

British power wants to imitate; but it will be impossible.[52]

Phaneng Haokip stated: 'The Japanese army arrived in our area (Gamnom Village), and set up camps. They spent time with us, and would often take rice and vegetables from us, which we readily gave. (Illustrates the affinity between the Kukis and the Japanese). There was no case of the Japanese harassing the villagers during their stay.

I was a young girl during the war. When the Japanese started retreating from Manipur,my (would be) husband, who was already a teenage boy, followed them and stayed with them (similar to Pu Japan Pakang) at Molnoi and Kaungkam area of Burma for some time. That was how he became a part of the Azad Hind Fauj (INA). Some people believe that he must have been forcefully used by the Japanese soldiers to carry their goods as a porter. (This was a common practice, current even in the Tangkhul hills). But the truth was that he followed the Japanese on his own, since he was really interested in joining them. Phaneng has referred to the Battle of Imphal as 'Japan Gaal' She has also mentioned that a couple of civilians were killed in air raids, but she believed them to be Government planes, as she could never imagine Japanese planes attacking their villages. [53] An accolade to the Japanese- the trust placed by the villagers in them.

Nemjahat Touthang's husband Shokholet Touthang was in the Burmese Army during the Japanese Gaal, along with his friend Haonoh, who surrendered to the Japanese. Haonoh's whereabouts remained unknown. Shokholet's unit fought a number of times against the Japanese; there were more Japanese casualties as their army was ravaged by hunger and disease. In death sadly, many of the dead bodies were left unattended, although much interest was evinced in their belongings by the locals- a similar reaction to the Tangkhuls who greatly valued Japanese guns, swords etc.

Nemjahat was about twelve years of age when the Japanese came to her village Khoikai situated on the Indo-Myanmar border, currently in Kamjong District. She along with others left home and sought refuge in Tangkhul huts built in the fields.[54] T. Holkhongam Songthu was only ten years old when he heard his elders refer to Japan spies in his village Khoikai. He refers to a Paokhomang who worked as a messenger and interpreter for the Japanese and refers to British and Japanese planes flying overhead. The villagers sought shelter in the jungle for a long three months and survived on their meagre stock of rice. He refers to a change in the demeanour of the Japanese towards the villagers- initially friendly, they became hostile -later on and appropriated the village stock of grain and livestock. What is significant in his account, is a reference to two villagers being blindfolded, dragged to many places and finally bayoneted to death. The reason for this action was not known but it does not accord with the statements made by other Kukis about the Japanese not harassing them. It is however similar to the incident already narrated about a Tangkhul Pastor who was killed by the Japanese.

Holkhongam also refers to the dead bodies of Japanese soldiers being left unattended. Again, there was no coffin or grave for the valiant soldiers, but perhaps this can be attributed to the nature of the war. As was customary, the villagers collected many articles left over from the war, but had to surrender them when one Haokholet, an Assistant Sub-Inspector took them away, probably to be deposited with the Government. Although every village Chief was given a muzzle-loading rifle to defend his village, the Chief of Khoikai did not get one.[55]

Because of the Japanese bombing in Imphal and other areas Mangkholen Misao who was studying at Kangpokpi Mission in 1942, returned to his village Makokching in Saikul sub-division as all schools were closed. Being aware of the approaching war, the villagers hid rice and other belongings in small huts built in the nearby jungle and dug trenches around their homes to hide in. When the Japanese soldiers arrived, Mangkholen's parents took his younger brother, two pots and a few clothes and sheltered at Tusam village; but he and two friends remained till hunger forced them to Tusam. The Japanese who brought horses, left two behind, so the boys played with them, until advised for safety reasons not to do so. They killed the horses and buried the horses, but the village was bombarded by the British. Mangkholen has also shown two sides of the Japanese soldiers' character. On the one hand, because of necessity(starvation), the latter appropriated food and livestock of the. villagers. But they were good people and provided effective medicines to the sick. There was heavy fighting and ultimately the Japanese retreated but not before begging the villagers for food- they put the rice in backpacks for their onward journey. This narration is similar to others, whose villages were invaded by the Japanese soldiers. Shelling by the British continued apace. One wounded Saheb unarmed, and in a 'terrible condition' came to the village, where Mangkholen treated his wounds with local herbs and stopped the bleeding. The Britisher was astonished and wanted to take him to Imphal, that was not possible, so he was taken to the nearest camp at Pukhao. The treatment and the conveyance of this Saheb by Misao was a splendid humanitarian gesture.

Misao mentioned that Kangpokpi Mission Compound was a stronghold of the Japanese. The Japanese soldiers used the houses and the Government buildings in the village. There were two hospitals in the area and the Japanese stayed there too. Trenches and bunkers were however built by both the Japanese and the British. In essence, the Japanese occupied all the built-up area of Kangpokpi, leaving its denizens to fend for themselves.

Misao's present house was built in Kangpokpi in 1946, and he recalled that many years after the war, some Japanese people came on a bone recovery mission and requested his assistance. He showed them a grave site, but they found bones which were not human. They gave a gift to Misao.[56]

There is a pattern in the statements made viz. that when the Japanese soldiers occupied the built areas of a village, the local population had to find shelter in the countryside or nearby jungle. The soldiers always requisitioned food supplies because they were starving but they were simultaneously courteous to the native population, who reciprocated this courtesy. Thirdly, the dead bodies of the soldiers were usually left where they were. This makes the search for the recovery of 'bones' a very difficult one.

Paojalhing got married at the age of seventeen to a man from Saikul. Within a week, the Japanese arrived at Saikul on horses and informed the local residents that they would capture Manipur in seven days (many soldiers must have believed that they were a part of an invincible army), and thereafter give the people, everything they wanted. But Government soldiers came and commenced bombing villages- the Japanese collected rice and also ate Ganja leaves from the Ganja farms; some died of diarrohea, after consuming wild plants like 'kege Manbi (bellyache). When fighting commenced, Paojalhing leaving behind her 'awonpot' (all the gifts given at the time of her marriage) fled to the hills. Her husband told her that a high-ranking British Officer had been killed, but the body could not be traced after the war. Because of continuous fighting, the villagers who had left were unable to even sleep.

She also mentions that the Japanese came and took food and other things from their village and were accompanied by Hindi-speaking Indian interpreters. The last appears surprising as neither the tribal villagers or the Japanese would have possessed proficiency in speaking Hindi. This is evident from Paojalhing's statement that the villagers and the Japanese conversed through sign-language. Although the Japanese as Misao also stated were good and helpful and provided medicines, the villagers took the precaution of always being ready to move to a safer place, and cooked and ate their meals very early, so that the Japanese could not come and take it away

Ultimately, she and her husband moved to Imphal as the latter was working as an interpreter for the British. She however did not cite any reason why her husband did so. For her, 'the war was exciting as well as terrible at the same time'.[57]

Y.L. Joseph has a different story to tell about the Japanese soldiers who entered his village and searched every house for food. Such behavior could not be condoned by the womenfolk, so the menfolk went to the Japanese camp and complained. They were fortunate that the camp commander had a Pangal (Manipuri Muslim) interpreter. The officer castigated his men, made them return all clothes they had appropriated and slapped them. He apologised to the villagers and stated that the soldiers could beg for food, but never take it forcibly. Such honorable conduct impressed the villagers, who pounded rice daily for the Japanese, who paid them in Japanese money. The officer after fifteen days announced that they were going to attack the British forces and conquer Imphal. Surprisingly, he asked the villagers to offer prayers, and used a villager as a guide. The Japanese failed in their mission, but the villagers never came across any wounded soldiers. They were advised to move out by the retreating Japanese, and when they finally returned, they found themselves 'homeless'- their village on the Mapao Range had been completely destroyed. When Joseph ventured up the hill where the Japanese camp had been located, he discovered many guns and other war remains-he kept two Japanese rifles and one British rifle but preferred the former as it was lighter. Later, as was the practice, the villagers had to deposit all guns with the Government.[58]

L. Achung Kom who had studied upto class VI at Chinga High School in Imphal and who knew a bit of English, Hindi and Bengali was an intrepid individual, who upon learning of the imminent arrival of the Japanese, sent all women, children and elders of his village to safer places. Perhaps not knowing or understanding what damage a small bullet can cause, he took umbrage when he learnt that some Japanese soldiers looted things of a village girl. He demanded and retrieved the looted articles. He was then summoned by a Japanese officer who asked him if he spoke Hindi, and he answered 'a little'. The officer asked him to stay with him and Achung accompanied him and guided him to many places.' The officer entrusted him with the office of cashier, and gave him a certificate for his services. After the war, he too collected five Japanese rifles and five British rifles and some pistols, but later had to surrender it to the Government.

Achung recalls being arrested along with four other villages for helping the Japanese- he was regarded as the leader as he knew Hindi and English. Their hands were tied tightly with telephone wire and they were kept at Bishenpur. One British officer passing by commenced talking to him in Hindi and English, and he gave him information on the Japanese and their locations of a hospital and INA camp at Laimanai and army camp at Sadu. The British officer gave them food and set them free.[59]

The Japanese officer was Captain Teiyo who taught Kom some Japanese as also the sword dance. Casualties of war needed to be carried so Kom arranged for Kom, Kabui and Aimol men to carry the wounded and dead soldiers to Sadu and the Japanese hospital at Laimanai.

Achung took the initiative when Captain Teiyo suspected a road block was a trap for him and his men. Achung removed the bamboos blocking the road; the Captain impressed by his gallantry, took off his shirt and gave it to him. (This illustrates the high respect which Achung was accorded- similar in some manner to the Mughal Emperor of India divesting himself of a personal garment and placing it over a noble's shoulders as a sign of honor). After spending two and a half months with the Japanese, Achung went back to his village (upper Kom, Keirap) but shells of the British artillery fell continuously, so he and others went to meet and discuss the matter with a British officer, and stayed inside the British position. But as mentioned, they were arrested, bound and blindfolded and beaten black and blue. They were then confined in a small dark bunker for five days without food- a cruel inhuman punishment. Probably, they would have perished but for the intervention of a particular British Officer who freed them, once he got the required information from Achung about the Japanese.

Achung helped first the Japanese who initially he challenged and then the British- was he playing both sides of the fence for purposes of survival. Undoubtedly because the Battle of lmphal was not his war.[60]

Gachung Dangmei who was in his teens when the Japanese came to his village, Laimanai which occupied a strategic position. They set up a large hospital where many top-ranking officers were stationed. This means that the Japanese Army prepared for casualties and for treatment of the injured or sick soldiers. But it must have been quite a feat for them to construct a hospital in a foreign place, which they were not familiar with. Before the Japanese arrived, bombs destroyed the village forcing the inhabitants to flee.

But they first spent ten days with the Japanese-Why would they have done that? The Japanese as was usual started searching for rice and other food items, and even pounding the rice. Probably, not being adept in the latter, they were unable to feed their horses. They requested young boys to assist in the task and as customary, paid them in Japanese currency.

Gachung portrayed the Japanese as valiant and fearless- a people who did not indulge in harassment of women and children. They even offered the sick villagers medicine, but the latter were afraid to accept. Gachung and others sheltered at Khoupum but twenty died there- the result of the war. After the war, the villagers returned to their village and again as usual, collected what the Japanese had left behind particularly guns, which again had to be later surrendered to the Government. In later years, some Japanese armed with a device to detect 'bones' came to collect the bones of the fallen soldiers, and performed particular rituals.[61]

Th. Chomlal Aimol was about fifteen years when the Japan-Laan occurred. As the Japanese asked his village for rice, the village elders held a meeting and agreed to share their rice stock with the Japanese. But the Japanese also requested for shelter and were assigned a bamboo grove for that purpose. Although the village produced much rice, the continuous demands of the Japanese for 'Kome'(rice) created logistic problems. Some village boys gave assistance in carrying wounded soldiers to the hospital at Laimanai.

The villagers were forced to move more than once in their search for shelter, but they found the Japanese entrenched all over. They, out of deprivation, snatched food of the villagers and forced women to cook twice to meet their pangs of hunger. However, they were well behaved and killed nobody. The Japanese officers were armed with swords. After, they left, their possessions were acquired by the villagers who however had to surrender the guns. After the war, some Japanese came to find the bones of the dead soldiers, to bury them with rituals which aroused emotions of severe grief.[62]

Thanglengir Chiru at the age of thirteen, experienced much trauma when his father went to find out which soldiers were going to their village, and did not return for a considerable length of time. He had been forced to stay and also assist the Japanese in carrying their wounded comrades. The continuous fighting terrified the villagers; their woes were- exacerbated by the Japanese search for rice and killing of livestock. They were forced to flee. But Chiru's father was on one occasion disturbed by a Japanese soldier who came and ate his chicken curry- he complained to a Japanese officer, who penalised the soldier. The intense fighting forced the villagers to hide in trenches, but ultimately, they left for Thanjing Chiru. Thanglengir's father had to leave behind the boy's grandmother and aunt as they were too old and weary to travel- a heart wrenching moment; as when the family returned, they found only their remains. The villagers had to start life from scratch- build homes, wait to cultivate till the appropriate season. Agruelling task after the trauma, they had already undergone. In their village, they found many bodies but could not identity to which forces they belonged. [63]

In 1942, Hankholun Kuki was able to fulfill his ambition of getting recruited as a rifleman in 3rd Assam Rifles at Kohima. His training was condensed from 11 months to 2 or 3 months because of the impending Japanese invasions.

The soldiers were Indian, but the officers British, as was the case with Pu Lamkhothang who joined the Assam Regiment initially. After Hankholun's training, his unit comprising of two platoons was named as V- force, and once again, it was put under the command of a British officer. The force was provided with some food items, including cigarettes and rum but when supplies diminished, a half ration system was instituted and unedible rice was given to the soldiers to eat. They revolted, and the half ration system was discontinued. Henkholun served in Nagaland mainly and mentioned a valiant British captain who fought the Japanese alone. The Japanese used the same propaganda that they used in Manipur-that the Japanese and Indian people are one, and should join together and fight for India's freedom against the British. He says the Japanese attacked at night and their planes were fast and small and flew too high that they often missed their targets. However, Henkholun experienced extreme trauma and fear when sheltering in a trench for some days. The soldier's supply of water ran out as the Japanese cut off the water supply. For three days, there was not a drop of water to drink and biscuits could not be eaten as the mouths and the throats of the soldiers were badly parched. Relief came on the fourth day via parachutes from supply planes. The Japanese whom they gunned down from the trenches-their bodies piled up. After the Battle of Kohima, they marched for six months, till they crossed the Irrawaddy River in Burma. During these months, they encountered some Japanese soldiers and officers, who were weak and emaciated, and they 'finished' them off. Was this a humane gesture as the Japanese were already dying of starvation and would not have been able to survive much longer. He states that ' before. the kaidi (prisoner)'were taken by the prison guards in the Kaidi van to Imphal, his commander had told them in English "Remember, unlike the Japanese who tortured and kill their prisoners, we have not killed you". The Japanese officer did not say anything' - how could he after hearing such a demeaning statement. Japanese officers could usually understand and speak a little English.

After the war, Henkholun returned to Kohima to his headquarter, but though he fought like a regular soldier, he felt he was not treated as part of the army. He stated: We followed the rules of the police. He wanted to resign and got discharged from the Assam Rifles as a riflemam in August 1948. As he was discharged, he was not entitled to a pension.[64] A sad ending after a heroic career serving in wartime and going through a terrifying, gruelling experience.

Ngamjang Mate has provided a heart-rending account of the travails of his family and the villagers of Tengnoupal. Inevitably, because of its proximity to the Burma border, refugees from Burma were crowding the village looking for every kind of help- food, water, porters etc. His father carried two children on his back from Lokchao to Tengnoupal and was paid a meagre Rs.40. He stated that many refugee families died while others got separated. The villagers themselves had to flee and a lady who gave birth to a child a week back fled to the jungle, where she died. Sadly, the other family members left the new born with the dead mother. A tragic loss of life.

'During the early days of the war, the Japanese came to our village and collected food. Our rice stock for a week lasted only three days for them.' The Japanese had either no means or time to cook the rice, so they placed it in their helmets, pounded it, and ate it uncooked. This must have added to the woes of the Japanese soldiers. But the Japanese remained honorable- 'a Japanese lady officer who sat in a big trench meticulously recorded the rice stock collected from the villages, and gave a chit to the village elders saying that after two weeks, they could claim money from Imphal for the rice taken'.

The villagers sheltered in the jungle but when they cooked food in the. trenches, some smoke quite naturally escaped through the tree branch roofs and the British would commence firing. Japanese soldiers in the jungle would fight the British. One injured Japanese soldier was left in a hut in the midst of a paddy field, he was surrounded by a group of Punjabi soldiers, who killed him although he shot three dead before he succumbed: Why did these Punjabi soldiers kill the lone, injured Japanese- a tragic loss for that Japanese soldier's family. Perhaps it was not possible to capture him as a POW (Prisoner of War). His observations on the dogfights between the British and Japanese planes echoes the description given by Henkholun Kuki- the Japanese planes were small and flew very fast, the British planes appeared heavy and slow. So the former's technology appeared superior. Henkholun and three young men from his village were recruited into the V force by the British and instructed to stop Subhash Chandra Bose and his men from entering Imphal, and to arrest them. Some basic training was given, and although they were provided with cigarettes, they received no cash remuneration. Since others too have referred to receiving cigarettes, were the British encouraging the Manipuris to smoke? And if so, to what purpose? After being in the V force for a year, the four young men from Tengnoupal had to return their guns to the British, and were left both penniless and jobless for no viable reason. Their woes were exacerbated by having no proper food to eat. And for a war, which was not of their making.

Ngamjang also tells us of discriminatory practices in the collection of dead bodies: priority was given to the British soldiers, then to Indian and Gurkha soldiers. Sadly, the Japanese bodies were never picked up. And so after the war, some Japanese came to search for the bones of the dead soldiers.

A British Captain paid the villagers Rs.30/ for every truck pushed down a ravine- two to three trucks were pushed down every day. What a waste of usable transport. Guns collected by village elders were deposited with the Government through Himmat Singh, Chief Commissioner of Manipur. A box of Japanese currency was found, but destroyed as it was worthless. Ngamjang ends with a statement common to many Manipuris at the time: I am still wondering why the Japanese and the British came to our land and fought that 'gruesome battle'[65]

There are many commonalities in all the above accounts. However, F.S. Downs was of the opinion that the participation of the Kukis in World War II was due to political reasons, but some section of the Kukis who accepted Christianity remained loyal to their colonial masters. But to most of the conservative and traditional minded Kuki chiefs and warriors, the preaching of a religion of love at this stage was anathema to them. This new religion was introduced at a time when the traditional and age-old culture was threatened by the British administration. No wonder after World War II and by 1950, the Kukis had become one of the major Christian groups in Manipur.[66]

Whether the Kukis supported the British or the Japanese/INA forces in small or large numbers, they experienced the whole gambit of emotions during the war years. It is often said that there is no victor in a war because everyone who participates or witnesses a war is impacted in myriad ways. Fear, uncertainty, hope, despair were some emotions that plagued the Kukis as also the Tangkhuls and the Meiteis too, perhaps in different measures during the course of the war. Trauma as also bad memories severely impact every individual. But the Kukis who supported the Japanese/INA alliance were a dejected people when the Alliance they supported was defeated. On the other hand, it aroused a nascent nationalism in the Kukis- a growth of political consciousness. It gave birth to the Kuki National Assembly, a regional political party in the hills of Manipur on October 24th,1946. Its primary objectives were 'to build a consciousness of common identity, to cater to the political interest of the Kuki people in the post-Independence era, and creating a single political unit for the Kukis.[67]

Meitei lady, Yengkhom Ongbi Hemabati recalls her time at Thanlon village near Churachandpur (The largest settlement of the Kukis was at Churachandpur) when news reached that the Japanese were camping close by and a fight was imminent, despite fear, her husband told her, he would go and see the Japanese, as they were likeable, as were the British, and neither was an enemy of the Manipuris. He mentions that the Japanese soldiers wore ' phaneks' (women sarongs) in the daytime and through sign language communicated their hunger pangs- they relished the boiled eggs served to them. But the Japanese were not faring well, and the lady felt sorry for them- 'My husband was right neither the Japanese nor the British were our enemies. The war concluded while we were in Thanlon. The Japanese were thoroughly defeated and many Japanese died, everywhere in Manipur.[68]

The Meitei Encounters:

A Meitei Pangal Story

This is a story of a Meitei Pangal village which was extinguished during the Battle of Imphal. Its inhabitants were forced to flee and seek shelter/refuge in some other village. The story has been narrated by Ms. Salma of the village of Kwaktha: Salma's grandfather, Turab Ali Mayang Mayum lived in the idyllic, peaceful village of Kwaktha, not too far from Imphal. He was approximately fourteen or fifteen years of age at the time of the occurrence of the Battle of Imphal. As a child, Salma had listened to stories of how this Battle had adversely impacted her ancestral village and of the anguish, depression, grief and worry, that her grandfather, the family and fellow villagers experienced, in the trying times after the houses/homes they had built with hard work and diligence were destroyed, never to stand again. Disturbed and distraught by the sound of the guns booming and bombs falling, they had to flee, but before doing that the villagers themselves destroyed their own homes, as they could not bear the thought of 'strangers' residing in their homes they had so lovingly constructed and cared for. The only ray of hope was that the paddy from their fields had been harvested prior to the evacuation of the village. But the Meitei Pangals had to search for a safe place on foot, and this necessitated carrying only bare essentials necessary for survival- some food and a few clothes. The villagers had taken the precaution of hiding their rice stocks prior to their departure- the common practice was to bury it in the earth. They were afraid to collect water, as there were rumours circulating that the water of the pukhris (water bodies/ponds which abounded in the valley) had been poisoned: Salma's grandfather's family and others had to seek refuge with relatives, friends and sometimes, even strangers. They were filled with fear and anxiety, they were physically and emotionally weary and never certain from where their next meal would come- hunger dogged their steps and they did not know whether and when they would be able to return to their original village. The desire to return home was strong, even though they had to face the ordeal of constructing new homes. The British had issued orders that no houses should be left standing, as they could be used by the Japanese to hide in. After they left the village, their hidden grain was unearthed and burnt, so as to prevent it being acquired by the Japanese, who always were on a search for rice to allay hunger pangs.

These Meitei Pangal villages neither favoured the British or the Japanese. A few had come in contact with some Britishers, who had constructed a bridge at Kwaktha to facilitate their movements.

After the war was over, the villagers returned to their ruined village, tasked with the necessity of beginning life anew, building homes, restarting cultivation. They did receive some financial compensation from the Government but that did not assuage the pain of the trauma they had experienced, and they continued to retain vivid memories, and for years suffered from a sense of insecurity and fear, and recalled the happy days before that fateful Battle.

Salma's grandfather had narrated to her parents, that when all the original families returned to their village, they came across the remains of many Japanese soldiers which were widely scattered. The villagers, honest and godly, collected the remains, and buried them within Kwaktha itself after performing certain rituals.[69]

A graphic description of the Battle of Imphal was published in a local daily, a few years ago under the title of 'My Japan Lan Memoir':

'In Manipur in 1942, far removed from the concerns of posterity, the mighty Japanese began their relentless pursuit of a Japanese Empire in Asia. During 'Japan Lan', Manipur gloriously stood the test of time against the Nippon Army, that ploughed as a whirlwind from far away Japan. Japan Lan arrived in Manipur on May 10th, 1942, with the promise of destruction, it was going to wreck. After the Japanese gave 'Britannia rules the waves', a nasty shock in South East Asia, with their lightning attacks, they sneaked through the jungles of Burma to the outskirts of Imphal.

The war bewitched the Meitei nation, there was a natural movement modifying traditional beliefs in accordance with modern ideas, and deliberate rejection of the styles of the past, such as an increasing adoption of wearing trousers, and change in unmarried girls Mangka style haircut, to the universal. There was liberalism and relaxation in religious orthodoxy, such as allowing Muslim and Tribal people in Brahmin run restaurants. (Brahmins are usually engaged as chefs to cook food for guests invited to an asop (feast), most such events are associated with the Passage of Rites) and Meitei homes (from which they were earlier barred after the conversion of the Meiteis to Vaishnavism in the eighteenth century). By 1945, many Meiteis including me, (then a school boy) had a working knowledge of Hindi, (Meiteilon is the lingua franca of Manipur) because of the war. (Many

Indian soldiers from different parts of the country had come to Manipur). Exposure to Hindi and English helped Manipuris to develop an ebbing consciousness, that the world is vast, with different races, religions, practices and culture. Manipuris have experienced the exceptional which couldn't have happened without Japan Lan. Boys in Imphal including me, were innately mechanical and quick to learn- soon reassembled many trucks, jeeps, motor - bikes- by 1947, Imphal was full of them.

Manipuris owe a great deal to Japan Lan. Without it, Manipur would still be struggling for a while for Independence. (Manipur's Independence lasted only two years 1947-1949)Exploring the Impact of the Japan Lan on Meiteis, seventy-five years ago, with the end of British Colonial Rule, new geopolitical events, social and economic consequences, the mythological, philosophical and psychological effects of the war, one could see their craving for freedom with a relaxed attitude towards a secular world view. For hill dwellers, there was an intense arousal for a belonging, dreams of equality, fairness and justice.[70]

From the above account, it is apparent that the writer has focused on the beneficial impact of the Battle, the change in the world view of the Manipuris. But he has not made any reference to some of the devastating impacts of the war on Manipur- people forced to flee their homes, find shelter in inhospitable jungles, etc. Being a schoolboy at the time, he and other boys felt joy and happiness tinkering with war vehicles left behind after the event, reassembling them with pride in their ability to do so. But in an interview with Yaiphaba Meetei Kangjam, he has stated that a stunning change occurred in the town centre (Imphal), when the first Japanese bombs rained down. He has contrasted this with the normal, noisy, crowded market-place, which now was enveloped in an eerie silence, which evoked dread and fear. This fear was exacerbated by the fact that many Manipuris living in the town were compelled to in a very short span of time- two hours to pack a few essentials which they could themselves carry, and evacuate their homes. Fortunately for the doctor, his father was on cordial terms with the British Political Agent Christopher Grimson, and had made arrangements for alternative housing, in the event of war at Imphal. The family boarded a lorry but were soon forced to disembark and proceed on foot, as 'all hell broke loose.' The doctor being still a young child was unable to complete the trek, and had to be carried piggy-back by two older sister-in-laws. One can only speculate on the tribulations of the families, especially those carrying children on their backs, as they sought shelter in rural villages. There is mention of the travails of Marwari merchants of Imphal town centre, who too had to flee on foot to find some safe sanctuary. The doctor's family however, lived quite comfortably in their new-dwelling- an outhouse, which had before their departure been furnished. quite adequately with necessities. This stands in stark contrast to the discomfort and shortage of necessities experienced by others who were forced to flee their homes- especially the Tangkhuls and Kukis.

Nevertheless, a thick cloud of anxiety and insecurity, tightened the noose around those forced to leave their homes, as the deadly disease of Malaria was claiming many victims. The doctor himself contracted Malaria, and believed that he too would succumb but he made a fortunate recovery with the aid of 'quinine'. But his family home like other family homes at Imphal was looted undoubtedly every individual who suffers from an incident of theft feels sad and depressed. But its not just the worth of the goods stolen that causes distress- it is the fact that strangers have entered and despoiled their homes. The doctor's family had to stay away for more than a year, and they certainly would have had misgivings about the condition of their home.

The doctor too was exposed to brutality- he witnessed the stabbing to death of an English Captain by a Pathan soldier. This must have made a lasting impression on a young mind. Simultaneously, many small Manipuri children were engaged by British soldiers to run errands or to perform small tasks as for example making bamboo beds. They were not paid in cash but in the form of food items, whose novelty aroused their curiosity; besides the children relished the food. However, most Manipuris had a preference for American chewing-gum and Lucky Strike cigarettes, which they sometimes received from American pilots. They also liked the American dress.

The only private school in Imphal was the Bengali School, but it lay vacant, as all the Bengalis had fled to Bengal; it was converted into a military canteen, where Manipuris were able to buy items that were not available locally at low price. Both the gifts of food and cigarettes and the purchase of items from the canteen were appreciated by the Manipuris, as it was a time of inflation.

Those who fled the town centre had to wait a considerable period of time after the war ended, before returning to their homes, as they continued to be occupied by 'remnants of the army.' Cinema halls however remained open and screened both Hindi and Hollywood films.[71]

Personal Recollections are an important source of History. One such Recollection was posted by the Reader's

Collective, Imphal on the social media on the 7th July, 2020.

Paomi Post

'Everyone was a victim in that war. Manipur was greatly devastated by the Second World War/Japan Lan. I am ninety-seven years old now, and saw the catastrophe unfolding in front of me. The war did not determine who was right, but it decided who survived. It was people against people, and nations against nations. I survived, but thousands of innocent souls like me lost their lives, and history was written by the victor of the pageantry. This is my Memoir:

It was Kalen Tritiya, the third day of Kalen, a Sunday, when the conches (moibung/siren) of war was blown. Around 8 A.M. in the morning, a huge plane flew around for surveillance. Planes had been flying every morning for almost a week.

Then the horror started at noon; an air assault at Koirengei. I saw a single file of bombers and then one by one they separated 1-2-4-8. There were seventeen bomber aircraft, ashy like dragonflies. They said the pilots were all fifteen years old Japanese girls. Six days later another air-raid struck again- Khwairamband (where the iconic Ima Keithel or Women's Market is housed), Nagamapal, Khuyathong, Kangla were all bombed.

Within a short period of time, soldiers of all races thronged in: the Goras (Whites), the Koktumbis (Afghans), the Negroes (Africans), Pathan Punjabis (Sikhs) and others. And we left our homes due to the fear-mongering. I relocated to my aunt's house at Patsoi Khunou near Leitong with my family.

Then bombs and sirens became a routine thing. We were instructed to dive into bomb shelter pits with the first sound of a siren, and come out only with the second sound of the siren. If the siren sounded hasty(uu-uu-uu) three times, we had to take cover. If it sounded only once and long (uu-uu-uu-uu), it meant the danger was over.

A year later on Sajibu Purnima, in Khurai Konsam Leikai Chingangbam Gulap's Mandap, when Ras Leela (Krishna's dance with the Gopis) was being performed, another air raid struck, and three hundred people gathered in the Mandap died. Only my maternal uncle and the pujari survived, as they both jumped into ponds when the bombs fell. For five days, my maternal uncle collected wood from the locality and cremated the victims.[72]

It is apparent that the memories of the time of the Battle of Imphal were so deeply embedded in R.K. Tamphasana's mind, that she could recall with clarity so many decades later. She has graphically described the tragic loss of life at a peaceful cultural dance performance, as also the continuous siren warnings, and the necessity to shelter when bombs rained down.

Manipur's society was at the time conservative, and it must have been quite shocking to learn that the pilots who rained the bombs were fifteen years old girls. But the pilots if they were indeed fifteen, and indeed girls, were extremely young and inexperienced, and in doing what they did, they were only obeying orders from their High Command.

She also saw soldiers of different nationalities and countries, and must have experienced mixed emotions- she had the opportunity to see foreigners and observe how they behaved, but she also experienced grief because she along with the family had to evacuate their home, and nobody could be certain that their home would be still standing, when the war was over. But even in his anguish, loss and grief her maternal uncle performed the last rituals for the victims who had gathered to see the Ras Leela performance. Another insight into how the Meiteis felt was also posted on the social media in August 6th, 2020.

The Story of Koktumbi Siphai

Life in a war zone can really be a trying time for civilians, especially the vulnerable lots; children and women. Not a war of ours, Imphal was to become a battleground for two Antagonists- the Japanese and the British. It finally ended after a mutually devastating encounter. My grandmother, Smt.(L) Ningthoujam Ongbi lbempishak Devi was about fourteen, residing at Wangkhei, when the first Japanese Air raid took place. Her father was a high-ranking officer in the Department of Settlement during the time when Manipur was still a British protectorate. The whole family had to run, bag and baggage, fleeing Imphal, which was now considered unsafe. Rumours of the Japanese Army knocking at the door, also fuelled the anxiety. Her father managed to arrange a bullock-cart, that took the family on the run. They finally took shelter at the residence of Moirang Koireng in the town of Moirang, about fifty-six kilometers from Imphal. It was where the first Azad Hind Fauj flag was hoisted by Col. S.A Mallick on the 13th of April, 1944. Little did they know that this town would bear the brunt of a fierce engagement in the days to come. So naive and ill-informed were the folks back then. Simply they were rushing into the blazing flame.

The Imphal town was already home to about a lakh of

newly arrived troops: a part of Slim's build -up for the pro-emptive strike of Burma. Inflation was already an emerging headache for the administration, the prices sky-rocketed, and food was scarce. Nobody was eager to tend the fields; rather it was a run for one's safety and life. Stories of rape and looting were going around like wildfire. Imphal was already a ghost-town. The civil administration had collapsed. The Thanas (police stations/outposts) were empty, and devoid of Siphais or policemen. In the midst of this, life was hard for a young lady. There were threats at every comer.

Whenever I got the chance to meet her, I would encourage her to recount her memories from the war-time. Her recollection was quite poignant: One day she giggled and confided in me, that they were really scared of the Koktumbi Siphai, literally, meaning soldiers donning the pointed Headgear. No fairer sex was safe around them; such a reputation! I knew it had to be the wild and tough bunch from around the North-West frontier Region (so different in appearance and build from the Manipuris) or the present-day Khyber Pakhtunkhwa bordering between Pakistan and Afghanistan. Or could they be Pathans or the Balochis or Punjabi Mussalmans or Afridis? I don't have an answer now. Whatever, they were fiercely independent and wild. And often was a handful for the immediate commanding British Officers. Yet, they were fiercely loyal and brave too! The pointed part of the Headgear is called the 'Khulla', made out of quilted fabric, which was conical in shape with a thick band inside to hold on the wearer's head. A nine foot cloth would then be wrapped around to complete the 'Pugree' or 'Turban.[73]

It is obvious that war impacted all sections of the local population, even those holding higher positions- they and their families had to also face the trauma of leaving their homes and sheltering elsewhere and apparently in this case, their choice of shelter was far from ideal-akin to jumping from a frying pan into a furnace

The arrival of almost one lakh troops in Imphal drastically altered its demography. The 1941 Census Report states that the total urban population of Manipur was 99,716. And Imphal was then the only town in Manipur. Inflation was a natural result as also food scarcity, as the town was not geared to provision double for its population overnight. Administration- civil and police collapsing was also an expected outcome of the abnormal increase in population.

Fear of fierce looking soldiers would only be natural to genteel Manipuri girls, though the realisation that their headgear and physical appearance frightened the young ladies, would not have occurred to the Koktumbi Siphais. Communication is still a very real problem in Manipur how much more would it have been during the war years- it is not surprising that the civilians had no proper information channels.

In a similar vein, M.K. Binodini Devi had stated: The Allied troops began arriving in Manipur in endless convoys. Soldiers of different colours and build that we have never seen before, huge armoured military vehicles, tanks and anti-aircraft battery began filling up our roads. It all made up for a very awesome and intimidating picture.

Again, war impacted everyone, irrespective of status: I too, even though I belong to the Manipuri royalty, had harrowing experiences. We had to flee home along with my mother, the Queen, and a good part of the war years were spent as refugees in makeshift arrangement in somebody else's portico or some such places. (L) Ningthoujam Ongbi Ibempishak's account, is the fear experienced because of booming guns, terrifying explosions exacerbated by chaos, lawlessness, numerous gangs prowling- looting people and homes. Insecurity was the name of the game for everybody, even at home.

But Manipuris possessed the quality of Resilience. The lone cinema hall (previously mentioned) ran full house, Ras Lilas were performed on schedule (with no disruption unlike the event at Khurai), religious ceremonies never stopped.[74]

Another Meitei lady observed: What a tumultuous time it was! People having to vacate their homes and flee to rural areas, leaving behind much of their belongings, letting loose their pets and cattle, in the hope they would fend for themselves until the war got over and they could be reclaimed.[75] At least the Lady Yengkhom Ongbi Hemabati believed she could salvage something from what was left behind when fleeing.

M.K. Binodini Devi had stated that the war time administration bombarded the place with pamphlets, instructing the civil population of the Dos and Don'ts during the war. One of the many advices was to dig trenches to hide during bombing raids: But the airplanes shocked us all out of our complacency, pouring on us bombs that exploded like unending thunder claps. A lot of familiar landmarks were flattened. A refugee camp took a load and many unfortunate souls were killed. The spectacle of terror was simply beyond words'.[76] The words speak for themselves of the trauma experienced by the Meiteis during the war years.

Nimaichand Singh remembered that despite the hardships' the place or the form of cultural festivals and religious ceremonies relating to birth, death, new year etc. were not totally lost. Festivals like Yaoshang, Kaang, Janmashthami etc. had their normal observations carried out almost everywhere with religious norms and gaiety.' Obviously, this continuity was the silver lining in the cloud.

The Resilience of the Manipuris is also attested to in The Administrative Report of Manipur State, 1943-44: The behaviour of the Manipuris in the face of these whirlwind advances was in remarkable contrast to their behaviour in May 1942. Nobody ran away, and except for the Ukhrul sub-division which had been overrun, all the departments of the State continued to function normally. During the second half of March, the auction of State Fishery leases produced bids ten times those of peacetime, the bidders being quite undeterred by the presence of the Japanese some ten miles away.[77]

Tongbram Sanahanbi Devi was a married women 17 years old at the time of the Japan Lan. She and other villagers were always ready to flee and not only had her family members packed an emergency kit, but they had packed up all their possessions and kept them outside their home, in the event of their home being bombed by what she termed as ' balloons'. One Koireng from Moirang sought refuge in her village-Thanga, and soon after he was followed by a group of 7 Japanese. The villagers pounded rice and sent it on boats at night to the Japanese base at Moirang and were paid in Japanese currency, which like the Tangkhuls, they regarded as worthless. The villagers could distinguish the distinct type of aircraft- sighter (fighter) and bomber- both of which they were mortally afraid of- they used to jump from their boats into the water when the planes flew overhead. Sanahanbi witnessed 2 aircrashes, one plane in flames crashed into a hillock, and the burnt bodies of the passengers fell into the Loktak Lake. The pilot of a second crashed plane survived and was rescued and brought to Sanahanbi's house before being escorted to Moirang.[78]

Nimaicharan Singh describes his experiences in his village Kangla Sifai near the Kangla Airfield. He says a cordial relation existed between the civilians and soldiers (of the Allied Forces), and barring some minor untoward incident, life was peaceful- the locals had adequate food provisions which they acquired from army men's stock. In similar vein Soibam Angangyaima Singh tasted delectable Western goodies- fish and meat cans, bread, biscuit, cream, coffee, butter transported by Allied aircraft.

Nimaicharan also refers to locals evacuating their homes which were requisitioned for the British, Indian and American army men. Many local families had to live in a single homestead of their unknown brethen. And wearied people trudging roads followed by bullock-carts carrying their possessions, was a common sight. As Yengkhom Ongbi Hemati stated: Some 25,000 people were given just two days to move out. Rice stored in granaries on timber piles were extremely vulnerable to fire, and rice hidden under mud floors or garden was dug sprinkled with petrol and burnt says Ian Lyall Grant, a sapper of the 17th Indian Division.

But at other times, local houses were burnt, and the local residents were asked to leave. One woman of a family which stayed behind gave birth inside a trench. In the evacuation, a child was left behind not to be seen again.[79]

Trauma certainly dogged the footsteps of the civilians.

Kangjam Mera Singh a carpenter worked at Kangla Airfield and observed the planes, the bombs falling, trenches being dug, the refugee camp for those coming from Burma etc. He also worked as a porter transporting refugees on improvised palanquins. When local goons attacked some refugees, he offered his services to escort the refugees up to Nambol. He saw people of different nationalities, and found the American soldiers to be the most disciplined. He admired a strong culvert built behind his house by African soldiers, and witnessed how big guns were fired. He also mentions novel western foodstuffs and clothes which the young children loved, although elders abstained because of religious and cultural taboos. The Manipuris were not partial to either of the warring sides, although one Potsangbam Tomal who left the village and joined the INA. He states as others too did, that most people were unaware of the reason for the Japanese invasion and for the fighting. He also says as others did that there were Japanese lady pilots.

Pukhrambam Birachandra personally saw lines of trucks, jeeps, ambulances, soldiers and witnessed fighting, in the course of which his village Ningthoukhong was destroyed by bombs. He speaks of rumours that the British dropped poison-laced food items in Japanese areas which caused illness and deaths. But the Japanese suffered from starvation, disease and casualties.

After the war he found his village ravaged and dotted with bomb craters, with scarce any trees. But ammunition, bombs and tanks littered the village and his uncle collected six to seven guns, sold them to some tribal people for a sum, sufficient to enable him to buy a plot of land.[80]

Ningthoukhongjam Moirang Ningthou of Keibi Village (next to Nungshigum) in the Iril River valley watched the Japanese occupy strategic hills and throw grenades upon British soldiers. The latter retaliated with guns, plane. attacks and tanks which the Meiteis called 'Iron Elephants'. While the battle was raging, the villagers were ordered to vacate the village; when they returned, they found body parts, weapons, canteens, stretchers, ammunition in big sacks and other items of which Ningthoukhongjam received a bottle of kerosene oil from the hills where the Japanese had been entrenched. In the paddy fields too, they found many Japanese items.[81] The Japanese met with an inglorious and sad death, and what they left behind was appropriated by the villagers.

Laishram Birendra Kumar Singh, a student, recalled the first bombing of Imphal, May 10th, 1942 by Japanese aircraft. Imphal was enveloped with thick smoke, so he and others armed with some money and clothes took shelter at Kwakeithel, but because of thugs looting people,they shifted from one place to another However, he got a job as an interpreter for the British forces and checked people passing on the Old Cachar Road, though most were refugees; Laishram did all the talking - the British officer watched him from his tree-top house. But he was assigned to sleep with Indian soldiers at night on the ground- Whereas the British slepts on scot or improvised beds. He was also asked to work at the Canchipur jail while the prisoners mainly local goons were interrogated by a British officer and beaten black and blue. Appalled by the Officer's callousness, Laishram refrained from going back to work at the jail after the first day. Laishram having studied Surveying, was assigned to assist the Corps of Royal Engineers at Thoubal in building bridges and roads. He spoke of a Manipuri clerk asking an African soldier at Thoubal whether Africans ate human meat and the latter replied in the affirmative- the clerk promptly hid in a cupboard!

Laishram describes the war years as hard- when he and the others returned to Imphal, they found that the walls of their homes had been knocked down to prevent intruders staying within by the British and Indian soldiers. But as was their way, the British kindly provided food items to the locals who addressed them as 'saathi' (friend). Laishram had a varied career. Since he loved music, and Manipuri women went to sing and dance at army camps- he played the flute at the performances- the most common form of dance was 'Marbak Jagoi'.[82] Jemadar Arambam Bidhu Singh was a soldier at the King of Manipur's palace. While escorting Maharaj Bodhchandra's wife, Maharani lshwari Devi to Ramnagar, he and three others were halted by Japanese soldiers and officers who specially harassed him, probably mistaking him for a Gurkha. He was ordered to pound rice in the rain- he refused, got into a fight and hit the Japanese soldier. A few days later that same Japanese soldier was killed in battle. It would seem that Arambam Bidhu Singh experienced some remorse, but it was also unusual for Japanese officers and soldiers to harass a Manipuri soldier and even try to kill him. Perhaps they did that because Maharaja Bodhachandra like his father extended all possible assistance to the British.

Soon after the Jemadar took ill with malaria and was left for dead by his 4-member team, two of whom soon joined the INA. Finally with the assistance of a man, he reached home where he found that his family believing him to be dead were performing his last rites. Later, he reported for duty, was promoted to Naik then Havildar and finally Jemadar. He later became the Commander of the King's guards. Khuraijam Nimaicharan Singh also refers to the planes and balloons and to pamphlets distribution on safety measures. Nevertheless, when the first Japanese planes bombed Imphal, he and his friends rushed home and hid under beds, because of a belief that any word starting with 'K' as 'Kangkha'(empty space under a bed) was suitable for taking cover. A rumour doing the rounds was that the Japanese bombs were laced with poison- so when hiding they covered their noses to prevent inhaling the poison. He saw many people with their belongings walking on the Ayangpalli road to take shelter in distant villages. Khuraijam's family followed suit. After a second bombing by the Japanese, Imphal town was deserted, except for escaped jail prisoners who indulged in crimes like stealing.

Thousands of soldiers in vehicles with 'strange equipment' and 'food items' began pouring in to Imphal and a refugee camp for those coming from Burma was set up. His account reiterates that the demographic map of Imphal changed, and the children were excited to see new people, strange equipment and never tasted before foodstuffs. He too noted the pathetic state of the refugees. The Manipuri children learnt the word 'OK' from English and American soldiers who used it frequently. After sometime Khuraijam returned home with his father to Khurai and noted that the Nepali soldiers had occupied most of the houses: they were friendly and gave him a book and mouth organ and used to buy cigarettes and pan (betel nut wrapped in a leaf) from elderly women sitting on the roadside.

On April 20,1943, a Gopi Chak Khangba feast was organised and Khuraijam's father went to attend it along, with others-200 in all. But around noon, guns boomed and bombs dropped: The impact of the Japanese bombing that day was so deadly and powerful that it will not be forgotten easily by the people who experienced or saw it. The Japanese bombing that day was said to have directly targeted and dropped bombs along the areas from Kongba Bazar to Chingarel on the Ukhrul road. Many houses were damaged and some civilians were killed on the road'. The venue of the feast, his father was attending lay along the line of bombing and the family were anxious and fearful. Some villagers informed them that most of the participants of the feast had not survived the bombing. "That terrible news made me feel that I had lost everything. Words fail to express the true extent of my agony and sorrow: It was too hard a blow to face". A family friend retrieved the clothes Khuraijam's father had worn to the feast. The father had been seriously wounded and had been transported to the Army Hospital at Sanjenthong, where he passed away. Khuraijam stated: I still regret that I do not know how and where my father's body was disposed'. So here we have a gentleman who received no 'closure'. May be the Khurai Chingangbam Mandap was destroyed because it was the only large structure with a tin roof. The bombing here was recorded as the largest loss of civilian lives in a single incident in Manipur during the war.

Khuraijam saw many planes including the big bomber nicknamed the 'Old Man of Koirengei', and the constructions of two airfields, one at Kangla and the other at Koirengei. The pilots of the 'Spitfire' planes used to give gum to the children and like the Britishers who gave the gum, they too relished it. Khuraijam admired the pilot's uniform- the pilots were friendly towards him as he could speak a little

English and condemned the Japanese who were responsible for his father's death.

Then he met American and Canadian Air Force personnel, and enjoyed interacting with them. That helped him to overcome his loneliness following the death of his father. Soldiers all liked children, but especially the US Americans pilots, who gave little gifts to the children, including cigarettes, as most boys smoked. The boys exchanged pineapples which the pilots relished for photographs.

Khuraijam was offered an airplane ride which he was excited about. But before the plane could take off, his friends urged him to disembark and later he regretted missing what would have been a great experience. The children not only chatted with the soldiers but also watched English movies with them. A Canadian Jack Hodge gave him some useful gifts like a khaki shirt, pencils, papers etc. and an English officer used to hum popular Manipuri songs, whereas Fernandez, another British officer taught Khuraijam some English songs and wrote down the lines of a song he loved. Many years later, Khuraijam understood the meaning of those lines:

If wishes could work magic

If wanting brought things near

Today, my love! I'd kiss you

And start with you another happy year. [83]

Gotimayum Ibotombi Shanna was twelve when the first bomb fell in May 1942 at Imphal. He too referred to the planes as ' balloons' and stated that when a Japanese plane crashed, his brother escorted the pilot who survived up to Loktak Lake from Samurou village. The villagers were forced to leave their homes and Ibotombi was even grazed by a bullet. When the villagers returned home after six months, they were greeted with destroyed homes and a destroyed mandap (covered pillared area adjoining a temple), American soldiers built an oil pipe line which ended in the local playground. He like Khuraijam admired the physique, features and discipline of the American soldiers, who gave gifts to the children, which they relished, especially the biscuits and salt which was in short supply. Festivals continued, and the pilots and the soldiers joined the locals in the 'Thabal Chongba' (moonlight dance during Yaoshang or Holi). They watched English movies with the Americans, but the Madras soldiers did not permit them to watch Hindi movies in the camp. Rather ironic- that one group of Indians denied another group the Manipuris, from watching Hindi movies?

The Americans relished beef, and cows were supplied to them by a Muslim man. But one Maisnam Kanhai from Imphal took umbrage, as the Meiteis were not permitted to eat beef. The matter was fortunately quickly resolved by the Political Agent. However, the incident made a lasting impact, in that as Dr. Mohendro had already stated, the food habits of the Meiteis changed: they ate all kinds of meat and drank liquor (traditional rice wines/beer was brewed in Manipur from the ancient times).

The 'black soldiers' at Tulihal Airfield were arrogant and ill- mannered and one of them was killed by the villagers, for chasing another villager with his 'dao' (sword) when drunk. In 1945, Ibotombi chanced on a number of human skulls when trekking the 'Red Hill', but he and his friends did not touch them.

Tourem Gouramuhon Singh was aged ten at the time of the war. As Irengbam village was famous for producing molasses which the Japanese consumed as they were low on rice stocks they also killed cattle for food. They disguised themselves carrying traditional tribal baskets and checking out British locations. Gouramuhon admired 'the clever and courageous Japanese'. But because of the fighting they vacated the village- the main battlefield was Maibam Lotpa Ching (Red Hill) close to their home. When they returned after the battle, they found that the British soldiers had occupied their home and outer shed and kitchen was used as their 'langar' and burnt all wooden objects in the house. The sight of their once beautiful house in such a sorry state compelled them to leave it again. Anguish must have been their companion for a long time. Yumnam Kullachandra Singh and his family also had to vacate their village during the war. But the villagers must have empathised with the Japanese because they constructed a 'Memorial ' to the Japanese soldiers who died in Irengbam village.

Khumanthem Kala was thirteen at the time of the war. In the early days of the war, his mother chanced upon a wounded Japanese soldier making his way to their house. The family assisted and sheltered him at great risk to themselves but they did it without dwelling on the consequences. Once again, like others, Khumanthem's family had to vacate their home, taking only a little food and belongings. Unable to take their livestock, they set their cows free. The war especially the bombings caused great damage to local houses. But being curious, the teenager went around the British camps and did petty jobs for them. He looked with awe at the ambulance trucks and the strategic sentry post erected. The Japanese however suffered from lack of supplies especially food and were always hungry. Some locals blamed the Japanese for their sufferings. Much after the war was over, a Japanese team came to search for the bones of the dead Japanese soldiers- they carried battle maps and could distinguish between animal and human bones. One of them compensated a villager for a cow he killed and ate during the war. Khumanthem appreciated this gesture. He also is the only one to state that some Manipuris blamed the Japanese for their sufferings; whereas other statements read: for most part the Manipuris were unaware of why the Japanese had come to Manipur.

Karam Jugeshore was also a teenager, fourteen years old, when on the day of Cheiraoba (Manipuri New Year) in April 1944, government soldiers ordered them to move out of their village. The elders who had spent time, energy and money preparing the special meal for Cheiraoba were saddened at this sudden departure, but the young children were excited to hear that the Japanese were coming: The family had moved to Keinou village, but were asked again to move on. Fortunately, they enjoyed a respite at their grandfather's house until the end of the war. The children witnessed the destructive havoc caused by bombs raining down. Their evening meal time was changed to the time of sunset, as fierce fighting occurred during the night time. The family suffered many travails, shortage of food and firewood coupled with continuous inflation of prices for all commodities. They did get to see but not to interact with Japanese soldiers.

The misfortunes of the family continued as they had to keep moving from place to place for shelter, till they returned to their village, which was completely denuded of its forest cover. They exercised ingenuity and collected used CI sheets, telephone cables etc. to build a new dwelling place- no easy task. They were forced to cook the spoiled rice they had hidden before fleeing the village; after some days, the soldiers gave them some foodstuffs including bully beef which they could not eat. As salt was scarce, they had to resort to using 'samor' which was fed to mules. At the end of the war, a lot of equipment was left around Bishnupur but the villagers were too naive to use it.

The war impacted the cane business of the Keibul Lamjao area and the balloons created fear. Villagers from other villages however, sheltered here after the Japanese arrival. Oinam Jatra Singh and his uncle were scared when they chanced upon the Japanese, one of whom was hiding behind a bush with half his body underwater. Soon after Sarkar planes flew over and dropped bombs and Jatra and his uncle realised that the Japanese was actually asking them to hide beside him. The bomb craters were visible for years after the war- these villages had been under Japanese occupation. When two Indian soldiers arrived, the villagers gave them food and sent them off as they were afraid of retaliation by the Japanese.

Jatra witnessed dogfights between the swift Japanese planes and the big British ones which were slow. At a crash site, villagers collected the pistols and uniforms of the dead men. Today, removing a uniform from a corpse would he viewed as sacrilege. After the war, people from other villages came to Keibul Lamjao area to buy bamboos, urgently required for rebuilding of destroyed homes. The bamboo business flourished as a result.

Naorem Kalimdhan saw what was nicknamed

-'Koirengei Hanuba'(Old Man of Koirengei) a huge aircraft, as also different airfields constructed in Manipur, and of course air battles. He and the other boys enjoyed watching the air battles- 'it was like watching a movie '. It wasn't until some people died because of the bombings that the villagers realised 'those things dropped from the planes, could actually cause death- in fact, some villagers in the paddy fields who ignored the siren warnings died.

Prior to the war the Pallel-Tamu (Tamu is in Myanmar) road was a dirt track- filled with mud in the rainy season and dust in winter. But the war brought about construction of proper roads required by the army- 'road building was a part of military strategy.' Young boys were used for collecting stones, assisting in road construction and by the British- 'Goras' as helpers and runners. They were paid in cash and given the usual British foodstuffs, biscuits, tinned fish etc. soap and cigarettes. Indian and Gora soldiers searched the villagers' homes in search of Japanese soldiers- simultaneously the Japanese and the INA soldiers destroyed aircraft housed in the 'aeroplanemahoom' (aeroplane nest) at Kakching Airfield.

When the American soldiers were replaced by African soldiers, the young village boys struck up a friendship with them- they always wanted ganja (cannabis) and wine (local rice wine), so the boys sold it to them for cash or articles in kind, including salt which was scarce. This contrasts with Gotimayum Sharma's description of the 'black soldiers being arrogant and ill-mannered'. An interesting exchange was iron nails supplied by the African soldiers who smuggled it out of their camps, often hiding it in their curly hair. The local people had gradually understood the importance of nails for use in construction.

The boys sometimes ate with the African soldiers-millet and a curry of dried sea-fish and potatoes. The Africans allowed them to watch movies and other performances in their camp. The Pathan soldiers tried to bar the boys, but the Africans had their way. Unfortunately, one black soldier was killed by the locals for misbehaving with a woman.' Unlike the 'Goras' (Whites), the black soldiers became aggressive after consuming liquor. As Gotimayum had stated the villagers of Kodompokpi killed a drunk black soldier who chased a villager with his dao. No such incidents have been recorded about soldiers of other nationalities.

As usual, when the war ended, the left-over items and equipment of the armies were collected by the locals and sold to scrap dealers.[84]

All these accounts have striking similarities proving that 'Oral History' is the first and best kind of History. Many locals were not aware of the reasons for the war, most experienced trauma, had to abandon their homes, seek shelter elsewhere, faced food scarcity and increasing inflation. After the war, the locals had to rebuild their lives and homes.

'There can be no doubt about the fact that Manipur took a very keen role in support of the INA Movement, news of the approaching INA under the able leadership of Netaji, had already created a stir in the Valley. A sense of extreme pride mixed with euphoric nationalism, resonated with many locals. This led to many Manipuris particularly, joining the Bahudar group, led by Col.S.A. Mallick, which was responsible for gathering intelligence, and conducting covert operations. And many more in the front lines, bearing the brunt of bloody encounters. In spite of ever-present repercussion, many families openly supported the INA Movement donating their meagre savings and secretly stocked grains. However, few of the active volunteers had to retreat back to Burma with the Japanese Army. Many were later apprehended, and jailed in Rangoon. They were later shipped back to Calcutta and released under terms and conditions of a general Amnesty.[85] This post of the Azad Hind Force, Imphal Front, clearly reveals that what motivated Manipuris to join the INA was a combination of pride and nationalism and the charismatic personality of Netaji. Despite deprivations, anxiety, fear uncertainty, the Manipuris were both happy and proud to assist the INA in different ways- they were the most knowledgeable about the topography of Manipur, and the psyche of the people. They suffered economic hardships and other travails voluntarily- they were part of a movement whose goal was to achieve India's Freedom. But those who had to retreat to Burma and were interned in Rangoon Jail did experience exhaustion- physical, mental, emotional, psychological and were definitely dispirited. The lot of POW's is never a happy one., and interned in a foreign country must have exacerbated their distress. Jails were then both depressing and uncomfortable with just a few basic amenities. But the silver lining were the words of NSC Bose - Supreme Commander of the Azad Hind Fauj: 'There are people who thought at one time that the Empire on which the sun never set, was an Everlasting Empire. No such thought ever troubled me. History has taught us that every empire has its inevitable deadline and collapse. Moreover, I have seen with my own eyes, cities and fortresses that were once the bulwark, but which became graveyards or bygone empires. But standing today, on the Graveyard of the

British Empire, even a child is convinced that the almighty British Empire is already a thing of the past.' They, (the defeated Manipuris of the INA-Japan coalition) must have also recalled the welcome of the People of Manipur to the INA and Japanese forces. Shouting' Banzai', they welcomed the 'heroes' as they crossed the area west of Myinthami range which was witnessed with great astonishment and profound respect.[86] This despite the fact that 'the Japanese Imperial Army- Indian National Army alliance had been routed by General William Slim's Fourteenth Army, with a little help from American B-29 bombers and the menacing monsoon (Traditionally wars were not undertaken in the monsoon season in India). Bose's struggle was all but up by early 1945, and the volatile world scenario only foretold more trouble for the INA leader. Nuked twice over (6th and 9th August) Japan had no option but to surrender to the Anglo-American forces. Subhas was informed in advance that 15th August would be the day of capitulation. Those surrounding him (Netaji) in his darkest hour were amazed by his stylish sangfroid. 'The worst they can do is to put me against the wall and shoot me. I am prepared for its. Speaking presciently, he told his close aides in Singapore that 'tremendous sacrifices made by the soldiers of the Azad Hind Fauj and civilian population will not go in vain.[87] And they did not go in vain; Manipur achieved her Independence on the 15th of August 1947. In fact on the 12th of December 1946, Maharaja Bodhachandra issued a formal order to constitute. a 'Constitution Making Committee to prepare a new Constitution for the governance of Manipur. Elections were held on 11 June 1948, Maharaj Kumar Priobrata Singh became the first Chief Minister of Manipur. The establishment of a Legislative Assembly with representatives elected on the basis of democratic principles was a landmark in the history of Manipur.[88]

The INA Movement in Manipur was so intricate and so closely interwoven with that of the Japanese campaign in 1944. It was not the original plan of the Japanese to fight the war on Indian soil, nor did they think it was feasible. This was modified later on the assumption that since the British defences in Manipur and Chittagong were probably unprepared, the capture of Imphal would rob them of the best base for launching a counter offensive against Burma. Bose also thought that the capture of Manipur and Chittagong which were considered strategically important was necessary for starting an Indian Revolution.

The Japanese and the INA forces started the military operations on 4 February 1944. Despite the capture of Moirang in April, Manipur was not liberated. The siege of Imphal was lifted because of the failure of the Japanese Air Force to reinforce its army and the INA troops. The total strength of the INA forces which took part in it was about 8,800, whereas the Japanese had 57,000 combatants and the Allied Forces 155,000. Surprisingly, no proper thought was given as to how the people of Manipur were to be mobilised for the movement. It would appear that the Manipuris seemed to have no connection or contact with the INA leader till 7th March 1944, when Bose's handbill containing documents and Gandhi's photo was given to them. As a result,only a small insignificant minority of Manipuris joined the movement. The population of Manipur according to the 1941 Census was, 5,12,127 excluding Jiribam (6139). This appears to suggest that the whole population was indifferent to the movement. This is in strong contrast to the stand of Manipur Government and the people to erect a proper memorial with the tallest Indian flag at Moirang in this the 125th birth year anniversary of Netaji. The British, because of their long contact with the Manipuris had the opportunity to get local supplies from villages, even when the Imphal-Kohima Road was blocked. Most people working under the British in the adjoining areas of Manipur fought with loyalty for the British. Bose suspended his movement in July, because of the loose conduct and corruption of his officers. But very few of them had received even a three months course at the INA Officer's Training School. Even the sympathetic Fujihara commented: As a revolutionary army its morale was high, and it was quite well organised, but the standard of its tactics, training and leadership was low. It lacked in particular, offensive strength and tenacity. Another serious drawback was that the INA had no wireless sets, no telephones, no transport, no weapons other than light machine guns. It would seem that while one cannot question Bose's patriotism, one has to see whether in such a sophisticated war 8,800 men without much training, equipment, ammunition and transport supplies could have been a force to reckon with. Even though the movement failed, the trial of INA men in the Red Fort evoked considerable emotion even among those sections of the Nationalist leadership which had no sympathy for Bose's alliance with the Fascist forces. India owes to them a debt, because their spirit of sacrifice hastened the process of freedom of the country.[89]

Despite the war occurring in the 1940's, there was certain consciousness in the army about psychological warfare. A Psychological Warfare Division dealt with (a) the question of Morale. Set up in October 1943, under Group Captain Bell, the division operated five Frontline propaganda parties- Indian Field Units raised by Force 136. Their technique--leaflets and news sheet, dropped during the campaign were confined to the Japanese, Burmese and Hindusthani, and the targets were the battle areas and lines of communication in Burma. Propaganda themes driven home to the Japanese:

(1) The implication for Japan with Germany's impending defeat

(2) Shortage of food and equipment in the Japanese Army (a sore point)

(3) Incompetence of the Japanese High Command.

The other tactic- promise fair treatment to the Japanese who surrendered. Propaganda to the Burmese-Japan was exploiting Burma- tried thereby to build hatred for the Japanese. Hindusthani Propaganda addressed to the lNA-Tried to dispel the Japanese legend that all INA personnel captured by the British would be shot.

In addition, Field Marshall Slim, drew attention to Japanese psychology, and the fact that when their rigid plans were disrupted, they became confused, and consequently easier to overcome, and that this disruption could be best brought about by mobility in the jungle, surprise and offensive action.[90]

There was a rise in both malaria and dysentery not just among the soldiers of both armies, but also the civilian population. One Indian soldier complained of immense discomfort and trauma (this was echoed by many others as well) caused by leeches constantly attaching themselves to a host, and attacking them. Dysentry and Malaria, relatively easy to treat today, in 1944, caused a great loss of lives. 'No matter which way you tum, you cannot be comfortable'.

It is apparent that both the armies and the civilians were subjected to such ordeals, but that is the nature of war.

The Manipuris, whether of the plains or hills for the most part did not actively participate or support either the Japanese or the Allies in the Battle. They nevertheless were impacted by the Battle in many ways- they suffered deprivation and discomfort, they were fascinated by and emulated in part some of the lifestyle features of the foreigners for instance in dress, food habits, world view. But the majority of the Manipuris, most especially the Kukis had great respect and empathy for the invading Japanese. They admired their courage as also the fact that they were never rude.

References

1. K.A. Nizami, *On History and Historians of Medieval India*, p.4
2. Interview with Ram Muivah, Indian Administrative Service (Retd.), Government of India, October 2020, Delhi.
3. Interview with Home Raikhan, Indian Revenue Service (Retd.), Government of India, October 2020, Imphal.
4. Home Raikhan, Naga History: Through a Clan and Tribe, pp.11-15.
5. Ram Muivah, *op.cit*
6. *Ibid, op.cit.* Source- SuisaRungsung, The Prophet, K. Wungnaoya
7. *Ibid, op.cit*, Interview
8. Arambam Angamba Singh, Facebook, 29th November, 2020
9. Home Raikhan, *op.cit.* p.15
10. *Ibid,op. cit.* pp. 192-193
11. *Ibid*, p.193
12. *Ibid,* p. 195 Steyn, Capt. Peter, *The History of the Assam Regiment*, vol.1, 1941-1947, Assam Regimental Centre, Reprint 1991, p.151

13. *Ibid,* p.195
14. *Ibid,* p. l96
15. Arambam Angamba Singh, Facebook, 22nd June, 2020
16. Answer to Questionnaire
17. Home Raikhan, *op cit.,* p. 196 18. Ibid, pp 192-196
19. Salam Irene, Ginneiching Simte, Thenkhogin Haokip, *Tribals of Manipur and Modernisation,* p.11
20. John S.R. Khathing, Indian Revenue Service (Retd.): The Life of the Unsung Hero Maj. Ralengnao 'Bob' Khathing, pp.11-12
21. Subedar A.S. Ninglam Tangkhul Retd.cit.in Yaiphaba Meetei Kangjam op.cit. pp.119-121. 22. John S.R.Khathing op cit., p. 12
22. John *S.R. Khathing* op cit. p.12
23. V.R. Azip, p.123- 125 cit. in Yaiphaba Meetei Kangjamop.cit
24. L.Ngaraipam, p. 127-129 op.cit
25. Hemant Singh Katochop.cit, p. 24-25, Interview with Shankazip Varu, January, 2014
26. Ibid, *op.cit,* p.25 cit.N. Luikham, Transformed Headhunters: The Pioneers of Tangkhul Education, Ukhrul: EI Shaddai Resource Centre,2011, p.75
27. Ibid, p.25 Lydall, Administrative Report of the Manipur State for the Year 1943-44 p.6
28. *Ibid,* p.26 cit. Singh, Manipur during World War II (1941- 45) op. cit. p.23
29. *Ibid,* p.27, Interview with A.S. Arthur, November 2014
30. *Ibid,* op.cit.
3l. *Ibid,* p.34 Singh *op.cit.* pp.20-21
32. *Ibid,* p.34-35, Lydall *op.cit.*
33. Interview with Dr. Michael Lunminthang, Asst. Prof. Ambedkar University, Delhi, 1st October, 2020

34. *Ibid, op.cit*

35. Hemant Singh Katoch, p.8, *op.cit* E.F. Lydall *op.cit,* p. I Note : The population of Imphal, the only town, was around 1,10,000.

36. Sonthang Haokip *op.cit* p.197-200 cit.T.S.Gangte 1993, *The Kukis of Manipur. A Historical Analysis, and Freedom Fighters of Manipur*, 1985 by Freedom Fighters Cell, MPCC(l).

37. *Ibid,* p.200 cit. L.W. Shakespear: *History of Assam Rifles* 1929.

38. *Ibid,* p.200-201 cit. Administrative Report of Manipur 1943-44 MSA p. 3

39. *Ibid,* p. 20 cit. J.Guite op.cit, p.307

40. *Ibid,* p.202 cit. Leaflets dropped in Manipur during World War II. History of Freedom Movement Papers, R-1, 49/3,NA l, p.86.

41. *Ibid,* p.205-206, cit."Notes on Kuki Situation", Assam State Archives, Dispur, p. l

42. *Ibid,* p. 228 cit. Rev. Zatanga (2010), Buaina Kara Eng Ropui: Japan Sipai in Saikawt, and the History of NEIGM (North East India General Missions)

43. Dr. Yoshihiro Kaburagi, 11th February 2020

44. Sonthang Haokip *op.cit.* p. 229, Kawlvel (Kolvella claimed that this officer was none than Netaji Subhash Chandra Rose), Lal Dena, *In Search of Identity*, p. 92

45. Priyadarshini M.Gangte: *The Kukis and the Indian National Movement for Independence* cit.in, Souvenir, 2006, *Anglo-Kuki War 1917-1919*, p. 63-64

46. Sonthang Haokip, *op.cit* p. 232, Japanese Propaganda, File No.29, Cabin NO. XLI, Manipur Secretariat Library, Imphal.

47. *Ibid,* p. 19

48. *Ibid,* p.253, Note: Onkholet Haokip was a Kuki chief (who developed love and affection for the Japanese for which he was nicknamed 'Japan Pakang' He followed the Japanese upto Japan during their retreat and refused to come back to his forefathers

land. This story collected from Pu Mangpithang Kipgen and confirmed by Pu Seikho Kipgen on 25th June, 2010

49. Ibid, op.cit
50. Ibid, p. 201: Reports of SI(FIB) forwarded by C. Grimson to Central Intelligence Officer, Assam, 25th November, 1944
51. Ibid, p.257 cit. JAC Memo of the Kuki INA Pensioners p,.8, December 1999
52. Ibid, pp. 258-259, J. Guite *op.cit* p.301
53. Phaneng Haokip cit.in Yaiphaba Meetei Kangjam op.cit. pp.131-133.
54. Nemjahat Touthang cit.in Yaiphaba Meetei Kangjam op. cit. p.135-137
55. T. Holkhongam Songthu cit.in Yaiphaba Meetei Kangjam. op.cit, pp.139-141
56. Mangkholen Misao, cit.in Yaiphaba Meetei Kangjam op.cit pp.143-147
57. Paojalhing op.cit.p.149-150
58. Y.L. Joseph, op.cit in Yaiphaba Meetei Kangjam op cit, pp.153-155
59. Hemant Singh Katoch op.cit pp.28-29, Interview with L. Achung Kom by Yaiphaba Meetei Kangjam, January, 2015
60. L. Achung Kom cit.in Yaiphaba Meetei Kangjam op.cit, p.61-65
61. Gachung Dangmei, cit.in Yaiphaba Meetei Kangjam op. cit, pp.67-69
62. Th.Chomlal Aimol cit.in Yaiphaba Meetei Kangjam p.71-73
63. Thanglengin Chiru cit.in Yaiphaba Meetei Kangjam, pp.75-77
64. Rifleman Henkholun Kuki, cit.in Yaiphaba Meetei Kangjam, pp.101-107
65. Ngamjang Mate, cit.in Yaiphaba Meetei Kangjam, pp.115- 117

66. F.S. Downs 1971, p.172, *The Mighty Works of God: A Brief History of the Baptist Churches in North East India.*
67. Sonthang Haokip, op.cit. p.278
68. Hemant Singh Katoch, op.cit, pp.26-27
69. Interview with Salma Annhaa, September 2020
70. Dr. Irengbam Mohendra Singh: *My Japanlan Memoir*, cit.in. The Sangai Express, 13th August 20 I7
71. *Ibid* cit.in Yaiphaba Meetei Kangjam *op. cit.* pp.39-47
72. R.K. Tamphasana, aged 97, Sagolband, Imphal-lnput provided by Surjalal Khuraijam: Readers Collective, Paomi Post on Facebook, 7th July, 2020
73. Arambam Angamba Singh on Facebook, 6th August, 2020
74. Hemant Singh Katoch, op.cit.pp.29-30
75. *Ibid,* pp.22-23
76. *lbid,* pp.19-20
77. *Ibid,* pp.21-22
78. *Ibid,* pp.22 cit. Lydall *op.cit,* pp.4-5
79. lbid, pp.20-23
80. Pukhrambam Birachandra, cit.in Yaiphaba Meetei Kan gjam op.cit, pp.90-91
81. Hemant Singh Katoch, op.cit., p. 29
82. Laishram Birendra Kumar Singh, cit.in Yaiphaba Meetei Kangjam, op.cit. pp. 9-13
83. Jemadar Arambam Bidhu Singh, Khuraijam Nimaicharan Singh, cit.in Yaiphaba Meetei Kangjam, *op.cit,* pp.15-27
84. GotimayumIbotombi Sharma, Taorem Gouramuhon Singh, Yumnam Kullachandra Singh, Khumanthem Kala, Karam Jugeshore, Oinam Jatra Singh, Naorem Kalimohon cit in. Yaiphaba Meetei Kangjam op.cit. pp.33-36, 53-55, 57-59,79-81, 83-87, 93-95, 109-1 12

85. Azad Hind Force, Imphal Front, 15th September 2020 on Facebook
86. Ibid, Facebook posted by Arambam Angamba Singh and Arambam Geeta
87. Anuj Dhar: What happened to Netaji, p.2
88. Laldena, op.cit., p.157
89. *Ibid,* pp.172-181
90. Col. M.G. Abhyankar, op.cit. pp.208-209.

3
The Japanese Voices

When a war such as a World War occurs, many men inevitably are fired with the spirit of patriotism/nationalism, and despite their enduring love for their families, they feel it to be their bounden duty to enlist or volunteer in such a war. This feeling is intensified when the Government of a warring country feels it imperative that all able-bodied men and even women should enlist themselves in the defence forces. Many who are afraid of enlisting are made to do so. But whether they enlist voluntarily or not, all those enlisting for the purpose of taking an active role in the war, know that their lives may be cut short at any moment by the enemy's fire, that they will be exposing themselves to all kinds of injuries, just not physical but psychological and emotional, that they will be vulnerable to exhaustion and diseases, that result in death. Their minds and hearts are filled with fear and anxiety – will they survive the war and be reunited with their families?

There is a revealing passage in a Japanese operations instruction dated 19 March 1944, issued by Col. Miyamoto of the 124th Regiment, Japanese 31st Division:

> Our enemies are the British and Americans. If you have to fight the Indians, persuade them as much as possible

> to surrender, and when they do, treat them kindly, they should be evacuated to the nearest INA headquarters. After crossing the Chindwin, treat all the natives kindly. Do not steal, and above all, don't get wrong ideas about women.[1]

The Japanese claimed that they came to give 'Swaraj' (Independence) to India. They carried pictures of Subash Bose addressing or inspecting the INA army; displayed Congress colours on arm bands, carried Congress flags and also uttered 'Jai Hind' as a sign of greeting. In order to get sympathy and support from the local people, the Japanese army used to respond to any of the genuine socio-economic problems of the people. For instance, they said there would be no 'house-tax' and 'forced labour' under them, and such propaganda certainly attracted the Kukis.[2]

The Japanese Story

This is not just a mere true story. It is one of the prime reasons for penning these words.

While delivering a lecture at Kobe, Yamate University, on 'The Battle of Imphal and its Relevance to Tourism', a member of the audience (all Japanese) came forward with a personal request. This Japanese national had been engaged for many years in a quest to discover the remains of a granduncle who had participated in the Battle of Imphal and was definitely a member of the Japanese/ INA coalition. The entire family wanted closure, but to get closure they wanted to find the bones of the granduncle, pray over them, perform the Last Rites, so that they could achieve some measure of peace of mind. The Japanese provided all details of the granduncle; personal details, educational background, name, rank, regiment, place of deployment, photograph and emphasised that the granduncle spoke English fluently and he possessed a degree in English. For many years, family and friends of the JIA casualties in Manipur had been visiting on a regular basis, to find the bones of family members and friends who had perished in Manipur during the Battle of Imphal. Some had been successful, but not all. Their visits increased approximately a decade ago, when a young researcher from Delhi began sensitising people on this important event of their history. This young man went on to establish a Battle of Imphal Tour, where the participants were taken to the WW II battle sites in Manipur and explained the details by Hemant Singh Katoch. About the same time, the Battle of Imphal was voted as Britain's Greatest Battle by the National Army Museum, UK on 20 April, 2013. A Second World War Imphal Campaign Foundation was formed and the Anniversary of the Battle began to be commemorated every year, with participation of people from both Japan and the UK.

The Japanese on the quest wanted help and I promised to do what I could, although I had never been involved in such a task. I requested Mr. Angamba Arambam to help as he and the 2nd World War Imphal Campaign Foundation were already engaged in this quest. What made it difficult to zero on any remains, was the fact that there were two different versions about the grand uncle's death.

The family had been informed that the granduncle was a regular soldier in a particular regiment. The family thereafter contacted families of other soldiers in that regiment, but to their shock and dismay, nobody knew of any such soldier with that name in their regiment; moreover all the soldiers in that regiment were personally known to one another and were certain that there was no individual bearing the granduncle's name. Disappointed and depressed, they took stock of the situation, in order to plan a new strategy to find their relative's remains. They had been told that he had died of malaria in Manipur. At that time, malaria was rampant, and many weakened Japanese soldiers did die of malaria, the explanation appeared plausible.The Japanese family believed that although the granduncle had come to Manipur with the JIA, he was not an ordinary soldier – because of his fluency in the English language, his services were required by the Japanese Command Administration not on the field but elsewhere. So he was a non-combat officer/soldier; unfortunately no precise details with regard to his duties and employment were available, and there was also a possibility that he may not have died in Manipur, but in erstwhile Burma.

The family representative who I had met had been searching for nine years, but with no success. She explained her dilemma in a correspondence with me:

> 'I do not yet know where you were. The granduncle seems to interpret Indian armed people. I want to look for an Indian knowing a Granduncle. Please tell me the group where a lot of soldiers of Indian armed people gather. Please.' (December 2018)

These sentences intrigued me. The family representative had never visited Manipur, we met very briefly in Japan, and she was not sure of where I resided, although I had given a visiting card. The words 'Indian Armed People' was not easy to understand. It may have been referring to the Indians who joined the INA, but Indians were also a part of the Allied Forces. But in 2018, most of the INA soldiers who fought in Manipur, would either be too old to recall the granduncle, or they may have also died, and in their reminiscences they don't seem to have mentioned him. The relatives believed that the granduncle was a kind of interpreter or translator, and associated with 'liason work' such as information on deployment of soldiers in the war.

Mr. Arambam Angamba Singh made a very earnest endeavour to find out all details pertaining to the person in question. After spending a lot of time and energy, he discovered the official record of this granduncle – details of his battle records along with the precise dates. The information also included the fact that he contracted malaria, and was carried to an army hospital in Burma where he subsequently died, as the strain of malaria contracted was severe and was compounded by dysentery from which he was suffering.

These details were relayed to the Granduncle's relative in Japan, and would have brought closure if the above details were correct. But the relatives of the deceased did not accept this explanation of his death or the details of his service record. There were reasons for the non-acceptance, but this presented a great dilemma, as the battle records would usually be accepted as a primary source of evidence.

The following are the reasons for the family's non-acceptance:

1. No one of his company, knows my granduncle.
2. On 24th (no month or year stated – presumably 1944 when the Battle of Imphal was fought), there were only 20 survivors' of his battalion. All the survivors' names were recorded, but my granduncle's name was not written in the name list.

3. Anyone (anybody) who took part in the operation said that it was impossible that only an infantry sergeant carried back over (on his back) 700 kms to Maymyo in that situation. (in the battle record sourced by Mr. Angamba Arambam, the granduncle was stated to have died in the army hospital at Maymyo in Burma)
4. When he (the granduncle) left (Japan), he said:

   'I will go to south front as a interpreter'. The language was English he majored in University.
5. As a result of the survey (Probably referring to the family's survey) I found it was the special organisation named 'Hikari', which had most hard needs of English translator in South front. The mission of Hikari, were the supporting INA, keeping relation and co-ordination with INA and JIA.
6. And then I found his sister's husband, the Director of his University, had deep relationships with special operation organisations of JIA.
7. And also, according to a testimony of Hikari member, they rewrited all the members record near the end of the war.

From these facts, I think my granduncle was a translator of a reason (probably the Intelligence Branch) with INA soldiers maybe. I attached my Granduncle's photo to this mail, Please use them.[3]

Less than a year later, on the occasion of the Platinum Anniversary of the Battle of Imphal, this family member formed part of group of Japanese nationals under the aegis of the Nippon Foundation, Japan to Manipur, for the Inauguration of the Imphal Peace Museum in 2019.

The members of the group were not allowed to meet with others, possibly because of security reasons, as most of them were visiting Manipur for the first time and were not conversant in speaking English, moreover they had a very tight schedule. On returning to Japan, this relative mailed me a brief but graphic description of the visit:

> "It's been a long time. It was the first time I visited India last year (2019) and was a miracle. I've be able to go to Manipur, Imphal, where my uncle wanted to go. It was a beautiful city, with lots of greenery, that I couldn't believe there was a fierce battle in the past. Unfortunately, I couldn't find the footprints of my granduncle, but I was impressed by the fact, that the people of Manipur still remember The Battle of Imphal, and they are keeping the Japanese military articles safe. I hope many people would visit the Peace Museum. I am grateful for Uncle's study from Mr. Anganbang Alambang (Arambam Angamba), last year. I can imagine various things from it, so I will use it for reference.[4]

There were few clues left. I didn't have knowledge only how to search the material about soldiers at the government office. In those days, I had few knowledge about war history. So I was a member of the Army Soldiers Friendship Association of Burma Campaign, and have made hearing (held interviews/ conversations) from many old soldiers. I found out a nurse in charge of the malaria ward at the hospital where my granduncle was hospitalised on (as per) his official record. I went to Myanmar, I searched out for members in the same company as my granduncle, and (they) said, he was never in our unit. Now I own, and research many books.[5]

This is a poignant story of a family seeking closure which eludes them. And as the years roll by, the task will become even more difficult. The relative who is conducting the actual search is a person of indomitable spirit, whose resilience must be admired; but the individual is an elderly person, not conversant in any language except Japanese. Nevertheless, she went alone to Myanmar to investigate. The flame within still burns bright, someday, the remains will be found. This story is the story of all Japanese families who lost a loved one in the war, and it illustrates the close enduring bonds within a Japanese family. The possibility also exists that the granduncle may have been a casualty in the last days of desperate fighting, where for various reasons, identification of some of the deceased may not have been possible. Yet this lone Japanese investigator on a mission, remarked on the beauty of People and the Land of Manipur.

The contrast between what the family searcher remarked about Manipur today (in 2019), and what it was seventy five years ago is factually correct. Seventy five years ago, the Imphal Plain was one vast military camp where thousands of Allied troops waited battle, as the Japanese army began their encircling movement. The Japanese soldier was always depicted (by the British), as a little bloke wearing long puttees, and running around shouting 'Banzai'. But as Richard Hill wrote: Now, we have a better understanding of what and where Nungsigum is, and how crucial the victory was. Today, every Japanese tourist who visits Manipur, makes a visit to Nungsigum. In June 2019, occurred the unveiling of the calligraphy signature 'Heisa' – 'Peace' by Shinzo Abe San, the then Prime Minister of

Japan, by His Excellency, Hiramatsu San, Ambassador of Japan to India at Red Hill, Manipur. At the inauguration of the Imphal Peace Museum at Red Hill were present, delegates from Japan, U.K. and other places, besides of course, the Manipuris. The Japanese delegation was large, and the Japanese contribution toward the construction of the museum, only reinforced and cemented, the special relation between Japan and Manipur. The Japanese believe that unlike what is done in many countries across the globe, the term 'war' should not be prefixed before the word 'Museum', as the word 'War', is associated with killing and death. For the Japanese gathered at Red Hill the inauguration of the 'Peace Museum' was something very dear to them. As one Japanese gentleman expressed it:

> The war is not over, until the thousands of lost souls can return to their homeland. (June-2019)

For many Japanese visitors who lost their ancestors in this epic battle, and for whom there are no grave and cemeteries to visit, the Imphal Peace Museum, funded by two Japanese Foundations, and inaugurated in June 2019 of the 75th Anniversary of the Battle of Imphal; it offers a chance for closure, reminding us, that in war, there are no true victors, only losers.[6] Maybe the Japanese will find the closure they so desire.

The bond between the Japanese and the Manipuris has been greatly reinforced especially in the last two decades, as the majority of the Japanese visitors to Manipur are eager to participate and do so in 'The Battle of Imphal Remembrance Tours'. Akiko Macdonald remarked: I feel personally sorry for the people of Manipur and their state, which became a battlefield, where so many fallen soldiers were left. I feel the Japanese Government were very late in acknowledging what happened in Manipur and just how much your people have endeavoured not just to re-establish your community over the years, but also the building of war memorials to Japanese soldiers.[7] The Japanese Imperial Army's War Crimes were presented at the Far East International Military Tribunal, where an Indian Judge, Radhabinod's view of tribunal was sceptical and questionable in regard to its legitimacy, and without his judgement, Japan could not redeem the nation's honor and dignity. The Japanese Imperial Army's war crimes were presented at the tribunal with evidence, but most of the pleadings by Japanese defendants were dismissed by the rest of the Allied judges. Justice Pal was convinced that there should be a correct way to examine and judge WW II as a whole under the international existing law.

Judge Pal explained how Japan engaged in the Great War in the Pacific and Far East, and argued that the evidence should be re-examined, as to whether Japan was guilty or not. His argument was based strictly on International Law, and not on sympathy for Japan.

After the Second World War, Japanese people became despondent and had mixed feelings: they felt that they had been unjustly treated at the war Tribunal, guilt and remorse for starting the war. Some of these feelings persist even today.

The history of WW II has never been coherently taught in schools in Japan. The Japanese post-war education system was greatly influenced by the American Military occupation, and young Japanese learned American values. American culture poured into Japanese old and rigid traditional society, which was turned upside down after the war ended. Talking about the war became a taboo subject amongst the wartime generation. Returned soldiers were despised as losers, whereas during the war, servicemen were feted as heroes fighting for the country. Many veterans felt guilt and shame about coming home alive, so they just put their heads down, and tried to get on with restoring the country.

After Japan had lost the war, the people repressed their remorseful feelings and memories, and many tried to forget about the war. Many veterans became heavy Sake drinkers, while others became taciturn, and focussed on working diligently every single day to rebuild the nation.[8]

One would certainly empathise with the Japanese. Smarting from the humiliation of defeat in war, the Japanese who actively fought in the war, and returned home from Manipur were treated harshly instead of with admiration and sympathy; they had risked their lives for Japan, they were mostly young people who fought in the war, but their contribution to Japan's war efforts was not recognised and they appeared to be treated as 'pariahs'. They must certainly have suffered from post-traumatic disorders, but as they were made to repress their memories, they probably did not seek any treatment, but sought to drown their sorrows in 'sake'.

Probably, this is the reason why a Japanese Professor stated that 'Memory' is an exceptionally sensitive issue today. The memories of that old generation (WW II veterans) have changed as time went by. The studies of the transformation of 'war memories' have been available in Japan. The famous monograph I know in this regard is the one below:

Ryuichi Narita, Zouho "Senso-Keiken" no Sengoshi: Katarareta Taiken/ Shogen. Kioku. Iwanami; Shoten, 2020.

(Ryuchi Narita, Post War History of War Experience: Narrated Experience/ Testimony/ Memory (Extended Edition) Iwanami Shoten, 2020.)[9]

If war memories had not been repressed, had the returning soldiers not been made to feel ashamed, these 'War Memories' would have become a very important source of 'Oral History'.

This book basically is divided into four chapters, excluding the Introduction and Conclusion. The first chapter entitled War as 'Situation' 1931-1945 gives 'three patterns of war description:

1. Soldier's Note narrating Personal Experience
2. Report by called up writer or correspondent, emphasising the situation as the outline of occupation, battle, etc.
3. Novel (War Literature) looking hard at oneself.

Record of war shows the war as an ongoing event with clear result of operation, but with unclear end of war itself. Positioning and meaning at the time of writing is completely different between wartime and post-war, when the dominant official logic is turned into the negation of war to change the view and description of words, in other words, the post war is born and begun, by denying the position during wartime. At post-war period, the description during wartime is tended to be adapted or hidden, so that the basic trend of war description goes toward the interest in existence.[10]

The second chapter recognises that 'each personal

experience will connect with Japanese nation overall. 'Biruma Senki' (Burma War Record: 1953 by Masaru Ushiro, staff officer, Regional Army of Burma): "The Imphal Operations were really of magnificent design, but timing was unfavourable. Fighting spirit and power of the opponent were much more beyond previous condition". The description remains only in hard work for commanders to proceed operations.

Imupaaru – Kaimetsu suru Biruma Homen – gun no Kiroku (Imphal – Record of Destroyed Regional Army of Burma: 1949 by Toshiro Takagi, correspondent of movie news) draws a rash and miserable end of the operations by writing from the interview of survived soldiers.

Okinawa no Saigo (The End of Okinawa: 1947 by Narumi Furukawa:

"Setting the dead aside, only we, survivors, can enjoy the pleasure of new life – is it good or not?

Tatakau Horyo – Sovieto Kikan – sha no Shuki (Fighting Prisoner – A Note of Returned Soldier from Soviet Russia: 1948 by Masao Ishikawa):

> "Keeping the return to Homeland as a big support. I am sure I can return to Japan to see my wife and children with the continuous feeling of nostalgic sweetness, and I will make up mind to reconstruct Japanese and Japan (the reformation of individual Japanese as well as the innovation of inner Japan)"[11]

Chapter 3:War as Testimony (1965-1990)

Shinpan: Inpaaru (New Edition: Imphal: 1968 by Toshiro Takagi)

The description of war record was amended to

boost the stressing points, and the whole image of the operations was strengthened by adding new books, viz. Komei (Protesting Order: 1966), Zenmetsu (Annihilation: 1968) and Funshi (Dying of Indignation: 1969) as a series of the Imphal Operations. Various relevant books were referred to, viz. Senshi-sosho: Inpaaru Sakusen (A series of War History: The Imphal Operations: 1968 by Boeicho (Dept. of Defence), verbal records, memories and diaries of commanders. The responsibility of reckless plan and evasive defeat should be owed not only by commanders but also by staff officers as "Hatred is to the war planner and crime is to the irresponsibility of concerned people of war." Sixty soldiers were interviewed for three days, to listen to individual experiences for writing Funshi, and small unit level activities were traced to reveal all possible factors of recklessness and contradiction of operations for writing Zenmetsu.

Kurashi-no-Techo Tokushu: Sensu-chu no Kurashi no Kiroku (Kurashi-no-Techo Magazine Special Edition: Record of Daily Life during Wartime: 1968): Common people did not recognise 'ruins of fire' and 'sufferers' as 'battlefields' and 'the fallen in War'.[12] Tokyo-Daikushu/ Sensai-shi (Big Air Raid to Tokyo and History of War Damage: 1973, 1974): Tokyo Daikushu/ Sensai-shi (Big Air Raid to Tokyo and History of War Damage: 1973, 1974): Tokyo Kushu wo Kiroku suru Kai (Association to Record Tokyo Air Raid) invited experience notes from survivors and also made use of circulating town bulletins and articles of magazines, by which the effect, was gained for testimonies to act in unison and reflect each other.

Personal Experience gives the first priority to the absoluteness of one's own experience, while Testimony delivers the narrative, to be conscious of others. In case of being mainly led by Personal Experience, the large factor lies in the difference of class, standpoint, and how to concern with war. In case of being mainly led by Testimony, the points at issue are the interpretation of event, and the original event itself, viz. the event happened or not, truth or falsehood, etc. to create severe rivalry, viz. progressivism vs. conservatism in history, innovation vs. conservativeness at present, etc. Testimony, is a form to talk to a specified object, or a practice through cooperative activity between narrator and listener, and the fact is not limited within the existence of fact, but inclusive of message to be presented through mutual interpretation and judgement. Many testimonies, before and after 1970 are records of recollection, as the recollection accompanies many conscious or unconscious transformation of fact by the mistake of memory, and the change of subjective or objective conditions in post-war period. (inevitable)

Taiheiyo Senso (Pacific War: 1968, 1986 by Saburo Ienaga), accumulates many different testimonies to be used commonly with undeniable emphasis, prepares for data carefully and critically, sublimates one's own experiences into common experience, to lead the description of a certain experience as typical universal experience (makes it easier to comprehend)[13]

Chapter 4: 'War as Memory' (1990 onwards)

The war image in Memory period is a trial: to place one's own experience into a context in post-war period. Interests are widened towards the double layers, and transference between assaulter and sufferer, being reflected by war painting, war movie, cartoon and popular song, as well as the consciousness of Imperial Japan, so that each aspect of recognition, objective, method and description is diversified and extended into multi poles.

Since 1990, trials (efforts) have been made to historize the post–war period through the war. It is searched more for the meaning of the wartime event at present post war time, rather than the investigation of wartime event.

Arguments concerning War and Imperial Japan – Colony or occupied area, emphasise the world wide commonness, rather than the investigation though passage of time. The post-war history (order under Cold War) is built into the description of war. Bearing in mind both consciousness caused by post-war and erased by post-war, the investigation of war, and the expression of war image are made, based on both the consciousnesses.

The period of Personal Experience created the common basis of post-war expression, the period of Testimony developed the post-war value and expression to show the post-war will, and the period of Memory reconsiders the post war itself along the main subject of war, as the post-war expression can be set up as thinking over an axis of war.

The period of Memory boosts the rivalry of interpretation, the axis of which emphasises more the point of issue on compositionalism vs. essentialism than such previous points as progressivism vs. conservatism and idealist vs. realist, and other point of view to question both War, and the relationship between Imperial Japan or occupied area is further required, as well as the simple rivalry between two concepts as exemplified above.

From 1990 onwards, war has been described from the view points of memory and subject of history, where the recognition of Colony and unsymmetrical others are considered, and then the counterpart to be talked and the position of one's own talk are realised or questioned under such concepts as war history or its theory and war image or its view.

Area wise, it is attempted to rewrite the regional history across Asia, not limited to the National History of Japan and Japanese as subject, in collaboration with digging out cross border movement or the new research trend of Colony or occupied area Time-wise, it should not be cut off by the end of war on August 15, 1945, but searched for views of 1940's. This enlarges the conspectus of history.)

The methodological connection between Oral History and Topos (the place like Okinawa, Hiroshima and Nagasaki) is attempted. The new proposal for recognition of history, narrative of war and war image, in relation to the redefinition of Early Modern and Modern Ages and Nationalism, is being examined in various ways.

The issue of War and Imperial Japan-Colony, or occupied area relation, is still under the dispute of Memory towards formulating historical image. War experience is now going into the process of being historicized through the periods of Personal Experience, Testimony and Memory. (This would certainly give rise to a new perspective on the events mentioned above).

This book 'War Experience' was commented upon (reviewed) by a Japanese novelist, Keiichiro Hirano, who analyses it thus:

War Experiences, talked and written, are divided into such three areas as Personal Experience, Testimony and Memory. Based on which area is dominant out of the above

Trinity, post-War information media are put in order into three periods when individual historical sources are allocated for trial:

1. The Period for Personal Experience (1950's in the centre), when one's own experience was talked in a society as a whole to share common experience. Then the concerned person writes oneself.
2. The Period of Testimony (1970's in the centre), when the concrete experience was told to be a specific counterpart. Then the other person keeps writing the hearing.
3. The Period of Collective Memories (1990's onwards), when each person who oneself did not experience war tries to follow quasi-experience, tracking the war experience talked and written so far, verify and reform the composition of its contents. Now in an extended line of this period, we are involved in the vortex of such a composition as if it is tampered with history to be mixed up with truth or falsehood.

Dr. Yoshihiro Kaburagi, who is well travelled and well informed not only about the history of Manipur but also that of India, has also commented on Dr, Ryuichi Narita's book:

> This book is quite useful and informative to find a way how to analyse the war records with various sources, so as to understand the war in Modern History overall, particularly for the people born and grown in post-war period like us. However, in case of our interested topic of the Imperial Operations, two authors are referred to, viz. M. Ushiro and T. Takagi, with a few comments only. Concerned books listed in Chronological Table are all

written in Japanese, mostly probably without English translation. Therefore, we have to pick up the relevant books written in English or Indian languages from other sources.[14]

The Current Japanese Perspective

'We Japanese shouldn't have started this war itself, where we had invaded many societies of other countries. I deeply regret this part of Japan's past.'[15]

Just as the last part of Dr. Ryuichi Narita's book is centered on the 1990's onwards, so two Japanese who were not witness to the Battle of Imphal, have written personal accounts of growing up in Post War II, Japan.

Kaz Nakajima's account though brief, is similar in many ways to the methodology adopted by Dr. Ryuichi Narita.

The Way to the Operation Imphal

In December 1941, Japanese forces attacked the British Malay Peninsula and Pearl Harbour in Hawai, U.S.A., began the war with countries such as British and the United States. This war which lasted for about four years, was originally called the Asia-Pacific War, but it also involved with the war in Europe and became the World War 2nd.

The war ended with Japan's devastating defeat, and killed a total of more than three million Japanese, soldiers and civilians. More than twenty million soldiers and civilians from the countries were killed at China, East Asia, Philippines and the islands of Pacific, which became battlefields for Japanese army. Why couldn't we stop such the war when it started, and there was a huge amount of sacrifice?

Looking back on history, in 1931, Japanese troops

invaded North-Eastern China and established Manchu Empire, in order to enlarge the new territory. Since then, Japan had been confronting against European countries and United States. In addition, there were many conflicts with China which leaded to the Sino-Japanese War in 1937.

Separately, the social situation in Japan in the 1930's, caused people to feel uneasy anxiety about famine and depression. In addition, people recognized that the Government failure of diplomatic measures, the rampage of the military, neglect of human life, hatred to Europe and the United States, and contempt for Asian people, etc.

Various factors had intertwined each other, and it was finally progressing to the war.

The Sino-Japanese War occurred in 1937, increased the political movement to exclude Western countries from Asian countries that had been colonized by them for a long time (for eg. India), and then the military priority policy, based on the political and economic co-prosperity zone centered on Japan, and Manchu was implemented by Japanese military without any permission from neighbouring countries. In order to spread this idea, military education and its training to create the Greater East Asia Co-Prosperity Zone led to the basic activities of the government itself. Military education to fight the enemy for the sake of Emperor, and for the Nation, became common sense in Japan, and it became a basic concept for all people in Japan to act in that consciousness without any exception.

In 1941, the elementary school suddenly changed its name to "National School", and the content of the study had changed completely, that even elementary school student had to work for the war. Especially, it was taught that the boy was going to the war ground sooner or the other (early military indoctrination). Under the conscription system, all men between the age of 20 and 40 had to go to the army. Thus warrant cannot be refused by an order from the nation. At that time, it was said in society that it was a great honor to go to the battlefield with this warrant. It was customary for all the people in town to celebrate and see off the soldiers, when they were sent to the army. Although the family members have to send the husband or child out with a smile, all they strongly wanted, was that husband or child would come home safely, from bottom of their mind, and pray for it quietly in their heart. (They were obviously wracked by a myriad different emotions.)

The Voice of the War Testimony

In 1944, there was a shortage of combatants on the front line, and students were finally forced to send to the front line as combatants. The age of conscription was also changed from 19 to 45 years old. In addition, the volunteers of the boy soldier over 15 years old had started. A thousand of the boy soldiers participated in it, from all over the country.

Before long, the atmosphere of willing to die on the battlefield for the sake of the Emperor and nation, spread nationwide. The Japanese Government forced all citizens to devote their lives to fight against enemy, regardless of what people thought.

Under the National Mobilization Act, the atmosphere that it was natural for even women and children to work in munitions factories and cultivate fields to increase food production had widely spread. However, the situation was getting worse and worse.

Since the loss in Midway Battle in June 1942, the Japanese Army had been defeated at each battlefield. In addition, as of May 1943, all supply routes to that combat basin overseas had been completely cut off. This had lost perfectly its victory for the Japanese Army. Nevertheless, Japanese Army did not come to the conclusion that war should be stopped. Even though, the situation was getting worse at every battlefield, Operation Imphal was executed, in order to break through the worsening situation.

In January 1944, the Japanese Army was deprived of the right to fly over Burma, and most of the planes flying over Burma were Allied aircraft. Therefore, the Japanese military had no choice but to carry all goods by land.

The location of Imphal was a key point between Burma and India. It was a major supply route to the Chinese army that Japan was fighting, as well as a major base for British troops stationed in India. As Japanese Army set up the strategy on the premise of capture at this territory in the short term period, the soldiers challenged the battlefield with small amount of food 'and few weapons which disregarded logistics, but focused only (on) spiritual theory. That was the reason why the operation Imphal was so-called "a reckless or the worst operation in Japanese military history" after the war.'

In like vein another Japanese stated: In modern Japan, we call reckless project or hopeless mission 'Imphal'. For example in April 2020, the Government have decided to distribute two masks to every household across the country to prevent Covid-19 outbreak. They spent 4,000 crore yen (2,500 crore rupee!!) only to distribute masks. It was huge money, but the effect was little. Once politicians and officers have decided to start any projects, they cannot stop to continue it, thought every citizen knew it is meaningless and waste of money. The mechanism of political decision making is totally same with what Imperial Headquarters decided in the Imphal Operation 76 years ago. Our mindset does not change at all after long years. We find many "Imphal operation" in our society. That's why we still remember the name of Imphal.[16]

The Voice of The Returning Soldier

'There was no food, no medicine, no medical treatment, and I was exhausted, while being groaned (wracked) by a high fever. It was a very mysterious that I could return to Japan, and I was able to live like this. I don't want to say a word of war. That was a nightmare.'[17]

My Life in Changing Japanese Society

I was born in Tokyo in 1947, two years after the surrender of Japan for the Allied Forces led by USA, and grew in Moji, presently a ward of Kitakyushu city. Fukuoka Prefecture, Kyushu Island, Southern Japan. Moji was a large seaport, prospered by the trade with Korea, China and South East Asia, especially till the end of the war, located at the north-eastern edge of Kyushu Island, across a narrow strait with the Honshu mainland. During the war time, most soldiers embarked at Moji port towards the battlefield in China, South East Asia and Pacific islands. In my boyhood, I could get several opportunities to listen various experiences during so-called 15-years war period (1931-1945), starting from Manchuria incident through China War to the Great East Asian War (The Second World War), from my parents, elder sister, relatives and other senior people, about the joining army in the war with China, the indiscriminate US air-bombings to major cities of Japan, and the estrangement of school children to rural areas. Particularly, I still remember my father having told us vividly such a story that he went out of a shelter with his colleague for survival just air-bombing crashed directly the shelter where all the hiding people were buried to death. During the war-time, he was engaged in serving National Shipping Association as marine expert, moving around several seaports. My elder sister alone was evacuated, to stay at her grandparent's house in a city of north-central province, but had to further escape to a nearby village, from which she clearly saw at night, the fires just like bright sunset to burn down the whole city by US air raid. I am the youngest child after an elder sister and an elder brother, while my parents got one more girl during the wartime, but she died shortly after birth, due to poor physical conditions under the shortage of foods (a tragic death). I came to know from newspaper and radio news the miserable retreat of Japanese migrants from Manchuria, suffered by the sudden invasion by USSR, even after the surrender of Japan despite the neutral treaty, the returned of imprisoned soldiers after struggle from China, South East Asia and Pacific Islands, and the soldiers under detention by USSR from Manchuria to Siberia and Central Asia as laborers,(58,000 died out of 5.75 lakh soldiers) and the accidents of blind shells and mechanical mines exploded to kill a few people, even more than a decade after the end of war. At towns, I often visited with my father and brother, the black markets with poor barracks, seeing often disabled soldiers, without leg(s), arm(s), and/ or eye(s), wearing one sheet of white Kimono (clothes), usually playing accordion to sing war song at an entrance of railway station, as well as in front of a shrine gate at festivals, to whom a few walkers donated a piece of coin into a small box, placed in front of them. One day in my elementary school, all the pupils were gathered at an assembly hall to listen the story told by a senior gentleman about his rare experience in Manchuria, before the war, as adventurers in the continent. (Tairiku Ronin) At an opening ceremony of Kanmon Strait Tunnel at Moji Gate, all the pupils were led by teachers to welcome Ten'no (Emperor), on a roadside, where old ladies sat down on straw mats in front and bowed to put their hands together in prayer upon Ten'no's passing through a road by car. At home, I often took such simple meals as porridge with hashed sweet potatoes, or rice mixed with a little butter or soy sauce, and enjoyed myself to boil water and sugar on a spoon, into candy, as sweets were so precious then. After I entered to work at a company, I visited Hiroshima Peace Memorial Museum, where many damaged materials were displayed by the first Atomic Bombing dropped in the city to cause the largest massacre of 1.7 lakh lives (0.7 lakhs in Nagasaki) at one time in human history, preserving destroyed building, so called Atomic Bomb Dome. I was surprised to watch TV news that two Japanese soldiers were found alive in southern islands viz. Gocho (the lowest non-commissioned office) S. Yokoi, in Guam Island of Marianas USA in 1972, Second Lieutenant H. Onoda in Rupang island of Luzon, Philippines in 1974. (This is similar to a post on FB maybe two years earlier showing a Japanese soldier who lived alone in a Manipur jungle after Japanese defeat) They kept engaged in war as the order to stop fighting under surrender, did not reach them. Near my house there still remained an air-raid shelter dug of cliff, used as store space then. I sometimes walked from my house up to a big Golden Pagoda built to pray for the souls of dead soldiers, in association with Burmese Buddhist Association, standing on a hill where batteries were located during the war time. At home, I enjoyed with my brother to make wooden miniature models of battleships, both Japan and US navies, playing a brave but a bit dangerous game to struggle for position at a small hill, by throwing pebbles to each other among neighbouring children (children invented war games). My father sometimes brought me and my brother a cinema theatre to watch Japanese battle movies, dramatizing the great victories of Admirals H. Togo and I. Yamamoto at the battle of Japan Sea in the Russo-Japanese War and the air-bombing from aircraft carriers at Pearl Harbor, Hawaii, in the Second World War, and other documentary films of war. (cinemas obviously were primarily screening war films)

Although people did not like to talk about the war and patriotism, torturing themselves the modern history with false activities under aggressive Imperialism, but sticking to the humanism for peace; on the other hand they seemed to long for the past difficult days during the wartime, to have overcome the crises by joint efforts and co-operation. This may show a kind of feeling of perversion. From around 1960's onwards, Japan developed rapidly, and prospered in a high growth of economy, boosting so many constructions of houses, buildings, highways and railways, that the memories and the remains of the war time faded away gradually in people's minds.

Japan changed politically and socially over all at the end of the Second World War, leading the change of people's valuation. In other words, there found a sharp discontinuity between pre-war and post-war societies. Before the end of the war, the Constitution of the Great Japanese Empire, prescribes that the Empire is ruled by Ten'no (Emperor, literally – Heavenly Royalty) with his line unbroken for ages eternal. Ten'no commands both army and navy, the essence of national framework is a single great family state with the ruler and subjects in one body, and Japanese subjects are charged duty to do military service. This was consolidated by such ideologies as Ten'no fascism or totalitarianism under the state Shintoism, the Imperial historical view appealing the Immortal God land and the greatest Yamato race in the world under Ten'no as the 'God Alive'. The flame of nation advocated such expansionist propagandas as: 'the syncretized would just like one house from eight corners of the world (Hakko-Ichiu) 'the new order of Greater East Asia' (Dai-towa-shin-chitsujo), 'the co prosperous sphere of Greater East Asia' (Dai-towa-kyoe-iken), to appeal the emancipation of Asia by the dogma of Great Asia-ism. The scheme of national totalitarian was by national mobilization, forced to mobilise 69.6 lakh soldiers (20.5% of total male population), supported by National Mobilisation for War Industry, Girl Volunteers (at below 25 years old), Student Labour Mobilization and University Student Going to War (at 20 years old and above). Accordingly, various unified organisations were set up under National Spiritual Totalitarian Mobilization Campaign viz. Great Political Enforcing Co-operative Party (Taisei Yokusan Kai), Neighbourhood Unit (Tonari Gumi) Village Unit, Town Unit, Great Japan Industrial Association for national service, Agricultural League for national service, Commercial Association for national service, Japan Shipping Association for national service, Great Japan Women Association, Great Japan Youth Corps, Great Japan Manhood Enforcing Cooperative Corps (at 21 years old and above), Rationing System of Necessities for life, Removal of buildings in major cities and Evacuation of pupils into countryside, against indiscriminate US air raids. The 15 year war ended with 3.4 million Japanese dead (inclusive of 8 lakh civilians.)

The Allied Forces led by USA occupied Japan for seven years from 1945 to 1952. The Constitution of Japan (so called 'Peace' Constitution) towards liberal and democratic society was promulgated in 1946, and came into effect in 1947. The selected paragraphs of relevant subjects are described as below: (to facilitate a better understanding).

(Preamble) We, the Japanese people, acting through our duly elected representatives in the National Diet, determined that we shall secure for ourselves and our posterity, the fruits of peaceful cooperation with all nations, and the blessings of liberty throughout this land, and resolved that never again shall we be visited with the horrors of war through the action of government, do proclaim that sovereign power resides with the people, and do firmly establish this Constitution.

(Article 1) The Ten'no. shall be the symbol of the State and the unity of the people deriving his position from the will of the people with whom resides sovereign power.

(Article 9) Aspiring sincerely to an international peace based on justice and order, the Japanese people forever renounce war, as a sovereign right of the nation, and the threat or use of force, as means of settling international disputes. In order to accomplish the aim of the preceding paragraph, land, sea and air forces, as well as other war potential, will never be maintained. The right of belligerency of the state will not be recognised.

The defence related government budget (5.3 billion Yen in 2020) has been minimised below one per cent of GDP, thanks to the alliance with USA under her nuclear umbrella. Japan Self-Defence Forces are maintained under volunteer system, eligible from 18 to 32 years old. However, people's consciousness for self-defence had been weakened, while the human rights are placed as first priority as each human life is evaluated to be heavier than the earth. Individualism or egoism prevails through Americanization in people's minds.

As I belong to a post-war generation, I am not a right person to answer the questionnaire (which I sent him), mainly touching about the feelings of people during the war time; yet I will make my own comments as student of history, to close together with people's minds then, taking my experiences into account, and referring to books.[18]

Akiko Macdonald has also written about 'Rebuilding Devastated Japanese Society after the War.'

During rebuilding of the nation, a new education system was established and women were given rights. Under the American occupation policy, (United States Education Mission) in 1946, the existing education system was restructured and improved, so as to democratise and abolish the Japanese elitist higher education system.

Some old traditions and values were abolished, such as worshipping the Emperor, which could have led to Nationalism, for example. The country embraced peace more than anything, in fact, if the truth be known, people were tired of war.

Japanese people in general were tightly controlled by the military, and the people hid away their feelings of dismay, disillusionment, and sadness, that the nation was engaged in war.

On the day, the war finally ended in August 1945, the Japanese people finally got rid of totalitarianism and militarism.

During the 1960's, 70's and 80's, the nation concentrated on building up its infrastructure, industry, high technology and exporting all manner of goods. Due to tremendous effort made by the war and post-war generation, Japan gained world-wide respect and established itself as a modern civilised country.

Only after Japan had becomes relatively wealthier and a democracy that took care of its own people did everyone look back at the war-time period and all the sacrifices.[19]

Many Japanese, especially in the last two decades have visited Manipur, in connection with the Battle of Imphal, primarily to find or locate the remains of loved ones, who died in the Battle, and if successful perform the Last Rites, either in Manipur or in Japan, so as to honor the dead, and provide some closure, and to visit the battle sites of World War II in Manipur. Even those who come as tourists want to visit the battle-sites. Hiroko Ozaki, wrote to me that she visited both Manipur and Nagaland, and in her hometown called Kochi, there were some soldiers who went to Imphal to fight, and as a result she often saw news articles related to the Battle of Imphal in her local news-paper, which aroused her interest in the subject. 'My impression of Manipuri people is very good. Quiet, shy and friendly. Perhaps because we Japanese and Manipuri, seem to have some similarities in our features, culture and characteristic. I feel very comfortable and close with Manipuri people.'[20] Dr.

Yoshihiro Kaburagi finds himself quite at home in Manipur which he visits frequently, and he is not afraid to move on foot alone in different parts of the state.

60,000 Japanese soldiers died in Manipur. Most of them were very young, some soldiers and pilots were mere teenagers, and this was true for both Japanese boys and girls who took part in the battle. There are references to young Japanese women pilots and lady officers, one of whom was described by Ngamjang Mate in the book compiled by Yaiphaba Meetei Kangjam (Refer to P.115). As Japan had been engaged in other theatres of war prior to the Battle of Imphal, their forces were stretched out, more seasoned officers and men had been deployed in war at other fronts, so the young and inexperienced came to Imphal and Kohima. But they believed as did other Japanese, 'that each of them who had sacrificed their lives for the nation, their souls reside in this shrine – Yasukini Shrine in Tokyo.'[21]

The features of the Japanese Constitution before the end of the war as described by Dr. Yoshihiro Kaburagi is in many ways similar to the theory of "Divine Right of Kings" which existed in India, China and many parts of the world in the ancient and medieval periods. In India in the ancient period, the King was held to rule by divine right and to be in a sense a God himself, being only tied to the advice of a Brahman.[22] The Muslim Sultans of Delhi called themselves Zil-ul-lah or 'Shadow of God on Earth'. The Chinese Emperor was similarly 'The Son of Heaven', and possessed 'the mandate of Heaven' to rule over the Chinese people and the encircling barbarians of the whole earth.[23] The idea of sacredness of Ten'no was endorsed by the 'Divine Will' as the title 'Devaputra' of Kusana Empire in Ancient India.[24] The Divine Right of Kingship entails both political and religious allegiance/ obedience to a monarch, and this theory has been used in different climes and times, to justify a monarch's actions. A mere glance at Mughal Indian paintings, will reveal the halo of light (divinity) around the Emperor's head. In Emperor Akbar's reign, there were four prescribed degrees of devotion to the King, but it was not incumbent even for the courtiers to accept these degrees. So there are differences between rulers who adhered to 'the Divine Right of Kings'. But a parallel could be drawn with Akbar's Four Degrees of Devotion and the Eight Virtues prescribed in the Japanese 'Bushido'.

Bushido of Japan – (Way of the Warrior), the code of conduct of the samurai or bushi (warrior), class of pre-modern Japan. In the mid-nineteenth century however, the precepts of Bushidos were made the basis of ethical training for the whole society. As such it contributed to the rise of Japanese Nationalism, following the Meiji Restoration (1868).

Instruction in the code was officially abandoned with the Japanese defeat in 1945. Elements of the code remain however, in the practices of Japanese martial arts and in the sport of sumo wrestling.[25]

Eight Virtues in Bushido:

Rectitude or Justice

Courage

Benevolence

Politeness

Veracity and Sincerity

Honor

Loyalty

Self Control.[26]

This is a Manipuri's understanding of the Code of Bushido. It is penned with reference to the Imperial Japanese Army WWII and shows the Code being practised by the Japanese Army.

'It was early March 1944. At the turn of the dawn, Company Commander Lt. Nishimoto of the 1st Batallion 58th Regiment 31st Infantry Division fixes his bayonet signalling the arrival of the final moment of triumph and tryst with honour for the children of the Nippon. In his deep resonating voice he announces to his men, that finally the moment has arrived to shine forever and if at all you were to fall you still fight on with your spirit... With the shout of 'Banzai' echoing in the air and the grenades exploding with the rattle of the machine guns, waves after waves of soldiers charges forward without the utmost care for the inevitable future lying ahead, thereby announcing the start of 'March to Delhi' campaign. A piquet manned by the Assam regiments commanded by British officers was stationed at this feature known as Harbak-hangai or Pt 7378. The fight continued till the complete silence this was the first major encounter that took place between the Japanese and the Allied force on Indian soil, and the latter knew that they were up against a far experienced and battle hardened adversary.

Great British dominion like Singapore the 'impregnable fortress', Malaya and Burma, were all crumbling like stacks of dominoes, under the weight of the idea that was the Great East Asia Co-Prosperity sphere, or plainly Asia for the Asian. The plan of co-operation U-GO or the March to Delhi was conspired within the Cherry Society, of which Lt. Gen. Renya Mutaguchi and the War Minister Tojo were prominent members. From the very onset, it was a very grand and optimistic plan with few takers. But tragically it ended as the greatest land defeat for the Japanese Army during World War II. The whole campaign ended officially on 4th July. 1944, having lost about 30,000 of soldiers, as a result of both battle casualties as well as diseases.

The tenacity and valor of an ordinary Japanese soldier has been passed down from the times of the Great Samurais. The Code Bushido is worth understanding. For years the public had been indoctrinated into the superior theories and the Divine Mission to liberate Asia. As the war waged on in Europe, Japan found an opportunity here. The nationalistic fervor was ignited once again. Preparation for war went on a scale never imagined. Citizens were hastily conscripted into the national army. The Generals were to be blamed for toying with the soldiers like pawns in the later campaigns. Poets in their paean have often compared these soldiers with cherry blossom, which is regarded as a symbol known for virtues such as purity, loyalty and patriotism.

The cherry is the first among blossoms

The warrior first among man...

The spirit of death before dishonour forms the very basis of Bushido Code.

As war raged on, there was more rapid conscription of youth into the army, wherein they had to undergo an intense three month introduction programme. This resulted into extreme fanaticism, ready to jump into death for the Emperor, for the country and for their own regiment. During the training, they are trained to endure extreme hardship and pain, which was to become a staple diet in the later stages of the campaign. Here, they are also made to understand that it was not necessary to command anyone of them to fight to the last man and to the last round. If necessary, save the last round for self. Or give a suicidal charge. They are also to understand that it is a sin to turn ones back to the enemy, which brings dishonour to one's family and the country. During the transformation period, death is often glorified to win the hearts of young recruits. Dying for the Emperor and the country was to live forever, and if ever to fall, the very soul deemed to live amongst Gods, and forever enshrined in the Yasukini shrine in Tokyo. Field Marshall Slim, Commander of the 14th Army once stated: 'we talk a lot about fighting to the last man and last sound, but the Japanese is the only one who actually does it.'

The ordinary Japanese soldiers were superb fighters with high proficiency in skills and cleverness. The overall effect of their competence in night attacks, their trickery and fanatical courage, had enveloped the Allied force in a sense of inferiority and the Code of Bushido had helped to earn a reputation of ruthless ferocity, and created a great impact. Japanese soldiers would often drive themselves to the extreme exhaustion point with total disregard for normal human feelings. Often, soldiers stood out in the open, with their guns, with total disregard to their safety. It was always a jaw-dropping scene, which often left one with amazement and psychological imbalance. This inherent trait also attributed to the extremely high casualty figure of the campaign.

It concluded: as one of the most bitter battles fought in the history of the Second World War, ... the Japanese army was one of the greatest fighting forces of the times.

'Whether I float as a corpse under the waters,

Or sing beneath the grasses of the mountainside,

I willingly die for the Emperor.'

(From a Marching Song).[27]

The Imperial Rescript on Education "Kyoiku Chokugo" has twelve virtues.

1. Be filial to you parents.
2. Be affectionate to you brothers and sisters.
3. As husbands and wives, be harmonious.
4. As friends true.
5. Bear yourselves in modesty and moderation.
6. Extend your benevolence to all.
7. Pursue learning, and cultivate arts.
8. Develop intellectual faculties.
9. Perfect moral powers.
10. Advance public good, promote common interests.
11. Respect the Constitution, and observe the laws.
12. In emergency, offer yourself to the State.

('Kyoiku Chokugo' published in 1890 by the Emperor of Meiji.)

The last virtue would be directly related to Japanese youth volunteering for army service during World War II. Many young Japanese who took part in the Battle of Imphal were young men – some mere boys (teenagers), with their whole lives ahead of them. 'Perhaps, (they took part) they believed that their actions would save the country, I would like to say that even if I had doubts, I think I was in a situation, where I could not escape from the act.' This is echoed in another respondent's reply: 'I think they believed that the act would protect their country and families' 'I don't know the truth, but I don't think that the fifteen year old soldier was forced to take part in Operation Imphal. It was true that fifteen year old boy soldier worked in the military during the war but not in Operation Imphal.'[28] 'Prior to the Second World War, the Japanese Government provided the youth from six to fourteen years old with the compulsory education at National Elementary and Senior schools. Total population as 73 million in 1940, as compared with 124 million in 2020. The average life span of male was 46.92 years old in 1935, as compared with 81.41 years old in 2019. People traditionally shared the feeling of fifty years old as active life span. The age from 19 to 40 years old, was to be conscripted for military service; besides from seventeen years old, by voluntary. During the War, the temporary calling-out paper (so called Akagami Red Paper) was handed over to the eligible citizen for military service at random. The eligible age for young Flying Corps was seventeen to eighteen years old, for pilot trainee and fifteen to seventeen years old, for engineer trainee. As one of the Rites of Passage (Sanskara) among Warrior, (Bushi or Samurai) clans till Edo era, boys took 'Genpuku-shiki'(official ceremony to fix up hair and wearing crown) to become grown-up adults at eleven to fifteen years old. This tradition formed the image of militaristic boys. (It is apparent that the age of mortality was as low as fifty, so perception of youth and adult was very different at the time of the Battle.)Flying corps mobilised from air bases in Burma from end February to end March, to guard the soldiers across Chindwin River, and to bomb British air bases at Imphal, Silchar and Tinsukhia, and oilfields at Ledo, not so much successfully due to unfavourable weather. Total number of mobilised airplanes was reduced from 41 planes per day in March, to 28 in May, only three times right upto Imphal, and ceased from mid-June onwards. The air supremacy in the region had already been dominated by the Allied Forces.[29]

Tomesaku Igarashi named 'Ace Over Imphal' was born in the province of Niigata in 1920; joined the army in 1939. Before he started flying, he was in the 89th promotion of NCO's from November 1942, and later he joined the 50thSentai in December 1943.

During his short career in the IJAAF, he managed to shoot down 16 confirmed killed, while in 50thSentai using his Ki-43, he engaged over Imphal against that fly across the Himalayas, to supply China and Burma. Between January and June, 1944, he claimed 16 enemy fighters (including 4 probable) 3 and C-47, as confirmed by a newspaper of the time. On June 6, it was over sky Meiktila to Arakan Yomas, he spotted many P-38, knocking one of the hunters. Having exhausted all his ammunition, he deliberately struck the rear of another aircraft, forcing the pilot to parachute. On 17 June, on patrol over Imphal, he shared in the destruction of a twin-engine aircraft. He was soon given the nickname Killer-P38, as he was credited with three P-38 twin engines heavy fighter kill. However his luck ran out as the RAF with their Spit-fires were waiting for the Ki-43 Oscar attack over the sky of Imphal. On that six Oscar were shot down over the sky of Imphal and Tomesaku Igarashi was among them, and was killed over Bishenpur. He might have been shot down by Flt, Stg. Bert. He was killed in action at the age of 24 on 17th June 1944 and remained to the last, true to the Bushido Code.[30]

'My father, Taiji Urayama survived the Imphal

campaign. He was 22 years old then. He went to Kohima in 1944. He led 150 soldiers who carried armour and parts for portable artillery on the back of horses. Often the soldiers as well as animals lost their lives on the way to get to the battle sites.

The Japanese Army's recklessness plan to march through the unexplored jungle to India, from North West Burma ended in total disaster. Japanese troops walked through mud in deep jungles, climbed 3,000 m. mountains and crossed rivers from Burma to North East India, often drenched and covered with leaches, encountering snakes, mosquitoes and tigers, all without sufficient food, medicines and ammunition, which made nature a major enemy.

I was told that my father rescued so many drowning soldiers, and horses, when he and his men were crossing rivers. He nearly died; he caught malaria, cholera, and dodged the bullets of fighters, and tanks and artillery shells. Boxes of food and miscellaneous goods meant for the British and Allied troops, dropped by parachute were sometimes obtained by Japanese troops. The soldiers realised in the end that medieval Bushi-do style fighting without proper logistics was ridiculously inadequate, and in their heart they knew they would never win.[31]

'They (the Japanese) fought for independence of Asian countries. They believed independence from Caucasian domination is very important for Asian nations, including Japan.' Japanese volunteered for this Battle, because skilful aged men were already inducted into the army in the early stage of the Sino-Japanese War (1937-45) and World War II (1941-45), and only young boys below age twenty, were left in the mainland of Japan, in the last stage of WWII. During the time of WWII, the great honour for Imperial Army to be killed in war. So, they (soldiers) could not express their true feeling that they felt fear in the battlefield. They (Japanese soldiers) were not volunteers, but forced to be kamikaze pilot, even if they were only fifteen. Of course, they must have been filled with fear, but had no choice to reject under coercive system of full-scale mobilisation.' In a similar vein: So many young Japanese volunteered for this Battle, because they didn't have any choice, but to go for the battle. Their parents must have been very proud of their sons, to give their lives for the country, as 'Die for your Country' was a main philosophy in Japan.' A different perspective, is that the Japanese volunteered to fight because their curiosity was stronger than fear. This is similar to the English adage 'Curiosity killed the cat.'

Japan was under huge pressure not to lose WWII against the Allied Forces, and all young citizens, even below ages 16, were urged to join the war, to help Japan to win. 'The Japanese who participated in the Battle of Imphal were not volunteers. They were forced to join the army, because the number of soldiers in need (needed) was getting less and less. The Government ordered them to go to the battlefront. Meanwhile, members of the cadre stayed safe in camp far back away from the frontline, giving orders. 'During the 2nd World War, the Japanese believed (regarded) the Emperor as a 'Living God'. Young volunteers had been educated to die for the Emperor. Of course, they must be filled with fear, but military education paralysed their sane thoughts.[32] Moreover, military indoctrination, and the fact that the Japanese Emperor was revered as a 'Living God', would have compelled the Japanese soldiers to fight to death for the Heaven-Born-Emperor – a binding religious obligation.

An analysis of the stated views of Japanese individuals tends to lend to consensus, as the young Japanese who fought, died, were injured in the Battle of Imphal, took part in the war because not only was the Japanese Emperor clothed in sanctity but it was both religious and civil obligation to obey the mandate of the Emperor. Moreover being young, the soldiers were impressionable, and they were also fired by a spirit of patriotism which caused them to sacrifice, liberty and life for the 'Heaven Born Emperor'. Moreover, the family of the soldiers enjoyed honour and respect, because their sons were ready to give their all in the service of the Emperor and their country. The soldiers became 'heroes' especially those killed in action. Moreover if the average lifespan in Japan was 50, teenage soldiers was not an anachronism, rather the Rites of Passage among Warriors considered boys between the ages of 11 and 15, to be adults, albeit young adults. All efforts were made by the Government to encourage young men to enlist or to volunteer for military service. It is possible that some individuals were given no choice in the matter. Japan was engaged in war, before the Battle of Imphal, and the experienced war veterans, who had proved their mettle, were ageing, younger people were required to step into their shoes. Whatever may have been the reason for young people to enlist/volunteer, the general belief prevalent in Japan at the time was, that if an individual was killed in war, the sacrifice of life, added to the honour and glory of the JIA – the soldiers were martyrs for a noble cause. The deceased soldiers' families would definitely be grief-stricken at the loss of a loved son/daughter, but they also experienced the feeling of pride – their children remained true to the Bushido Code and would in fact be venerated for their sacrifice. For instance, at the Battle of Shangshak, in Ukhrul District, Manipur, the Japanese Company Commander Lt. Nishimoto fixed his bayonet signalling the arrival of the final moment of triumph and trysts with honour for the 'Children of Nippon'. He announces to his men that finally that moment has arrived 'to shine forever', and if at all you were to fall, you still fight on with your spirit.[33]

Moreover, in the din and clash of arms, rival contestants although fearful of being killed, rally forth courageously, because in the heat and fire of war, the desire to conquer dominates the heart and mind.

'Live in the great loyalty and patriotism of eternity.' 'Die and become demon to guard the nation' 'Never get the humiliation of prisoner alive in the battlefields'.

(Senjin-kun, teaching in battlefields.)

Bearing these mottos in mind under the ultimate situation of no ration or ammunition at all, Japanese troops dared to take the final performance to cut their way into British camp with sword and rifle at night – brave, heroic, yet anachronistic, presented the aim, made bows of definite farewell to the Imperial Palace and Motherland, and offered prayers for a firm conviction of victory and welfare of the Empire, and dashed to occupy the British positions crying; "Ten'no Heika Banzai" - 'Long live the Majesty, the Emperor, and died in honor, - Gyokusai, not dying a day's death, but making demons wait'.

What did the Japanese Army and Air Force personnel experience when they were risking their lives and facing sure death. Although fully conscious of the risks and the possibility of death, they did so, because the entire nation/

society was brainwashed at that time and believed that they must sacrifice their lives to the Emperor and Japan. Such (a) tendency was much strong among the supreme leaders of the army. 'From the hierarchical military management point of view, there was no choice but to obey the orders of the first priority, without any consideration (hesitation). There were only two options on the battlefield, 'Live or Die'. Then the officers had always been taught to give their lives for the Emperor and for the nation'.

All the students and the people during the war were thoroughly taught to behave, that they must always be prepared to die 'for the sake of the nation and the Emperor'.

No one could go against the orders of their officers, so they went out to the battlefield ready to die. In their mind, they didn't want to die but wished to come back, and so hoped to meet their family. However, they were never allowed to speak out anything, such (say) a real honest word to anyone.

The soldiers did not neglect their lives though, the times and social environment made them that way. Those who had common sense felt that the plan (invading Imphal) was nonsense. Because by that time Japan was economically collapsed, and people were starving. But difficult to claim (say) that Japanese army system was such a hierarchal organization.[34]

National slogans prevailed among Japanese soldiers as the national service by thorough loyalty and unselfish mind – Jinchu – hokuku and Messhi – hoko, the devotion to the nation even though seven time cycles of birth and death – Aichi – sho – hokuku, and exterminate the devilish and brutish Americans and British.[35]

The Japanese when risking their lives experienced a lot of emotions. They were scared. They would have been saddened by their relationship with their families (that they may never see again). However, I think that their own death will save the country and the family, and died with pride.[36] An echo of the same sentiments: The Japanese must be very scared. But all the Japanese did it for family and Asian nations, I think it is a kind of Samurai spirit.[37] (Here the sacrifice is made more for family and Asian nations – not for the Emperor and Japan). "They felt scared to death in such a situation.[38] The Japanese had to fight for the Emperor and the Japanese Empire. They could not go against the policy of the Imperial Headquarters, otherwise they were put in jail. If they escaped from the battlefield, they could never go back to their native place, as neighbors would blame and treat him as unpatriotic".

The Imperial Japanese Army and Air Force were so oppressive and merciless that they felt nothing for their lives, especially at the last stage of war. They might have thought them just as the pieces and parts to be replaced. People were cultivated to worship the Emperor as a 'Living God'. (Oft repeated by the respondents) they were supposed to fight for a 'Living God'.[39]

No one could manage the fear (of war) with the normal mindset but most of the people got 'desensitized', due to the mind control by the Commander. If they (Japanese army and air force personnel) were scared and tried to run away, they would have been ashamed, and there would be no place to go back to.[40]

'What I know from my readings about the Battle of Imphal, the battle plan was faulty and impossible to carry out, as the Japanese army did not have a secured provision of supply. The higher level of officers knew that it was almost impossible to win this battle but they carried out the battle. I think the Japanese leaders of the Battle did not care about the lives of their subordinates nor the lives of local people, totally lacking the ability of making rationale judgment. If they had that ability, they would have cancelled the battle soon after they realized the impossible situation.'[41]

'In the face of death, I think, I finally realised that the operation (Imphal) was a failure. It's my subjectivity but since many Japanese people value their physical conditions, I think it was not possible to cancel the strategy once decided'.[42] (This is similar to the parallel drawn between the Battle of Imphal and masks being distributed in Japan during Covid 19).

They (the Japanese) were trained to fight to the last, and ready to die at any moment for the Emperor and the Motherland. They had been educated so.[43] All soldiers were educated and trained to become a weapon (human bomb) by themselves, when there is no other means to fight the enemies. So most of them were not scared to die, as it was a great cause (honor) for the country they had to fight for.[44]

These statements make it clear that the Japanese who participated in the Battle of Imphal were faced with the choice of 'Do or die'. They had no choice but to fight – the political clime was such that they had to believe that if they died in the fighting, their deaths were for a worthy noble cause which gave honor and distinction to the Emperor, the Motherland, and their own families. No individual is free or devoid of a fear of death, but the thought of death as a martyr for the cause, would have blunted perhaps some of the fear. Moreover they possessed the fighting spirit of the

Samurai, and those who died were revered and respected and prayers were offered. The word 'Cowardice' was alien to the Japanese; they also knew that if they refused to fight or abort their mission, they could not return home, as there would be no place for such people in the Japanese society. Moreover young soldiers, airmen and pilots were not given choice, and so they fought till the bitter end. They also possessed reverence for the Emperor, and put death before dishonor.[45]

'Those Japanese families, who suffered the bereavement of a member, must have felt very sad. However, I think it was not possible to express that feeling in Japan at that time'.[46] This statement emphasizes or highlights that families who lost a husband, father, brother, son, son – in –law, daughter, could not grieve openly, they were to find comfort and consolation in the fact that their loved one had sacrificed his/her life, for the greater good of the Emperor and the Japanese people, and take pride that the loved one had died for a noble cause. 'After the war, various facts became clear, and the families felt doubts about Operation Imphal for the first time, and I think they were disappointed.[47] Another respondent concurred with this statement, but added: 'I think they (the families) were very sad but proud of them too'.[48] The prevailing ideology of service to the Emperor and the country, pervaded both thought and action.' I think it's a families' sacrifice, and they felt that as unacceptable, and to ask about 'death' was just a wrong. How could they stop the invaders (probably meaning the white people) from domineering, without the sacrifice of their young lives. (A paradox) 'Death' is not a word common use in Japan. The Japanese had witnessed the phenomenon of many Asian countries being colonized by western powers, and they wanted to halt or put an end to such colonization. This would ensure security for future generations of Japan, 'I can't express how devastated the families of each fallen soldiers were, but many Japanese think that there is a peaceful Japan, at the expense of them'.[49] This implies that the deaths of the fallen Japanese soldiers were not in vain: their deaths ushered in a new era of 'Peace' in Japan. The Imphal Peace Museum is a symbol of this ideology.

Other respondents have expressed similar sentiments. 'The families must have felt a great loss when they learnt of the death of their son, brother or husband. But they could not express their true feeling publicly. Instead they must say, they were honored, as their son had sacrificed his life for the nation'.[50] Families were forced to bottle up their grief. 'They (the families) have no choice other than accepting their death in front of the society. If your son died for the country, you could live without shame for the rest of your life, as not contributing, for the good of the country was against their (the Government's philosophy).[51] Nevertheless, despite the fallen soldiers being honored as a 'martyr', the loss of a family member inevitably brings sorrow and grief in its wake. They (the families) who lost a member in the Battle have never come to terms with the loss (although time does dull the pain). Some of them have prayed and talked, giving water or food to the mini – temple at home almost everyday. Some have visited big shrines and temples regularly, to pray for their soul and World Peace. Now a few people have been visiting about the memories of them, and contribute to the books that feature the testimony of war. Among them, some refer to the case of the Imphal Battle.[52]

Prayers and charitable deeds do assuage grief to a considerable extent over a period of time, but although time is supposed to heal wounds, the memory of a lost one can never be obliterated and the memory becomes a part of one's consciousness. "I read some articles about the bereaved family members of the fallen soldiers of the battle of Imphal. I think they could not tolerate the loss of their loved ones, especially when they come to know how savage and inhumane the battle was in the harsh conditions. But I think, they must have sensed at the same time, some kind of feeling of relief, as they must have felt that they could understand to some extend the reality of the battle in which their loved ones fought and lost their lives.[53]

An example of a War Testimony:

Father receives the notice of his son's death in the war. He asks whether my son was killed in action or disease, which one? When he understood that he was killed in action, he said that it was good! At that time, there was a feeling, that death in war of disease (which was rampant) was shameful.[54-55] In general, family would pretend to look calm, and boast of their son being killed in the war. Also family tried to behave thus: 'My child had fought well for the Emperor and the Nation'. Separate from this attitude (public image), the regret of losing a child was to remain in the heart of the family left behind.[56] The families prayed for soldiers to be fortunate for long in war, while at the same time, they longed for them to return home safely when they were departing for the front, they handed over to the soldiers Sen'ninbari (thousand stitch cloth belt), an amulet to protect the body from enemy's bullets. (Meiteis also wear amulets to keep them safe from different kinds of dangers or misfortunes) People tried to concentrate on defending the country by themselves behind gunfight, during the absence of soldiers. However, ladies hearts, struggled worriedly over death and 'parting from their beloved' as preached in Pains of the Four Noble Truths by Shakyamuni Budha, though they were praised as the mother or wife of wife of soldiers in a militarised society. The family of a dead soldier rested assured that the death would be reported as death in the battlefield, not by disease or accident, and so could reach a state of mind which enabled them to face the neighbors with pride, as the soldier had proved himself and devoted his life to the nation. However, the emotions of sorrow and pain were reserved for the soldiers who fell for the nation, but their bones lay scattered without burial, and no loved ones could give them 'a farewell with honor'. The pension was given by the Government to the families of dead soldiers, as also to injured or deceased soldiers directly.[57] After the war, the Japanese Government provided some kind of pension for the families who lost someone during the war.[58]'On the surface, I think I regard it (death of soldiers) as a good, killed in action, but I don't think I could accept (assuage) my inner feelings. It's sad, considering the feelings of the families who later learned that they (the Japanese soldiers) were involved in an operation that was unlikely to succeed'.[59]

"It's very difficult to imagine how desperate and miserable the families were. The families were prepared that their beloved son or husband maybe killed in the battle, and they would have exclaimed officially: 'I am honored that my son or husband, sacrificed their lives for the sake of the Emperor and the Motherland'. But I do not believe they were saying so from the bottom of their heart".[60] In the same vein: 'Obviously many of them were sad about loss, however they were proud of their son who fought bravely for the country and lost their lives'.[61]'As the entire nation/society had been brainwashed, the death of a soldier was considered an honor, he sacrificed his life for the Emperor. However, individually, a loss was obviously a sad incident for the family. The loss of a breadwinner of the family, meant loss of income to survive in society, though some pension was paid afterwards'.[62] It is clear from the above expressed views that a dichotomy existed – families of fallen soldiers could command respect and hold their heads up with pride; inwardly they grieved the loss of a much beloved son/husband.

Families/relatives, friends of soldiers who died in battle, and have visited the battle sites in Manipur, felt both sadness and regret.[63] But together with sadness, they experienced pride. This was because, Asian countries could not get independence from the Caucasian domination without their (the Japanese soldiers) deaths.[64] Some families are full of gratitude to know how valiantly their loved ones fought for their country, sacrificing their lives.[65] In contrast, and speaking in present context, a respondent stated: Now every Japanese knows that the deaths of their ancestors were meaningless, and they lost their lives for nothing. The Imperial Army should not have charged forward to Northern Burma and Manipur, with so little supplies. It was the lack of strategy of the Imperial Headquarters, especially Gen. Mutaguchi which killed many young armies in Manipur.[66] "The Imphal Battle has been said to be the most tragic battle in the war history of the world. I hear, Japan's strategy was the worst. So the family members would feel (experience) the cruelty of war, praying for the soul with sorrow and grief.[67] Family members feel differently depending on the generation. No single attention was given to their lives during this period. No proper battle strategy was planned, even though most of the commanders knew that there was very less (little) possibility to win the battle. As a grandchild, I have to see the place where our ancestors fought and lost their lives unnecessarily. We have to accept the fact, and teach what happened to the next generation.[68] I think those family members who visited Imphal must have felt sad, because they could now realize (visualize) how difficult the battle was in the harsh conditions. But I think they must have sensed at the same time some kind of feeling of relief, as they must have felt that they could understand to some extend the reality of the battle in which their loved ones fought and lost their lives.[69] The family keep on praying, that tragedy never happens again – Battle of Imphal.[70] A historical Geographical approach has been used by Kaz Nakajima and Dr. Yoshihiro Kaburagi: Steep mountains (1000 to 3000m in height above sea level) and deep valleys (100 to 200m in depth from the river bed), run across the Indo – Burma border, mostly from North to South, while the Japanese troops made painful efforts to cross mountains and rivers from East to West, within thick jungles under the world's heaviest rainfalls during the monsoon season. Several tribal villages are scattered on the ridges in 2 to 5 km distances.

My major interest in this region is focused on its periphery, among India, China and South East Asia, a headstream of Japanese culture, and the battlefields of Imphal operations. For the last ten years, I went alone for fieldwork in February – March and August – September;

mostly during the dry season, except one group tour with a few participants in North – East India and the Japanese Cultural Symposium (held in Manipur) in February 2018. By trekking around mountains and hills, or walking around cities and villages viz. Japfu Peak (behind Kohima), Zuko Valley (spread over Manipur – Nagaland border), Dimapur, Merema, Jotsoma, Khonama, Kohima, Chakbama, Theniyizu, Mon border village (the above all in Nagaland), Motbung, Kanglatongbi, Ukhrul, Shangshak, Imphal, Kakching, Pallel, Moreh, Red Hill (Maibam Lotpaching) Bishenpur, Moirang, Churachandpur, Japan 'Lungpui' (the cliff rocks where a Japanese General hid from an air raid, located in the slope around Saidan village near Churachandpur (the above in Manipur), Silchar, Jorhat, Digboi, Margarita, Ledo (all in Assam) Tamu, Kalewa and Kalemyo (in Myanmar) etc.

Several fine war cemeteries and memorial towers are built in the 'fierce' battlefields by the British or the local governments. The Japanese Government together with the Indian Government has built the Peace Memorial Monument beside Red Hill. Some Japanese groups have erected memorial towers besides Red Hill and Shangshak, and inserted a bronze panel at the basement (base) of the Maria (Mary's) statue at a church in Kohima. Further, I remember my visits to the Japanese cemeteries in Yangon in Myanmar, Singapore, Tashkent in Uzbekistan (For Japanese prisoners brought from Manchuria as forced labourers) and Comilla in Bangladesh. (some unknown Japanese soldiers buried within the British cemetery), and memorial towers erected by Japanese survivors in Monywa, Sagain, Mandalay and Pyay in Myanmar (some have already been deserted/abandoned, and the war museums in Kisama, Lotpaching (Imphal Peace Musuem), Moirang (INA War Musuem), Digboi (Oil Musuem), Margarita (Coal Museum), Guwahati (War Memorial Park), Thambyuzayat in Myanmar (Death Railway Musuem), and Sentosa Island in Singapore, together with the remain of a pill – box (tochka), along the seaside.

Japanese families might feel lucky enough to reach grounds where their husband/son/brother laid down (died), and fold their hands with a string of beads, to pray for the souls of the dead soldiers with tears, sincere gratitude and deep reverence as they can be alive here thanks to devotion of soldiers, offering, flowers, burning incense and chanting 'Namu – amida – butsu' (amitabha – amitayu - ssaranagamana), a phrase of the Buddhist sutra, in front of a memorial tower, surrounded by great natural environment, desiring to pick up by chance from the ground and take home, the bones or remains of soldiers.

The Imphal Operations were really the most magnificent expedition in the furthest (farthest) distance (around 5000 km in a bee - line) from Japan in her history; being carried out under racial fanaticism and megalomaniac expansionism. (These are the words of the respondent which may perhaps be phrased in different words by other Japanese people) Racial power or energy was enormous to unite all the wills of the Japanese who would not know themselves; yet the crushing defeat proved the over – estimation of themselves, and under – estimation of their opponents, the omnipotent idealism cracked down by the almighty materialism, and the mismatched among Ten – Chi – Jin (occasion, place and human being) which transformed the life and the fate of relevant nations, societies, races and inhabitants, whether the results came to be favorable or not'.[71]

'I think, the families of the war dead will feel sad and regrettable'.[72] 'Of course they will feel very sad, and they must have complicated feelings, difficult to express in words'[73] 'Many of the members (family members) would feel proud of the ancestors as all of them were fighting for the country.'[74] "Of course they feel sad (seeing battle - sites). There is no great justification – just – their ancestors died in vain. All because of the Japanese Army's incompetency. Family would feel 'sadness, grief, and pray for peace'."[75]

The Japanese Imperial Army (what was left of it) that returned home after the Battle of Imphal experienced different emotions, 'it varies from person to person', 'I can't imagine what they felt'. "Many Japanese veterans took pride in fighting. However, it is a pity that the Japanese knew the war as self – deprecating due to post – war GHQ education".[76] "I do not know well, but they must hate the military officers who ordered them to go to die (the Japanese Army Commanders knew that they could not win the Battle), in the Battle of Imphal. They must feel sorry for not having saved the lives of their colleagues who died in Manipur or Burma". These two statements are an expression of divergent views. Moreover veterans for the most part did not take part in the Battle of Imphal. The majority of those who took part in the battle were young and untried, inexperienced combatants. 'They had no hatred of the Allied Forces after the battle, because they were not willing to fight, but just forced to fight through (because of) conscription system, even if they were opposed to the war. 'The soldiers who returned home would have struggled to come out of the trauma. I heard that no one would want to disclose what exactly happened'.[77]

Probably many of the returnees suffered from PTSD, but

were unable to access proper healthcare as the environment would not have been conducive for them to do so. So they buried the trauma deep down. And psychiatric treatment as also medication available then cannot compare to what is provided by medical science today. And till very recently, in many countries, people visiting a psychiatrist or clinical psychologist were usually dubbed as a 'basket case'. Even today in Manipur, very few people take the help of professionals to deal with trauma – they feel both fear and shame, and also fear ostracism, which would lead to greater depression and despair. The condition in Japan may have been similar following the Battle.

"It is said that 'Operation Imphal' was so called, because it was a reckless battle that ignored the logistics, but emphasized only psychiatry to the soldiers, so that the soldiers who survived have stopped talking about the events there, even after returning back to their home. Survivors did not speak out of their feelings of sorrow for their friends who died in the war, and to the bereaved families".[78] This echoes in great part what Akiko Macdonald had stated in 2014. (Refer to Souvenir)

Because of the New Education brought in by the US., most of the events related to WWII could not be told. Half a century after the end of the war, people who went (participated) to the war, finally began to speak out about the experience, little by little. And most of them are ninety years old. (This would not have been easy because of their advanced age and suppression of memories for a period of 50 years).

"The Voice of the War Testimony, Mr. Nishizaki Nobuo at South East Battlefield"

In about 1944 there were boys who became 'Navy Special Young Soldiers' at the young age of 14 or 15. As the situation began to deteriorate into serious, even boy soldiers were sent to the battlefields without sufficient military training; as a result, many young boy soldiers were killed.

Originally, the Special Juvenile Soldier System was set up to train the talented young boys over the age of 14, from all over Japan, for the development of future senior Navy officers. One day when the leader asked a young boy at (during) the training time, 'What is the essence of the spirit of the soldiers on the battlefield?' he immediately remembered his Mom's words and said: 'I was going to go home alive', and immediately regretted it. Sure enough: 'Why didn't you answer that you were going to die for the Emperor?' And he was punished without (not given) dinner. Now I think that I had been thoroughly taught the education (principle ideology) of (to be) willing to die for the sake of the nation. When we were on the go, food and fuel were piled up along the way and it was told: After shooting out the bullet, you should be crushed. There were about 3200 first year students of the Navy Special Soldiers, but about 2000 people were killed in the war. In 1947, he returned to his hometown for the first time in five years. When I raised my voice, 'I'm homc now', at the front door, my mother saw me and said: 'Were you Nobuo?' as if she were looking at a ghost, And it (she) seems to have greeted it (me) with the body (face) with a lot of tears in the eyes, saying: 'I came back alive like that'.

The Voice of the War Testimony at his six years

In 1945, June, I watched the air raids in Osaka from the evacuation place with my mom at my six years old time, and recognized that we had lost everything. All the yard of the school where I was evacuated, became the potato fields. Among the elementary school students, they always talked about which I went to: the Navy or to the Military. However, no one in the family wanted to talk about war.

As far as I understand from my reading of the articles related to the Batttle of Imphal, the ordinary soldiers who could return home felt deep grief for their comrades who were killed, and also felt anger and indignation towards the leaders of the Japanese Army who ordered and forced them to fight in the battle.

In the Imphal Operations, 86,000 Japanese soldiers followed the army, out of which 60,000 crossed the Chindwin River with 50,000 animals of horse, cattle, elephant, sheep and goat; 30,000 died by battle and of disease, and 20,000 sent back because of injury and disease. Two thousands, each died, and hospitalized among 6000 soldiers of INA. Only 12,000 soldiers could return home. Whereas, in the British and Indian Empire armies, 1.5 lakh soldiers joined, out which 18 thousands died or were wounded, and 47 thousands were diseased. Three lakhs Japanese soldiers participated in the Burma Operations inclusive of Imphal, out of which 1.8 lakhs died and only 1.2 lakhs could return home.

In the beginning of the campaign to Imphal, soldiers were encouraged triumphantly, 'Lets reach Calcutta with glory after occupying Imphal and Kohima.' However, after the survival from the 'Hell on the Earth', they surrendered in Burma, were disarmed and committed to the concentration camps as Japanese Surrendered Personnel to put up with forced labour and cruelty under insanitary conditions for one to two years, and finally, could be demobilized back to Japan by vessel. However, at concentration camps, some soldiers committed suicides, never forgetting the Senjin-kun not to be prisoner. The suspected war criminals were shut in jail in the worst conditions, with a very scanty supply of rations, and then several accidents occurred as starvation, jail-breaking, going mad, committing suicide, and some accused soldiers were judged death by shooting to end at no return to homeland.

Returned soldiers felt so sorry for dead comrades left behind Arakan Mountains, while only they could return home alive, and folded their hands in mind to pray for their souls peaceful. Around one hundred soldiers decided to stay in Burma as monks, to pray for the souls of dead comrades. Some soldiers became heavily wounded physically or mentally in PTSD (Post Traumatic Stress Disorder), taken care of by their families or hospitals in Japan. Although the country is ruined, yet the nature of mountains and rivers remains unchanged. They willingly made a fresh determination as a new life of rebirth to contribute to the social reconstruction with the spirits of preserver, docility, self-sacrifice and struggle for betterment fostered in army life.[79] They sincerely wished that beloved Japan will remain in a peaceful and green archipelago where the prosperous and cheerful life will get back to continue forever, never forgetting the sorrow and resentment of the families of dead soldiers who devoted their lives to the nation at young ages.[80]

"Some of the returned soldiers felt that the Battle of Imphal 'was the most foolish and daring' of all battles, in light of the 'scarce food and guns' (ammunition). There was no hope at all to win (the Battle) against the British.

But some of them felt satisfactory (experienced feelings of satisfaction) that they had fought against the common enemy, the British, along with the INA."[81] By seeing some of the interviews of them (the returned soldiers), I could see that many of them were reluctant to discuss about the Imphal Battle, as their nightmare continued even after the loss of the Battle. They did not want to remember seeing many fellow soldiers going home by (with) diseases, hunger. And eating them for survival.[82] In times of dire necessity, human beings are driven to do things, they would never have dreamed of otherwise.

"Some returned soldiers wrote books about the war (maybe a form of catharsis). They claimed (revealed) the nonsense plans of the upper rank/people of the Army (Japanese Army). They wrote about the difficulties experienced because of climate (monsoon rains) malaria and starvation.' 'The Battle of Imphal, specifically was an utter waste: a meaningless, stupid battle which should not have been enforced. That was the affection (perspective) of most of the soldiers who fought at the battlefront and survived.[83] It is obvious from the above statements that the Japanese who fought in the Battle, were forced to go to a place where angels fear to tread.

A fairly large number of Japanese people have been visiting Manipur especially in the preceding decade. Most of them are desirous of participating actively in war tourism. Manipur is the first state in India to have organized 'War Tourism'. The first Battle of Imphal Tour which commenced in 2013 started by Hemant Singh Katoch, was participated by the faculty and students of the History Department of Manipur University. Hemant, an erudite scholar, presented a running dialogue on the events of the Battle which fascinated the participants. Subsequently, many foreigners, mostly Japanese and British, individually or in groups, went on this tour of the battle sites of World War II in Manipur. Though the Battle of Imphal Tour continues, the Imphal Battle Remembrance Tour started by Arambam Angamba Singh, covers a wider terrain, Manipur, Nagaland and Myanmar, and provided a more detailed account of the war and particular occurrences during the Battle.

'The tours are well organized. However, although the description of the Battle and the Battlefields by the guide was very much in detail, it is very difficult to memorise or understand everything (the commentary is in English), especially for a tourist. For example, chronological tables of battles, more detailed maps of camps, and sizes of armies of both the Allies and the Japanese at respective battlefields etc. would be more appreciated. (The founders of these tours and the guides are not historians, but are doing an admirable job nevertheless). 'Keeping (maintaining) the natural landscape is very nice. There is no need to construct any monuments except the Museum. At the time of the tour (undertaken by a respondent), the Imphal Peace Museum had not been constructed. Short films about the Imphal War are very necessary.' 'The guide knew well the history of the Battle, and I received a lot of information during the tour. But it was unfortunate that I could not see any written documents and photographs; except for the oral explanation from the guide, as the Peace Museum had not opened in 2018 when I visited.' (This lacunae has been partly resolved with the opening of the Imphal Peace Museum).

With regard to the attitude of the Manipuris towards the Japanese Imperial Army (JIA): 'I don't know what the Manipuris' attitude was towards the JIA during the Battle. I am sure that they would have been very disturbed by them. However, what I learned from the books is the Manipuris are currently Japanophile. I have a doubt – how is it possible for the Manipuris to feel good for (towards) the Japanese.' But as stated in Chapter Two, most Manipuris found the Japanese soldiers to be both well-mannered and well disciplined. 'All other countries spoiled their place (Manipur), though it was a very calm and simple place, before it was considered an operation base in 1942. It is because the Imphal Battle had given the infrastructure, goods supply due to the battle, and both are trying to maintain the peaceful relationship till today.[84] This is a fact – in fact Manipur can be a good example or a case-study for Indo-Japanese relations. 'The astonishing remarkable recovery of Japanese economy post World War II, aroused admiration and the innate courtesy of the Japanese is a quality that appeals to the Manipuris.

"I hear their (the Manipuris) attitude was very kind and supportive to the Japanese Army that had nothing to eat. (their rations were exhausted at the beginning of the campaign) for which we (the Japanese) offer gratitude from the bottom of our hearts. We are so sorry to have put the Manipuris to so much trouble.[85]

In like vein: 'I heard from Manipuri people that they were sympathetic and helpful towards Japanese soldiers. I think that is true, because I met some Manipuri people who have been helping Japanese people to collect the remains of their family members who were killed in the battle, and also I heard, local Manipuri people commenting about the Japanese soldiers in a positive manner, despite their invasion to the place which must have caused huge damage/ destruction to the local people. So I think Manipuri people were kind and tolerant towards the Japanese soldiers.'[86] This is corroborated by the fact that at the time, many Manipuris buried corpses of Japanese soldiers strewn over the battlefields and other areas of Manipur.

The Japanese secret service named Hikar-i-kikan (literally light machinery) worked to collect local information, and to appease and pacify several tribes around the border area. They specially trained INA soldiers to smuggle themselves into India for intelligence as well as military maneuvering but resulted unsuccessfully. Indians, Gurkhas, tribesmen, and prisoners were trained at a hidden house in Homalin, riverside of Chindwin, Burma. They were expected to break the V-force (the British tribal unit) and Gurkha soldiers as counter-spy. The Japanese utilized tribesmen en route to advancing routes to conceal rations, salt and vegetables, removing village people forcibly. INA soldiers went into intelligent service to collect geographical features for military use successfully in a short distance across the border to lead the swift occupation of Kohima. Further advancing to open up the routes, they pacified village people. Village chiefs around Kohima and Ukhrul were mustered to organize the Japan-India War Cooperation Unit to cover up self-guard body, consumer co-operative union, education committee, save-refugees committee, and carrying out hidden rations and ammunition, on top of providing intelligence, supplies and labour. However, the confiscation of unhusked rice and the shortage of labourers resulted in difficult cultivation.

In order to win over the Manipuris for the alliance with the INA, the Japanese made use of propaganda that they came to give Swaraj (independence) to India as greeting of Jai Hind (Long Live India), on top of the prophecy among the Manipur is that 'Eastern Gate will be opened', was interpreted as the Japanese represented the eastern power. Japanese tried to emphasise on racial similarities and got some support, especially from the Kukis, appealing that they descended from Chongji brother of Chongthu, from whom the Kukis claimed their descent. Many Kuki songs have been preserved about Japan Gal (War) with full praise of the Japanese. In Japan, the Kuki (literally nine demons or originally nine trees symbolizing winding lay of land) is a warrior (Bushi or Samurai) class based in South-eastern seashore of Kii Peninsula, south of Nara, in Kansai area, who were active with strong naval power around the 14th to 16th centuries AD during the medieval war times. There is no historical evidence, but as an imagination only, if the Kuki clan people had penetrated into an international trade with South East Asia in the 16th century AD under the license of Goshuin-sen (red-stamped vessel) as trader, shipping agent or guard they would have stayed at Japanese port towns in South East Asia, contacted with the Burmese, assimilated with the Chins and the Kukis, and finally migrated into North-East India together.[87] There is no historical evidence of trade by Kukis is South East Asian ports. In fact as early as 1434, the Great Chinese Imperial Missions exploring the shores of the Indian Ocean came to an end. There were also late fifteenth century decisions to abandon coastal towns in Southern China in the face of Japanese piracy.[88] Meanwhile, the ancestors Kyrgyz people in Central Asia are said to have migrated towards the east and the west, and then became Japanese and Europeans.

After the Japanese occupation of Ukhrul, a local chief and all leaders met a Japanese Commander who said friendly (frankly) that Japanese and Tangkhuls are brothers of the same Mongoloid stock, and presented cattle and foods. Japanese soldiers were reminded of a basic discipline. "Our enemies are British and Americans. If we had to fight Indians, persuade them to surrender and treat them kindly. Also treat all the natives kindly. Do not steal and do not get wrong idea about women." Later, however, they became more desperate to seize any available paddy and killed livestock, paid by Japanese Burma notes, forged British India notes, or nothing. Local people served as coolies and porters carrying rations and ammunition to the Japanese camps in hills, but later treated harder to carry loads in long distances. They pounded rice for Japanese soldiers.

One young tribesman stayed at Japanese camps and went around together to guide several places, and was appointed as cashier, being handed over lots of Japanese currencies, and granted a certificate of service.

'It was not our war. We made friends with the Japanese and the British. The Naga and the Kukis of V force supported British by gathering Japanese information e.g. their location, for pinpoint bombing. On the other hand, many Manipuris actively supported one side or the other. The Maharaja of Manipur firmly supported the British. Many Meities and the Kukis worked to support INA by supplies and intelligence, while most Tangkhul Nagas did not help the Japanese – INA. Many arms and ammunition abandoned by the British were collected by Manipuri volunteers and handed over to the INA-Japanese. Netaji Subhas Chandra Bose gave a slogan 'Give me blood, I will get you freedom! Chalo Delhi!' The Manipuris gave full co-operation to INA with its operational headquarters, the Provisional Government of Free India in Moirang, by providing supply of food, donation and necessities for three months. Two hundred Manipuris joined INA Movement. (This is a small number which illustrated the meaning of the first sentence in the paragraph – It was not our war.)

The Japanese kept away the escape of tribal people from guide and labour services, by confining females and children upon reaching villages (Holding family members hostage, albeit temporarily is a strategy used in war throughout history – for example in Medieval India Sultan Alauddin Khalji resorted to that tactic to ensure success of his Market Regulations). A few acts of violence caused the alienation and protest of villagers by reporting the activities of the Japanese to the British, guiding routes, and attacking to kill sentries.[89]

'I suppose they (the Manipuris) were very co-operative and subordinate. They were very tolerant. In other parts of the world, anti-Japanese riots would have occurred.'[90] The Manipuris were certainly tolerant and even showed great empathy to the Japanese especially the Kukis but they were not subordinate except when they were forced to pound rice, provide livestock and grain; many were ignorant of the cause of the Battle and moreover, it was the Japanese who invaded their land. Perhaps co-operation is explained in the statement: I believe they were very supportive, evident from the screening of the documentary film about the Imphal Battle.[91] "I heard that the people of Manipur were very kind to the Japanese soldiers. People might have felt sympathetic because they look similar." Including those of the Nagas at and around Kohima battlefields, as far as I have heard, the attitude of the local people was rather friendly and intimate because of physical similarities of the Japanese soldiers. At the same time, I heard from several, very aged locals, of both Manipur and Nagaland, who were witnesses to the Battle, that the Japanese soldiers were always so hungry, and in need of food, and they felt very sorry for them, and also sympathy. Some soldiers did steal animals and food, etc. but there is no or very less incident of killing of the locals.[92] 'My impression of Manipuri people is very good. Quiet, shy and friendly. Perhaps, because we Japanese and the Manipuris seem to have some similarities in our features, cultures and characteristics. I feel very comfortable and closer with the Manipuri people.'[93] Post-war, it is apparent that cordiality and respect are shown towards one another by the Manipuris and the Japanese.

A film 'Imphal 1944', directed by Junichi Kajioka was screened in Imphal in April 2019 at a reconciliation Meet between the British and the Japanese, organized by the WW II Imphal Campaign Foundation. There was a fairly good representation of British and Japanese delegates, most of whom had some link with the Battle, as relatives, friends, well-wishers, etc. Manipuris comprised the bulk of the audience, and the Manipuris who were present all had a keen interest in the proceedings. The purpose of screening the film was articulated in the statement made by a Japanese: the film 'was a great film. We can reconcile after a long absence and we can start a new life with each other. I could renew my recognition of the futility of war. The message of the film was Reconciliation, Reconciliation between former bitter adversaries, by forging a new path of 'Friendship' and 'Peace'.

In answer to the question: what could have been the dying thoughts of soldiers who perished in the Battle:

'Well-being, security, peace within their family. No more war, ever.'

'All soldiers might remember their family and be vexed (sad, desolate). They wanted to do many things.'

'We Japanese shouldn't have started this war itself, where we had invaded many societies of their countries. I deeply regret this part of the Japanese past.'[94]

'During the real battle they probably thought: 'We are dying for the country', but when withdrawing, they must have thought 'Why are we dying like this? It's so sad.'[95]

"It is unavoidable to some extent that as time passes by, people forget. But we should not forget this historic incident. We should learn the lesson of World Peace from this silly war.[96] 'I think they were disappointed.'[97]

'All soldiers had received military education to give their lives for the nation and for the Emperor, but when they were really about to die on the battlefield, it was very natural, that they were screaming desperately for help, because they didn't want to die. Some of them might have been screaming 'Mom, help me'. And then they died. I have heard an exact story from one of the returning soldiers.'

One day, the soldiers' friend visited the house of the dead soldier to tell that: the senior officer of the soldier in the war explained that he (the dead soldier) did not say 'Mom' but 'Majesty', and appreciated that he had done his best for the nation and the Emperor. This was the standard style in Japan at that time.[98]

'They must have thought it was unreasonable that they were going to die in that way. They must have wanted to live and go back home to reunite with their family. They must have felt angry with the leaders of the Japanese Army and the institution of the Japanese army, which did not care about protecting the lives of soldiers.'[99]

'By the time they died in the Battle, they wouldn't have a proper mentality, as they needed to kill, and to eat each other to fill their tummy. I hope they would have been proud of themselves and died. However, they would have been disappointed and frustrated, and also, I am very much sure, that they would have been missing their parents, friends and loved ones in the last moment.'[100]

'They were the victims of the worst strategies. They were controlled by air supremacy of the Allied Force, but had no food, no weapon. They died in the desperate situation in vain. So their dying message would have been a deep-seated grudge against the top Commanders who were said to have (been) enjoying lives in the distance'.[101]

'The Japanese soldiers feared death'.[102]

An analysis of the above statements reveals a dichotomy. On the one hand, the young Japanese soldiers already indoctrinated with the ideology, that Emperor and Country come first, would have been proud to sacrifice their lives for a noble cause. But being human they must certainly have not wanted to jump into the fire, as they knew that the JIA were fighting a losing battle, they were starving, malnourished and wracked by disease; they were dying in a foreign land with nobody to bury them, or mourn their deaths, and at such a young and tender age, they had to accept that they would never return home and be reunited with their families. Nobody would have wanted to die but during the Imphal Campaign, death constantly stared them in the face.

As mentioned in Chapter one, the Battle of Imphal was often referred to as 'Japan Lan' or 'Japan Gal'. The explanations offered are:

The Japanese Army came and fought in Manipur, or perhaps many Japanese soldiers died in vain.

The Battle was begun by the Japanese for the Japanese. For the Manipuris, the period from 1942 to 1945 was the days of Japan Laan, because the Japanese Army was the new invading force in the land next to British and Burmese in the modern era. The Manipuri experience of Japan Laan can be divided into four phases: viz. The first phase is the early 1942 when many refugees arrived from Burma towards (going to) Assam, mostly Indians, but some retreating British troops. Japanese warplanes started bombing Imphal from May 1942 onwards. The second phase is from late 1942 to 1943, when the British started building airfields, roads, bridges, military camps, etc. where many Manipuris became a part of the workforce. Manipuri experienced a huge inflow of soldiers and other personnel from different parts of India and the world for the first time. The third phase is March to July 1944, when Manipur saw the actual fighting. The last phase is July 1944 to mid-1945, when the war related activities continued, even after the end of the battles. Imphal still remained as the main base for the British operations in pursuit of retreating Japanese to Burma, as many Allied soldiers continued to pour into Imphal en route to Burma. Inflation was at a peak due to booming commodity markets for soldiers.

Local people suddenly found themselves at the front lines of the Second World War. People dug trenches as shelter to hide from Japanese air-raids. 25 thousand people were given just two days to evacuate out from Imphal. The British burnt all rice stocks left behind in villages, and fired (destroyed) houses. As agricultural activities were disrupted people could not eat normal rice but half-burnt rice with water chestnut only. Six thousand village houses across Manipur were destroyed. Cholera, dysentery and fever grew rife in some areas.

The war opened the eyes of local people to develop Manipur. During the war time, Manipur transformed at all levels – politically, economically, socially and psychologically. After the end of the war, Manipur was forcibly moved into a modern era by dramatically improved infrastructure and massive money economy to lead new business chances. Meanwhile, the battlefields left a large number of arms and ammunition which were possessed later by tribesmen and communists. Once when I took a train from Dimapur to Guwahati, one old Naga tribesman approached my seat to tell me his memory, that at the end of the war, his father collected several rifles and other weapons left in the battlefields, and handed them over to the Naga guerillas struggling for Independence. A churning soon started to get underway all over North East India, seeking for independence and autonomy, partly by the politicization and militarization experienced during the war time. Despite a meaningless war for most local people, yet their life styles were significantly changed in dressing style, eating habit and cultural mindset, especially for school education in English language.

At the Imphal Operations, Indians fought each other, separately between INA and the British sides. Some Kukis and Nagas joined the British, while very few Meitei civilians. The war brought irreparable physical and psychological damages to many families, while it excited young minds by the introduction of many new things and technologies.[103] A respondent not aware that the Battle of Imphal was also referred to as 'Japan Lan', thought that 'perhaps it was because Japan claimed that' by defeating the British in this battle, Japan would help liberate India from the British rule. Another stated: I don't have much idea why Manipuris refer to this (Battle) as 'Japan Lan', as many countries got involved with this battle, and there is no need to mention (it) as 'Japanese War'. As (from) the negative side, I can assume that the Manipuris refers to this as 'Japan War', because the Battle of Imphal actually contributed for (to) India's independence. The Japanese Imperial Army was (on) a joint operation with Chandra Bose (Netaji) and the INA. Though the battle was thoughtless, and not practical in terms of victory, but still Japanese Commanders pushed as they were impressed by Chandra Bose's charisma. In spite of losing the battle, it might be a trigger for India's Independence. "Arrogant Japanese troops suddenly came and stayed for a long time, and made use of the Manipuris, for which we feel awfully sorry". "Japan had to fight with a small amount of resources and military from the beginning of the war and I think that only this operation, but all operations were reckless. But they still had to fight. The mainland will be attacked if supply to China is cut off by blocking air routes. However, it is possible that the Commander made the wrong decision, because mental theory alone cannot win the war. I think the impact of this withdrawal is a major factor in Japan's defeats."[104]

The Japanese Perspective on their country fighting the fiercest battle of WW II in a foreign land like Imphal:

> "I will answer on the assumption that it is not something to do with war. I think that the Japanese Army analyzed the war situation calmly, and put it in the viewpoint of what to do to win, and how to protect the soldiers. I think that Japanese Army continued the fight, but did

not prepare enough supplies in advance to win, or put troops in, without understanding the situation of the war, especially the latter half of the war". "I feel proud that they fought for Asian countries". "What happened to the country that gave up the fight? Japan is treated as a loser, but before that, most Asian and African countries were colonized by many economies and people. It's even more dangerous to say that textbooks still didn't. As a Japanese, I am grateful for the Battle (fought by) my ancestors. Before the Meiji era, Japan was isolated, and had (fought) no war for nearly three hundred years. It is a Battle, in which the general public of India, who had nothing to do with the war, also died. We pray for the souls". "It was a total failure and a reckless operation for the Imperial Army to go on an expedition all the way to Imphal to attack bases of the UK, but nobody could stop the operation at that time, as Japanese citizens who believed the bogus news from the Imperial General Headquarters, expected it. The situation of Japanese society is almost the same, and remains unchanged even after 76 years. We know the policy of the present Government is wrong, but nobody can stop it. That's why, the name of 'Imphal', continues to be known to every Japanese even now." "Japanese invaded so many countries. We fought in the foreign lands, not in Japan, for which we feel very, very sorry. We must apologize heartily and compensate in every way. And cultural and economic communication would be the most important from now on." "As a Japanese, I feel ashamed of disturbing/spoiling a foreign land, and focusing only on their target, and we shall not repeat the same forever. At the same time, I have a strong opinion that the history which we learnt was so much controlled by the country. Today, I cannot agree that: 'Die for your country' which was taught during WW II Battle. No human should be treated as a 'piece' and no life should ever be disrespected." "I think it was sheer stupidity and lack of rational judgement, as well as lack of the global perspectives about the world, that propelled the Japanese Army to start WW II, to continue the war even after it became apparent that Japan will lose, and to head straight into the Battle of Imphal, which was the impossible fight. As a Japanese person, I feel ashamed of the Japanese invasion of the Japanese Army in Imphal, and also, I despise the leaders of the Japanese Army, like Mutagachi, who did not take any responsibility for killing so many lives, unnecessarily, for his faulty plan. The top leaders of the Battle of Imphal who did not take any responsibility after Japan lost the war were shameless and cowards I think it was the tragedy of Japan to be led by those military leaders lacking the capabilities and integrity during WW II. Those leaders survived, and lived comfortably after the war, and innocent soldiers were killed in the fight like the Battle of Imphal. Unfortunately, not many Japanese people, especially young Japanese people, know about the Battle of Imphal. Therefore, I do feel it is necessary for us who know about the history of the Battle of Imphal, to talk and write about the Battle, so that people would know what happened in Imphal, and learn from the history to make a better world.[105]

'It seems too difficult to find the person who can convey the real history, and correct regognition of the war. There were very few opportunities to talk in detail about the

Operation Imphal too. As a matter of fact, schools in the moment, have not prepared sufficient time to study about the history and its background, why various wars related to WW II had happened. Because, education on War, still tends to be regarded as taboo. On the other hand, the mass media has come to take up the topic of Operation Imphal of WW II. It's a happy trend for mass media to do so, though how far can they uncover the truth of war. I'm very much afraid that what Japan learns from the bitter experiences of the past, and whether we can promise not to repeat again.[106]

We feel that we need to pay more attention to the loss of overall interests for the benefit or physical condition of individuals, or some group. I think the current situation in Japanese politics is the same. We feel that the current Japanese policy makers seemed to have the same tendency to seek solutions for the benefit of some politicians for their own pride. If they had seen and analysed their situation based on the facts, they could have avoided such prolonged war of fighting an obvious losing battle.[107]

'War is nothing but tragedy, it repeats itself in human history. In fact, warfare revolutionised Science and Technology to invent new machinery, transportation and communication with which civilisation keeps on with development. Yet, the Human Spirit wishes for Peace and Happiness continued in everyday life. So it is highly essential for humankind to harmonise Moral Culture and Material Culture, so as to extend Co-Existence and Co-Prosperity to all creatures living in this great nature of the earth."[108]

"It was unjust, and a big mistake of the then rulers of Japan. It is against 'humanism' to invade a foreign land.

But Lieutanant Mutaguchi did not feel his responsibility for the defeat and loss of many subordinates in vain. On the contrary, he wrote many excuses and tried to justify his failure to fight against the British Empire soldiers. I despise such an irresponsible army leader. He is against the traditional Japanese chivalry-Kshatriya Dharma.[109] After learning of the facts, the Imphal Battle was a big mistake, as there was no chance of winning the battle, even before it started. But the decisions at the time were made at the Headquarters in Tokyo, where information about Manipur was limited. And they needed to stop the invasion by the Allied Forces. So it was inevitable.[110]

"Nonsense! (The Battle of Imphal) We should not repeat the same thing." "There was no explicit and distinct plan for carrying out the battle in such a mountainous land, but only poor commands, based only on spiritualism. The death of soldiers was merely dying in vain, a wasteful sacrifice of life.[111]

The story of the search for over a decade of granduncle's remains in both Myanmar and Manipur is poignant and is an indicator to the myriad emotions, especially grief and despair, of the Japanese, especially those who lost family members, friends and others in the Battle of Imphal. After the Battle ended, and after India became independent, teams of Japanese nationals have visited Manipur, to see where their ancestors died and fought, and to excavate if possible the remains of the dead soldiers. These excavations came to an abrupt end with the pandemic Covid 19 in the early part of 2020. Some teams were successful and were able to offer prayers and perform rituals at the excavation sites. For example: A dream came true for a man Yoichi Murata San who kept his promise made fifty years back to his once senior friend, veteran of Kangpokpi Battle, WW II Sergeant Toidoi, Engrs. Matsuri group, 15 Div Japanese Army, that 'he would one day stand beside the bridge they blew up at Kangpokpi MS 105 in the midnight of 28 March, 1944. Recruits of Matsuri group are generally from the Kyoto area of Japan. Murata San has also undergone military training while still in junior school during the WW II. He also lost many of his close friends in this battle. He now prays for all the lost souls, irrespective of Nations and Race, and also offers apology for the unfortunate incident at Kangpokpi.[112]

Whether the excavating Japanese teams have received closure, is something else, as is evident from the testimonies of the Japanese. These testimonies/memories are written in 2020, almost eight decades after the Battle, they are stark and vivid descriptions of the Japanese psyche, perspective and feelings – most important is the crucial element of the truth behind these revelations. They provide a new insight into how the Japanese perceive the Battle today, especially its repercussions. They know that the Battle was a battle which the Japanese could never win, as right from the beginning of the battle, the Japanese Army suffered from a shortage of food, supplies, ammunition. Moreover the soldiers were for the most part young and inexperienced – their military training was brief, as a result they went through 'a baptism of fire', in which many lost their lives. The paradox lay in the fact that these young soldiers had been taught to believe that it was an honor and a duty to fight for the Emperor and country; at the same time they wished to be able to return home after the battle to their families, and throughout the ordeal, their overriding emotion was 'Fear' – would they survive the battle? Their deaths were unnecessary, the Japanese war strategy was wrong; and the current generation of the Japanese (not the young, who are unacquainted with the history of this Battle) have made sincere apologies for their kinsmen invading Manipur and disrupting the life of the indigenous people. The testimonies/Memories are replete with the innate characteristics of integrity and courtesy that the Japanese possess.

The paradox has been written about by Akiko Macdonald: Anomaly of Japanese Militarism consisted of Rule, Obedience, Discipline and Violence.

Prejudice and Misunderstanding: I have heard that some British POW's complained because the Japanese Army gave them 'root' to eat. In fact, it was 'burdock'. In Japan, it was commonly known as a healthy vegetable. The Western diet is based on meat, potatoes and bread which differ to the Japanese diet of fish, rice and all sorts of vegetables. Also Japanese food portions are again different; they eat smaller portion as compared to the big-sized westerners.

Feeding large number of POW's (80,000 + is a massive challenge). They were not guests. Japanese forced the POW's to obey, no matter what; otherwise they received severe physical punishment. During the war, humanity and basic individual human rights can sometimes disappear, including Japanese to Japanese.

Japanese military discipline and obedience was another large cultural difference which created a huge misunderstanding between East and West.

'Surrendering to the enemy' was just unthinkable to them. Laying down their sword and gun is absolutely "dishonourable" and they were taught to take their own life, rather than let themselves be captured. If they were captured, their name would be disgraced in their own family and country.

Hatred: (POW's suffered traumatic experiences during their captivity.)

British POW's, who came back to the UK, naturally held a grudge for a long time about the Japanese soldiers and their army's brutality. Their hatred towards Japanese was so great that British former POW's boycotted Japanese products in the UK after the war. Post-war Japanese industries developed, which helped Japan economically, and Japanese export goods flourished in the world market. Most British veterans saw with bitterness that despite defeat, Japan managed to prosper.

As I married an Englishman and moved to the UK from Japan 25 years ago, and in that time, I have never encountered anti-Japanese feeling by British people. I was astounded that British veterans still bear a grudge towards Japanese, fifty years after the war ended.

In 1983, Masao Hirakubo, (founder of the Burma Campaign Society, initiative of Anglo- Japan reconciliation activities in the UK) met two Welsh Burma veterans, Gwilyn Davis and Hirwen James in Wales. One of them was a former prisoner of war. They talked and talked, and British veterans were initially furious in expressing their anger. But they gradually softened up, and realised that the Japanese also suffered so much during the war. Masao invited them to visit to see the real and present Japan. From that point, they became fond of Japan, and started to understand about Japanese people and the country's history. Eventually, they became good friends till their death.

Since their dramatic meeting, the message was spread by word of mouth amongst British Burma veterans, and at the peak, more than 150 British Burma veterans and nearly 2000 Japanese Burma veterans reconciled in Tokyo. British veterans visited the Yasukuni shrine, some went to Hiroshima as well, and Japanese veterans visited Imphal barracks in York where the 2nd Infantry Division was based. Masao organised also a trip to Kohima-Imphal in India for both parties, and held a massive joint Anglo-Indian-Japan Reconciliation ceremony, and prayed for peace at a Cathedral in Kohima in 1991. Masao was awarded an OBE from Queen Elizabeth, for his relentless work and dedication to achieve reconciliation between UK and Japan.

Akiko Macdonald's Personal Involvement of Reconciliation and Building a 'Peace Bridge' between countries and sustaining hope for the future of all humankind.

'Reconciliation activities are very important and necessary to promote peace, and make sure there are no more world wars. It is very important that we acknowledge the different cultural values and traditions of each country, and take account of the geopolitical aspects.

I became involved in this activity, since my father fought against Britain, and I married an Englishman, and have two grown-up children, when my children think of their identity, either English or Japanese, it will be most difficult to determine who they are.

I became very close to Masao as soon as we both realised that my father and Masao had fought at Kohima. Masao naturally and immediately persuaded me to help his activities.

My father was a troubled man after Japan's surrender. I wanted to know how the war had affected my father's character, and so many of those men who had traumatic experiences during the war.

Since I joined the Burma Campaign Society, I have had excellent opportunities to meet British Burma veterans.

In the case of Britain, I am very fortunate that I have been given the opportunity to express my thoughts, even if they are different from the British view of the Second World War.

War produces heroes as well as evil on both sides. On the evil side, human beings can sometimes become arrogant, cunning and sly, people who have evil ambition, desire to gain power.

War produces so many orphans and widows, destroys family, society and country.

I believe that all the nationalities involved in WW II should share their war stories and their experiences with each other. In this way, if we keep talking and communicating to create peace and stability for future generations, rather than provoking each other and creating violent conflicts, it is possible that reconciliation and peace can be achieved.[113]

References

1 Hemant Singh Katoch. pg.33. citing Intelligence Summary No. 140, April 1944, War Dairy of 'G' Branch HQ 5 Indian Division File No. 601/221/WD/Part IX-B, History Division, Ministry of Defence, New Delhi.

2 Ibid., op. cit. p. 36

3 Personal testimony in the words of a relative of the Granduncle mailed to me in December 2018 from Japan.

4 Ibid op. cit., September 2020

5 Ibid – Note – Produced Verbatim

6 Ranjan Pal – Kohima – Imphal – The Stalingard of the East cit. The Sangai Express. 8th Oct. 2020.

7 Akiko Macdonald, daughter of WW II Veteran Taiji Urayama, a Lt. of the Mountain Artillery of the Imperial Japanese Army cit. in Souveniur – 70th Anniversary Battle of Imphal, June 2014 pg.30 Note – She is the daughter of WWII Veteran Taiji Urayama, a Lt. of the Mountain Artillery of the Imperial Japanese Army.

8 Ibid pg. 30-31

9 Answer to a Questionnaire – Japanese national residing in Japan.

10 Note - This is corroborated by several Japanese in answer to a Questionnaire mailed to them.

11 Note - The defeated Japanese soldiers of the Battle of Imphal who returned to Japan may have experienced similar sentiments and emotions. But they were treated more like 'pariahs' than soldiers who had given their best in the fighting in Manipur.

12 Note - Probably this was not possible in the environment prevalent in Japan following Japan's defeat in World War II.

13 Note - Much of the above information does not pertain to the Battle of Imphal but enables a better understanding by comparative analysis.

14 Note – The book 'War Experience' authored by Dr. Ryuichi Narita was recommended to me by a Japanese Professor. As I could not access it, and as it was written in Japanese, Dr.YoshidoKaburagi summarised the contents of the book and mailed it to me, October 2020 from Japan – a magnificent gesture for which I am very grateful.

15 Answer to Questionnaire mailed only to Japanese Nationals – Note – All answers by Japanese nationals are recorded in the exact words they have penned and sent to me between October-November 2020.

16 Ibid.

17 *Ibid* – Respondent - Kaz Nakajima-October, 2020.

18 *Ibid* – Respondent - Dr. Yoshihiro Kaburagi 16th October 2020. Note – These are his personal views.

19 Akiko Macdonald, *op. cit.* p.31

20 Answer to Questionnaire, Respondent, Hiroko Ozaki

21 AngambaArambam Singh. 29th October 2020 on Facebook

22 Kanwar Muhammad Ashraf – Life and Conditions of the People of Hindustan.pg.35

23 Tapan Raychaudhuri and Irfan Habib – The Cambridge Economic History of India Vol.I-C.1200-C.1750, pg.139

24 Dr. Y. Kaburagi op.cit.

25 Enclyclopedia Britannica

26 Inazo Nitobe-Bushido-The Soul of Japan

27 ArambamAngamba Singh, Souveniur 2014, op.cit.pp.48-49.

28 Answer to Questionnaire sent to the Japanese. Note – Some respondents do not want their names disclosed.

29 Ibid. – Dr.YoshihiroKaburagi

30 Tom Thounaojam, Souvenier 2014 op.cit.pg.47

31 Akiko Macdonald op.cit.pg.32

32 Answer to Questionnaire, op.cit.

33 ArambamAngamba Singh op.cit. pg.48

34 Answer to Questionnaire, op.cit.

35 Ibib.- Respondent – Dr. Yoshihiro Kaburagi

36 Ibid. – Shinchi Iriyama

37 Ibid.- Tabe Kiyoshi

38 Ibid.- Hiroyuki Ishida

39 Ibid.- Japanese Respondent

40 Ibid.- Japanese Respondent

41 Ibid.- Mika Hisada

42 Ibid.- Hiroko Ozaki

43 Ibid.- Noriko Yoshida

44 Ibid.- Tomio Mizokami

45 Ibid.- Hidehito Jay Araki

46 Note – These are answers to the Question – How did the Imperial Japanese Army and Air Force feel as they fought and risked their lives or when they faced certain deaths? The answers are reproduced in their original form.

47 Answer to Questionnaire – Japanese national

48 Ibid.- Shinichi Iriyama

49 Ibid. - Tabe Kiyoshi

50 Ibid.- Hiroyuki Ishida

51 Ibid.- Japanese National

52 Ibid.- AtsufumiMikami

53 Answer to Questionnaire

54 Ibid – Kaz Nakajima

55 Note - At the time the soldiers were malnourished, starving and vulnerable to dysentery, malaria, typhoid, fungal infections, etc

56 *Ibid.*- Kaz Nakajima

57 *Ibid.*- Dr. Yoshihiro Kaburagi

58 *Ibid.*- Answer to Questionnaire

59 *Ibid.*- Noriko Yoshida

60 *Ibid.*- Tomio Mizokami

61 *Ibid.*- Hideto Jay Araki

62 *Ibid.*- Answer to Questionnaire

63 *Ibid.*- Shinichi Iriyama

64 *Ibid.*- Tabe Kiyoshi

65 *Ibid.*- Hiroyuki Ishida

66 *Ibid.*- Answer to Questionnaire

67 *Ibid.*- AtsufumiMikami

68 *Ibid.*- Maki Hisada

69 *Ibid.*- Hiroko Ozaki

70 Ibid.- Answer to Questionnaire

71 Ibid.- Dr. Yoshihiro Kaburagi

72 Ibid.- Noriko Yoshida

73 *Ibid.*- Tomio Mizokami

74 Ibid.- Hideto Jay Araki

75 Note - These are answers to the Question – How do the families feel when they see, where their ancestors fought and died in Manipur.

76 Answer to Questionnaire – Hiroyuki Ishida

77 Ibid.- By Japanese nationals

78 Ibid.- Kaz Nakajima

79 Ibid. op.cit.

80 Ibid.- Yoshihiro Kaburagi

81 Ibid.- Tomio Mizokami

82 Ibid.- Hidehito Jay Araki

83 Ibid.- Answers to Questionnaire

84 Ibid.- Maki Hisada

85 Ibid.- Atsufumi Mikami

86 Ibid.- Hiroko Ozaki

87 Ibid.- Dr. Yoshihiro Kaburagi

88 Tapan Raychaudhuri and Irfan Habib op.cit. pg.138

89 Answer to Questionnaire – Dr. Yoshihiro Kaburagi – Note – What was the attitude of the local people towards the Japanese?

90 Ibid.- Tomio Mizokami

91 Ibid.- Hidehito Jay Araki

92 Ibid.- Answers to Questionnaire

93 Ibid.- Hiroko Ozaki

94 Ibid.- Answers to Questionnaire

95 Ibid.- Hidehito Jay Araki

96 Ibid.- Answers to Questionnaire

97 Ibid.- Norika Yoshida

98 Ibid.- Answers to Questionnaire

99 Ibid.- Hiroko Ozaki

100 Ibid.- Maki Hisada

101 Ibid.- Atsumi Mikami

102 Ibid.- Hiroyuki Ishida

103 Ibid.- Dr. Yoshihiro Kaburagi

104 Ibid.- Answers to Questionnaire

105 Ibid.- op.cit. Note – One respondent wrote: 'I hope your work will be read by many Japanese people as well as Indian people.'

106 Ibid.- Kaz Nakajima

107 Ibid.- Noriko Yoshida

108 Ibid.- Dr. Yoshihiro Kaburagi

109 Ibid.- Answer to Questionnaire

110 Ibid, Hideto Jay Araki

111 *Ibid.*- Answer to Questionnaire

112 ArambamAngamba Singh, Imphal War Museum 14th April 2017 on Facebook.

113 Akiko Macdonald, Souveniur 2014 op.cit. 31-32 Note – Her father Taiji Urayama survived the Imphal Campaign. He was 22 years old then.

4
The British Story

The British story is very different, in that, while the Japanese probably encountered the Manipuris for the first time in the Battle of Imphal, this was not the case with the British. It was the British East India Company which laid the foundations for British rule in India, and a popular adage in line with Britain's Imperial policy was: "the sun never sets on the British Empire". The drain of wealth from India to Britain in the colonial period did not impact Manipur. So what was Britain's interest in Manipur?

The strategic location of Manipur, which was the gateway to S.E. Asia and East Asia, was definitely of great interest to the British. Moreover, the British were determined to conquer Burma which shares an international border with Manipur. Even after their conquest of Burma, the British needed Manipur not just as a frontier defense base but to ensure smooth commercial exploitation of both Burma and Assam. And as Alexander Mackenzie pointed out, Manipur played and continued to play a prominent part in the politics of the North East Frontier; British strategists wanted to use Manipur as a spring board for controlling the unruly tribes in the frontiers.

Manipur was an independent kingdom in the nineteenth

century— Manipur was never "colonized", nor did she ever form an integral part of British India. She established diplomatic contact with British India— the first treaty, essentially a defense alliance was signed in September 1762. The Treaty of Yandaboo February 1826, recognised the Independence of Manipur by both Burma and British India.

The appointment of George Gordon as the first Political Agent marked the formalization of the relation between Manipur and British India. But Manipur was not a protectorate (as stated by Alexander Mackenzie). Historically and theoretically, protectorates and protected states were independent states. But, after the Anglo-Manipur War of 1891, the situation underwent a change— Manipur lost her independence. The British Imperialists became king-makers by asserting their right to settle successions, and also by raising the doctrine that resistance to Imperial orders constituted rebellion, and the right to inflict capital punishment.[1]

The Anglo-Manipur War had ended Manipur's Independence and Sovereignty, which was so long preserved through the centuries, had now been lost. One need not enter into the justice or injustice of the British action; it was an application of an old adage that "Might is Right", which was the foundation of British Imperialism throughout the world.[2]

The Government of India declared that the state of Manipur had become forfeit to the Crown, but the Queen Empress of India had been graciously pleased to forgo her undoubted right, and to permit re-establishment of native rule under a minor Raja on suitable grounds.[3]

This action was certainly not appreciated by the Manipuris, and loss of their Independence would have rankled, and been one of the factors that decided their attitude towards the British in the Battle of Imphal.

This was just the beginning. Churachand was selected as the future ruler of Manipur. The Regency administration continued for sixteen years, during which the British officials introduced whatever changes they wanted to do in the state administrative structure. Reinstallation of the young Rajah Churachand Singh in 1907 was a mere formality.[4]

The task of placing the administration of the state on a firm footing, could not be isolated from that of mobilization of the military forces, which was a necessary condition of an Imperial Power. The fact that Manipur was placed in such a commanding position between Assam and Burma, demonstrated its advantages as a military base. For this reason, the British adroitly collaborated with the state of Manipur, and the latter played a great role in the colonial expansion of the British power in Burma. But did Manipur of its own accord offer assistance? It was the insensitivity of colonial officials in Manipur to the people's sentiments that invited protests and challenges. In 1904, the first Nupi Lan (Women's Agitation War) broke out challenging the Political Agent's order, which compelled the male folk of Imphal to re-build residences of British officers which were destroyed by fire in mysterious circumstances. The womenfolk came out in thousands spontaneously, paralyzed the whole administration and got the order cancelled. When the First World War broke out, the colonial officials in collaboration with the ruling Maharajah and his vassal tribal Chiefs, raised the Manipur Labour Corps of two thousand Nagas and Kukis, to be sent to the war zones in Europe, particularly

France. Not satisfied with this, the second recruitment was afoot, and in protest, the Kukis rose in open rebellion from 1917 to 1919.

In fact, from the very outset, the hill people were antagonistic towards the British. The Hill Administration all through the colonial period did not form an integral part of the general administration of Manipur State. The extension of British administration over the hill people who were strongly averse to any kind of administration was not without disturbance. And with the outbreak of WWI, the yoke of imperialism became heavier. Apart from the imposition of land revenue, forced "coolie" and the "pothang" system[5], the people were now forced to fight on the war frontlines. The Labour Corps recruitment which became more a question of compulsion, constituted the immediate cause of the outbreak of the Anglo-Kuki War.[6]

It was literally, the last straw on the camel's back. The Anglo-Kuki War ended on the 20th May 1919. The British assumed the administration of the hill-tribes, and justified their action on the ground, that only by maintaining a decent standard of administration can peace be preserved.[7]

Yet, the Manipur kings as recorded in the "Cheitharol Kumbaba" (Royal Chronicle) had carried out this task with great acumen for centuries. The result of the Anglo-Kuki War was that the Kukis were not well disposed, and were in fact antagonistic towards the British in Manipur.

But it was not just the Kukis who grew hostile towards the British. Equally intense and irksome was the Zeliangrong Naga Rebellion in 1930-1932 under the charismatic leadership of Haipao Jadonang, who tried to establish a Naga Raj in place of British Raj. Then came the

Second World War followed by the Second Nupi Lan of 1939, and the movement for the establishment of responsible government in Manipur. All these show the unpopular and weak foundation of the colonial rule, built on the support of teetering semi-feudal elements.[8]

With the near approach of the formal transfer of power into the hands of the Raja in 1907, the Government of Assam wrote to the Government of India on 16 May 1907: The arguments in favor of retaining a garrison of regular troops at Manipur, and that the people of the country are not well disposed towards the British Government, that the minor Raja is of weak character, and that disturbances are not unlikely to arise from intrigues regarding the succession, that a police force would be more likely than regular troops to join hands with the people against the Government, or with one section of the people against another section, and that there is more danger of mutiny in a police force, than in a regiment of regulars.[9]

The Period of Regency was fully utilised by the British for making all major political decisions, and also introducing several changes in the administrative set-up of the native state, which the Raja, even after his formal installation of the "Gaddi" (throne) of Manipur with full power, would find impossible to change. Churachand's installation took place on the 15th May 1907, but the Raja had no sovereign powers; all vital functions and powers of the state were taken over or controlled by the paramount British power. The Political Agent was the "de facto" head of state.[10]

This must have been gall to the Raja as all his actions were circumscribed. But simultaneously, he had been selected by the British as the future ruler of Manipur after the Anglo-Manipur War of 1891. And so on Tuesday, 4 December 1917, The London Gazette published: Central Chancery of the Orders of Knighthood, St. James Palace, S.W.— "The King has been graciously pleased to give Orders for the following appointments to the Most Excellent Order of the British Empire for Services in connection with the War:

To be Commanders of the said Most Excellent Order:-

His Highness, Raja Churachand Singh, Raja of Manipur"[11]

The Maharaja reciprocated by supporting the Allies throughout the war period (WWII). In September 1939, Maharaja Churachand Singh who remained on the throne until September 1941... placed the resources of his State at the King Emperor's disposal for the prosecution of the war, the Durbar, a year later, voting Rs. 85,000 from the State funds as a gift to His Majesty's Government towards the purchase of aircraft.

His successor Maharaja Bodhchandra Singh continued to extend all possible assistance to the war effort, including—through his leadership of first the Manipur State War Fund Committee and then the Manipur State National War Front.[12]

The cordial relation between the Maharajas of Manipur and the British were strengthened during the Battle of Imphal.

When Imphal was encircled, the military authorities suggested to Maharaja Bodhchandra Singh that the royal family be evacuated and take shelter at a safe place in India. They arranged an aircraft for the purpose. But the Maharaja politely turned down the offer and preferred to stay with his people. The Maharaja said: "I can't leave my people and the State at this hour of danger. I shall fight to the last".

The Maharaja had a secret verbal agreement with Lord Louis Mountbatten, the Supreme Commander of Allied Forces in South East Asia. The latter promised to do everything to defend Imphal during any Japanese offensive, while the former vowed not to abandon the city under any circumstances.

The then Viceroy Lord Wavell thanked the Maharaja for his support during the Battle of Imphal in a telegram in August 1944:

I send your Highness my cordial congratulations on expulsion of Japanese armies from Manipur soil. During the arduous campaign which has now ended so satisfactorily, my thoughts had been much with your Highness and your subjects. I was particularly pleased that your Highness refused to leave Imphal, even when the capital was under serious threat from enemy forces. As you are aware, the Central Government have arrangements to give your people ample assistance, and I am sure that normal conditions would soon be restored in Manipur.

The Maharaja also received a message of thanks from the British King Emperor on 8 October on 8 October 1945, after the surrender of Japan:

In recognition of your Highness's and your people's services towards Allied Victory, the tribute of Rs. 50,000/-, payable by your Highness since 1891 is remitted in perpetuity forthwith — George R.I.[13]

The delighted Maharaja went on to declare October 8 as a State holiday and called it "Bodh Leisemba" (nation-building) Day.

It is evident that both the Manipuri Maharaja as also the British Viceroy in India maintained a relationship that was mutually significant to both.

In addition, the British had local support from the V Force. Though the V Force comprised a few thousand of hillmen, the hillmen were generally antagonistic to the British, but fortunately for the latter, the hill people never put forth a combined resistance against the British, for they were a divided house. Inter-tribal war was common. The British viewed these as acts of extreme barbarity or inhumanity. At the point of the sword, the local offices levied forced labour and collected a hill-tax of Rs. 3/- per house. The main concern of the British was the collection of land revenue and the conduct of expeditions into the wild border hills to punish villages which carried out head-hunting raids within British territory. They also began a task of disarming the hill people which alienated them all the more. The reconstituted Manipur State Durbar had no representation of the hill people. The British administration wanted to create a barrier between the hillmen and plainsmen and even among the hill people themselves by carefully emphasizing inter-tribal disharmonies and superficial differences in terms of religion and employed the well known policy of "Divide and Rule"— a policy that played a crucial part in ensuring the stability of nearly every colonial system.[14]

In his instructions to the English navigators, Edward VII, stressed that the service of Christianity must be the chief interest of such as should make a foreign discovery.[15]

The British Government in India actively encouraged Christian Proselytism in the hill regions of North-East India.

Reverend William Pettigrew was the pioneer Christian missionary in Manipur. A. Porteos, the acting Political Agent, had insisted that he open a school at Imphal, and Rev. Pettigrew commenced his operation in Imphal on 6th February 1894. Not surprisingly, the Vaishnavite Hinduised Meiteis who had converted to Vaishnavism only in the reign of King Garib Niwaz (early 18th century) construed Pettigrew's teaching as a deliberate attempt to impose upon them the Government's religion (Christianity). Maxwell, the Political Agent, on his return from furlough, believed that if Rev. Pettigrew was given licence to preach among the Hindu Manipuris, it would mean waging war against the state religion.

The peculiar position in which the British were put to administer the state on behalf of the minor Raja (Churachand), perhaps, made them hesitant to interfere with the religion which occupied so much of the Meitei's time and attention. The British officials decided to maintain the status quo, and Rev. Pettigrew was asked to desist from his missionary activities in Imphal. Maxwell suggested he should work in the North-East area at Ukhrul, and the foundations of the Baptist missionary movement was laid in 1907, when the Church of Ukhrul was established. Some years later, another missionary Dr. Crozier joined the Baptist Mission, but Crozier took interest in the Kuki churches, whereas, Pettigrew took greater interest in the Nagas.[16]

This policy of Divide and Rule is clear in the statement of Sir James Johnstone: I pointed out that the Nagas had no religion, but they were highly intelligent, and capable of receiving civilisation, that with it they would want a religion, and that we might just as well give them our own, and make them in that way a source of strength, by thus mutually attaching them to us. Rev. Pettigrew was considered to be part of the colonial establishment, in so far as he was acting both as a missionary, and officiating state officer, in all matters concerning the day-to-day administration of the hill areas.[17]

By the time of the Battle of Imphal, the majority of the hill tribes had converted to Christianity, and their acceptance of a major world religion created a divide between them and the Meiteis.

The British conquered Manipur in April 1891, and the advent of Christianity in the state is a significant factor of the British rule in Manipur.[18]

One must not overlook the fact that the colonial powers in many cases more or less directly exploited missions for their own ends. It was the colonialists strategy to try to clothe their colonial enterprise as a divine mission— that of taking up the "white man's burden" to the subject peoples. The mutual binding between missions and colonial politics was at its strongest, where the two accepted the "white man's burden" as a "genuine responsibility". The theory of operational unity was put in such a way as to give the impression that colonisation and missionary work were two sides of the same thing. James Johnstone, the Political Agent of Manipur also thought in terms of the stabilisation of the British Empire, and regarded Christianisation of the people as the only effective means for mutually attaching them to Government. He concluded that a large number of Christian hillmen between Assam and Burma would be a valuable prop to the British.[19]

But the question arises whether the cultured Manipuris,

accepted this concept of "the white man's burden", and of Christian evangelisation. The first was certainly not acceptable, and with regard to the latter, the first few years of Pettigrew seemed to be quite dull and unpromising, although in the course of the next few decades, the majority of the tribals in Manipur had converted to Christianity.

All of the above certainly had a bearing upon the attitude of the Manipuris towards the British. Manipur was used as a battlefield by both the British and the Japanese, but other than a few hillmen joining the V Force, Manipuris did not side with the British— rather they stayed aloof. The Second World War suddenly appeared on the quiet hills and valley of Manipur. C. Grimson, Political Agent in his letter dated 10th December 1942, briefed the Maharajah Bodhchandra that Manipur might be an operational area because she was very near the frontline and also the possibility of declaring martial law in the state anytime. Also, it was not the original plan of the Japanese to fight the war on Indian soil, particularly in Manipur, nor did they think that was feasible when they declared war against the Allied Powers on the 8th Dec. 1942.[20]

The British Story begins with a poem penned by Christopher Johnson whose father fought in the Battle of Imphal.

The Box of Lions
Kanglatongbi twixt Imphal and Dimapur
Was the place my father fought at during the War
Already he had seen seventeen years service
A Company Sergeant Major no need to be nervous

To 20 Reinforcement Camp he was sent

And proudly on his way he went
To stop the Japs was the given order
Before they crossed the Assam border.

In early April of '44
The Japs were knocking at Imphal's door
So a defensive box was formed
And to hold their ground the troops were warned

The defenders were a motley crew
Mostly non-combatants but fighting men too
Sappers and Storemen and clerks were found
And to a man they stood their ground

Jap jitter parties were the first to appear
The inexperienced troops they were trying to scare
More determined attacks were later sent in
All being repulsed by the men of the Admin

Ordnance and Sappers formed a mobile patrol
The course of the battle they hoped to control
Wherever the Japs tried to break through
They were met with bullets and bayonets too

For four days and three nights fought the gallant band
But gradually the Japs gained the upper hand

Tanks and infantry were sent to help out
But t'was a losing battle there was no doubt

On Good Friday morning the evacuation began
Withdrawing in good order according to plan
Father got out along with his men
Back to Imphal to fight again

At the "Lion Box" many men died
But all the Jap plans they had defied
The Siege of Imphal for three months had begun
A long war ahead and battles to be won.[21]

The poignant poem tells the story of a brave, proud, experienced British officer who when pitted against the Japanese, did his very best along with other British officers and men to direct the course of the war: the Japanese however were the victors; despite this defeat Christopher Johnson's father never lost heart, he and the others marched to Imphal, where they participated in a long and difficult Battle.

Christopher Johnson has also provided a graphic description of the Lion Box which is a pointer to understanding what the British felt when they fought in Manipur. Their experience also changed their personalities and emotions, "My father hated the Japanese, but he did not instill this emotion into the next generation. Many POW however were unable to do that."[22]

"Seventy years ago, the Imphal Plain was one vast military camp where thousands of Allied troops awaited battle, as the Japanese army began their encircling movement, cutting off the British IV Corps from all ground routes for supplies and reinforcements. Supplies were now at a premium for the Allies and Japanese alike, for the latter depended on captured foodstuffs and equipment, and the large Ordnance Depot at Kanglatongbi was in their sights."

When the Japanese cut the main Imphal-Dimapur road at Milestone 105 on 29th March, all administrative units in the area were ordered to Lion Box, a secure defensive position, for their protection. It covered an area of scrub jungle on either side of the main road. The defenders were from the transport and labour companies of the Royal Indian Army Service Corps and Indian Pioneer Corps, and the Sappers of the Royal Engineers and Indian Engineers.

The large and normally non-combatant force was commanded by the Box Commander Lieutenant Colonel Henry Wells Cole– a decorated veteran of the First World War.

By the 4th April, the Japanese 3rd Battalion of the 60th Regiment was massing to the north of the Lion Box and began probing the defences with "jitter parties to encourage the inexperienced troops to open fire, giving away their positions". Ultimately, the Ordnance personnel, engineer and transport units were forced to leave for Imphal. Several men were captured by the Japanese, as they tried to escape into the jungle. They were later killed as a reprisal when the Japanese realised that it was just usually non-combatants that had thwarted their plans. When the last of the Box evacuees arrived at Sengmai, at Kanglatongbi, the Japanese surveyed their prize. The scene at Lion Box was one of death and destruction, as the dead from both sides, laid strewn about amongst the blackened and burnt out vehicles, tents and bashas. The Japanese had learnt a hard lesson, that the capture of Imphal would not be an easy task. The casualties were:-

British killed 27, wounded 33+, Indian killed 47, wounded 45+, Japanese killed 70, wounded unknown.[23]

Yumnam Rajeshwor Singh in an article titled "How Manipur's Battlefield Diggers are unearthing stories from World War II", published in The Indian Express in 2020, told his story.

Like many others, he grew up in ignorance about the WWII battlegrounds. More than seven decades ago, this hill was one of the many sites in Imphal that the Japanese and the British skirmished in — the Japanese lost more than 30,000 men in a defeat so decisive that it ended their imperial pursuits in Asia. But it was only in 2013, when a vote by the National Army Museum of Britain termed them "Britain's Greatest Battle" that the Battles of Imphal and Kohima entered public consciousness. Till then, the battles were buried in the hills of the Northeast, unknown, save for some literature by military experts, war veterans and historians. In 2005, Rajeshwor chanced upon one such book: The Forgotten Army's Box of Lions: The True Story of the Defence and Evacuation of the Largest Supply Depot on the Imphal Plain (2001) by Christopher D Johnson.[24]

"It was set in Manipur and focused on the battle of Kanglatongbi, I was surprised that I knew nothing about it. Growing up, we only knew what our grandparents told us... that there was a war...the Japan laan."

Over the years, he struck up an unlikely pen friendship with Johnson, whose father fought in the war. "Christopher started sending me books, war diaries — material I would devour late into the night," he says. Soon, with Johnson's cross-continental guidance and encouragement, Rajeshwor graduated from books to battlefields. "They were all around me . . . all these years, I had no idea," he says.

In time, many friends joined in. Before they knew it, weekends or holidays became sojourns into history. "We would go from battlefield to battlefield, spades and shovels in hand. Even years later, there were things to find: helmets, shrapnel, cartridges, personal artifacts such as buckles and combs and even bones," he says. In 2013, Rajeshwor and his friend, Arambam 'Bobby' Singh, founded the Second World War Imphal Campaign Foundation to formalise their weekend expeditions in digging up a forgotten battle. Since 2017, the Japan Association for Recovery and Repatriation of War Casualties has been collaborating with the foundation on missions to recover the remains of Japanese soldiers killed in the war. "But I am not allowed to talk about that," says Rajeshwor.

What he can talk about are the personal requests he gets. Through Johnson, Rajeshwor was introduced to descendants of a number of war veterans seeking information about the last days of their family members. "It started with someone wanting me to lay a wreath at their grandfather's grave in the Imphal Cemetery," says Rajeshwor. Over the years, the requests became more elaborate: someone from the UK enquiring about the location of a tank blast their grandfather died in ("Could you please find that spot and lay a wreath there?"); another 78-year-old from the UK whose dying wish was to locate his father's remains in Imphal. "I have done all that – climbed a hill, laid a wreath, put a poppy cross," says Rajeshwor. When last June, Sharon Gibson, a 40-year-old nurse, reached out to him from Edinburgh, with a request to "find" her long-dead great-grandfather, with only a name (David Tod) and a photograph (black-and-white and faded), he told her: "No problem. This is a big thing for you, but a small thing for us. We will do it."

When we reached the top, Rajeshwor and his team get to work at once — the metal detectors and shovels are out, tents are being pitched, wood is being collected to cook lunch, and "toilets" are being "constructed" — unperturbed by the fact that it is raining, a bitter cold wind sweeping away the glorious summer day we left behind at the base of the hill. The British codenamed it the Pimple (because it resembled one), and Rajeshwor and his friends refer to it by the same name.

It is a terrain he has studied for a year — first, through documents he sourced from the British Library, then through a drone he flew over it and by trekking to the spot last November. "We followed the exact route mentioned in the British war diary of the time. It maintained the events of the episode — who shot whom, the direction of the attack, etc," says Rajeshwor. According to records, 16 Allied soldiers had fallen at the Pimple. "According to protocol, they were buried with crosses. But when the Imperial War Graves Commission unit came two years later to collect the remains, the area was an overgrown jungle and the markers were gone," says Rajeshwor. "Of the 16 bodies, only 12 were recovered, and four were left behind."

One of them was of Tod, Gibson's great-grandfather. The family believed that he was "lost in the jungles of Burma (now Myanmar)", since these battles fell under the British's "Burma Campaign". "That the battlefields transcended the boundaries of Burma is something they have come to understand now," says Joseph Longjam.

"We were really expecting a jungle in Burma and not a hill in Imphal," says Gibson later, over an email. Last year, she dreamt of a man, who she thinks was her great-grandfather, telling her: "Find me in Burma." Gibson got herself on a Facebook group, comprising families of war veterans, scholars and historians. Her queries led her not to Burma, but to a man in Imphal. That month, Rajeshwor pored over war diaries, got in touch with researchers in the UK and managed to track down Tod's regiment, and, finally, the location where he died, by painstakingly superimposing map references of the time to Google Earth to pinpoint the rough location of 25 yards. Finally, in November last year, they did their first trek.

"We just started digging anyway in the location we identified. Suddenly, we found the personal effects of soldiers in a pit. For us, it was a eureka moment because it meant that the four remaining bodies were around that area," he says. At Gibson's request, Rajeshwor had lugged up a memorial plaque and a remembrance poppy cross. In a small ceremony, the team laid the plaque at the spot where they believed Tod was killed, and live streamed it to her in Edinburgh. "It was a very emotional sight. I was afraid to even blink in case I missed any of it," she recalls. "Rajeshwor dusted off the layers of time and brought a little-known part of history to light. It is amazing what he has done for me, a stranger from across the globe."[25]

What is amazing about this story, is that Christopher Johnson's meticulous research at the site Kanglatongbi where his father was stationed, led him to write a book, that ignited a flame in Rajeshwor, leading the latter into a rich historical discovery which he continues today. He and his team have brought to light many untold stories about the Battle of Imphal and have undertaken a significant humanitarian work, unearthing the remains of dead soldiers as also their personal artifacts and the ammunition and equipment used in the WWII battle. This provides a new insight and a valuable perspective of the Battle of Imphal. He and his team have tried to assist descendants of war veterans to find closure through their outstanding excavations, so thoroughly researched. Usually the work of excavating war sites is a work carried out by archaeologists who are trained to perform such tasks. But here we have humane and self-taught Manipuris performing this task. So despite the fact that the Manipuris never sided with the British in the war, decades later, they are bringing closure to British families who were and are in urgent need of such closure.

Several British and Japanese soldiers died in the hills of Manipur during some of the fiercest battles of WWII. They do not lie there forgotten. Why? Because, a team of battlefield diggers, has been scouring this terrain to find their remains and bring some closure to the families seeking answers about their final days in a foreign land.[26]

How does the intrepid Manipuri go about the task? On a full-moon night, atop a hill in Manipur, Yumnam Rajeshwor Singh reads the names of the dead. They may have been gone from this earth for 76 years, but time is relative for Rajeshwor, a man with a plan — and dozens of maps.

"We are on this ridge," he says, tracing a finger along a route on an A-4 size copy of a map from 1944. "And there — there were the Japanese bunkers! From where they fired."

He points a little further away, in the direction we had trekked from — carrying everything from pressure cookers to metal detectors, tents and canned fish — earlier that morning. Of the 10 who had embarked on this journey, only nine made it, after one took ill en-route. The nondescript hill, about 15 km from Imphal was after all, one of the many battlefields where the Allied and the Axis powers fought between March and July, 1944, in some of the fiercest battles of World War II. Rajeshwor gets back to reading his list of the dead soldiers — aided by the flashlights of three phones — before he stops at one. "Private Tod D," he says, "This is the guy we are looking for."

In early March, when Rajeshwor drives me to the hill to look for the remains of David Tod, a British soldier who had died in the war, the skies are blue and the days are glorious. The newspapers have some news about the virus from China entering India but few in Manipur think of it as a threat to them. If China is far away, Delhi and Mumbai are probably even farther. Rajeshwor, who works in a telecommunications company in Imphal, has his itinerary chalked out.

For months, I have been persuading Rajeshwor to let me join his World War II excavation expeditions — where he and his friends travel the hilly Manipuri countryside, unearthing relics and remains, stories and memories from the twin World War II Battles of Imphal and Kohima.

Initially, he tells me that these are "secret" things that happen in the "complete absence of media." But earlier this year (2020), when I send him my customary monthly WhatsApp message asking him if he has changed his mind, he finally relents, but with a caveat: "Please don't mention the exact location in your news."

He did not need to worry — with my despicable sense of direction coupled with the wilderness of the hills, I have no idea where we are. "People talk about things they see and read in books, but neither of these battles have been included in school curricula," says Rajeshwor.

Ten minutes into the climb, I understand why Rajeshwor had told me: "I hope you are healthy." The hill is far from kind: my running shoes are not equipped for the terrain, and I slip, stumble, fall, and on certain portions, comically crawl up the hill. To think of men vying for each others' blood, with guns and bayonets in hand, seems a ridiculous idea. But I am less amused when I see the 72-year-old member of the group, trotting up the hill, way ahead of me, with the support of one thin stick.

(If this was the condition in 2020, what would have been the condition in 1944. That is why the Battle is described as "the fiercest battle")

Even before his first climb, Rajeshwor was certain about one thing: he wasn't here to make money off dead people. The excavation expeditions involve trekking up various hills (the Pimple is one of the more accessible ones), arranging for food, shelter and equipment for digging — but they are funded entirely by the members.

"While Sharon did insist on paying for the memorial plaque, I did not charge her for anything else. I do not want to earn a single penny off this".

"For me personally, I do not care much about historical dates," says Longjam, "But if what we do makes people visit Imphal, it means a lot."

Christopher Johnson has spent decades unravelling his father George Johnson's role in the war. He tracked down families of those who served with his father in Imphal. In time, he found out that George had to kill one of his wounded orderlies, Howard, in the war. "It was a case of mercy killing."

In his article "Lion Box – Kanglatongbi", when writing about the British withdrawal, he states that the Royal Air Force came over strafing and dropping 250 pound bombs on the Box. The retiring troops were mistaken for Japanese, and were gunned down, despite frantic efforts to show they were British, and many casualties were taken, including the runner of Company Sergeant Major Johnson. He had then left his trench with a message when he was hit by 20mm canon fire, and upon seeing this, CSM Johnson ran to his aid, but he was so badly injured that CSM Johnson, shot him to end his suffering.[27]

David Westgate, Johnson's nephew stated about the mercy killing, "My grandfather never spoke about it, but carried with him years after the war."

In 2017, Johnson managed to track down Howard's family, and in April last year, during the 75thanniversary of the Battle of Imphal, his great granddaughter, Ellie, flew down to Imphal. "We were there too, and with Rajeshwor's help we had a small funeral ceremony, bugles and all, where her grandfather died," recalls Westgate. "I don't mind admitting it but I started crying. I walked up to her and apologised. She told me, there was no need to say sorry. 'Your grandfather did what he had to do.'"

"Searching for a person's remains is like looking for a needle in the proverbial haystack," says Rajeshwor. The next morning, the hill is abuzz with the beep-beep of metal detectors, and the scraping of shovels. With Rajeshwor, are

Longjam, and Ratan. "All these years, we have not recorded our work but I am thinking of making a video repository on YouTube and naming the channel 'Battlefield Diggers'," says Rajeshwor.

"We have never felt the need to. Our satisfaction comes from connecting people to their forefathers. Some families just want to know where their fathers or grandfathers went, what kind of places they stayed at, what they did. For them, this is a part of the world they know very little about." (Longjam)[28]

Last October, the team chanced upon a mass burial site, the recovered remains of which they have handed over to the Japanese. "But personal bone collection missions, like that of Sharon's great-grandfather, can take years too" (Rajeshwor).

At the end of the dig, they have shrapnel, a few buckles, a comb, parts of a bullet, tail fins of mortar shells, but no bones. Before the team starts their descent down the Pimple that afternoon — unaware that a pandemic will keep subsequent ones on hold for some time —Rajeshwor calls up Gibson, and informs her that the excavation was unsuccessful.

"That's okay," she says, "At least, we now know where great-grandfather Tod is. He is no longer lost."[29]

This beautiful story illustrates the friendly relationship of the Manipuris with the British.

Another Britisher, but one who participated in the Battle of Imphal viz. Malcolm L. Connolly has also written an account of his experience during the war years:

"My regiment, the 3rdCarabiniers arrived in the Imphal

Valley, India in December 1943, immediately taking over the village of Yairipok, some ten miles south east of Imphal where we started to train with 23rdIndian Division, mostly the Seaforth Highlanders.

In late February 1944, it was reported that the Japanese were converging on Imphal/Kohima. C, Squadron, the one of which I belonged, were ordered to take up position North of Imphal astride the Imphal/Kohima road, just south of Kanglatongbi.

This, I remember, as a lovely situation, it even had a freshwater stream running through, also it was here that Lord Mountbatten came to welcome the regiment to his army, telling us that we would not be running away anymore, we would be supplied by air — then he was gone. The Squadron at this time were given the task of patrolling the Kohima Road as far as the first L of C Post, each troop would take their turn leaving early in the morning, drawing rations for the day of 'Hard Tack Indian Biscuits' and a tin of bully beef, practicing the art of giving covering fire to the tank in front as they went around corners of which there were many. This was quite an enjoyable task, an escape from the petty disciplines of army life, most times making the war seem quite a long way away."

This description gives an idyllic graphic presentation of Manipur, basically a "little Paradise" endowed by nature with a beautiful terrain. Similar words have been used by the early colonial ethnographers and anthropologists in their writings during the colonial period.

What followed this brief period of enjoyment, was stark in contrast. Connelly writes:

It would have been towards the end of March, that

my troop, 7 Troop was employed on this duty, but the traffic coming from Kohima seemed very light, and as we approached our destination, had stopped completely. Pulling up at the entrance of this post it was very apparent that all was not well, all in there had been killed, but there was no sign of the Japs, they were probably watching from the jungle covered slopes that surrounded this post, quickly we turned around and traversed our 37mm gun in the turret to cover our rear, and started to make a hasty retreat, it was then that a lone military policeman emerged from the side of the road still wearing his red cap, he was quickly dragged inside.

Returning back to our squadron after dropping our Guest into a MP post at Kanglatongbi, leaving our Troop leader to make his report. It was here that there was a big flock; the Squadron tanks were being quickly loaded onto transporters and returning to our previous position at Sengmai. It was at this time that many rules and regulations were being inflicted and enforced upon the Squadron. All badges of rank were not allowed to be worn, saluting of officers discontinued, it seems that the Japs or Nips as they were called would rather shoot an officer than another rank, information of what was going on was scarce and our officers told us very little, perhaps they didn't know but occasionally our wireless operator managed to tune into All India Radio which was very difficult, because of the mountainous terrain in which we were situated, but we did manage to know that the Nips had crossed the Chinwin river, and were heading for Imphal, also that the reinforcement camp to the North-West corner of Kanglatongbi had been evacuated, and the staff were being used for the defence of the very large Ordnance supply depot at Kanglatongbi, now known as "Lion Box".

What stands out in this account, is that badges of rank were not allowed to be worn, saluting of officers was discontinued. This has been a glorious tradition not just of the British army but of all armies across the world. In fact, army officers wear their ranks and medals with pride – it is also mandatory for them to do so at official functions, as is so well illustrated in the funeral of Prince Philip, the Duke of Edinburgh in April 2021. And Connelly has provided a very real description of the problems of communication in the 1940's in Manipur. In a post on FB on the 2^{nd}Sept. 2020, Arambam Angamba had outlined the importance of communication during the WW battle. He wrote:

The medium of communication is a very crucial link in winning a war. As such, the Indian Army, the largest volunteer force primarily consisted of Punjabis, Gurkhas, Marathas, Dogras, Kumaonis, Jats, Pathans, Tamils, and Rajputs with a few sprinkling of tribes from the North Eastern belts. It was a huge challenge for the British Officers commanding Indian Units. And Urdu was often the accepted medium of communication. In one instance, Slim was to make an appearance at two camps located adjacently, of which one of them belonged to the Gurkhas. After having finished with the Gurkha's Camp he went on with the other in Urdu. Later he inquired his ADC what he thought about his grasp of Urdu and to his utter surprise, he was told that he jumped off after two lines in Urdu to complete the rest of the talk in Gurkhali!

But it was certainly praiseworthy, that Field Marshal Slim, Commander of the 14^{th}Army had a good command over not just Gurkhali but also Urdu. And Urdu emerged as a camp language in Medieval India.

Connolly explains: "This Depot (Lion Box) was apparently indefensible, manned by mostly Indian administration troops, no plans had been made for its protection, the decision was made to evacuate it, C Squadron and the 2ndBattalion West Yorkshire Regiment, were sent in to engage the Nips and hold them until all the administration troops had been evacuated. This action started on the morning of 7thApril '44 (It was also Good Friday) with a slow trickle of the admin staff leaving, carrying as much of their personal belongings as they could. Later the battle with the Nips started to hot up, and they were as close, that the Tanks could not depress their guns low enough to shoot at them, they had to rely completely on their supporting infantry who were fighting hand to hand keeping the enemy soldiers from climbing on to the backs of the Tanks. Also there were many occasions when Tank Commanders were having to defend themselves with pistols and hand grenades."

A graphic account of hand to hand combat and the importance of "Good Friday" for the British Army. "Good Friday" has been mentioned by Connolly as also Christopher Johnson because it is a very significant day in the liturgical calendar of Christians, not just the British, but Christians across the world. Quite obviously if they started "action" on "Good Friday", Easter Sunday which followed a day later would and could not have been celebrated.

As mentioned previously, Connolly has also referred to the courage of the Japanese. He writes:

"The punishment inflicted by C Squadron and also their supporting infantry on the Nips, was extremely heavy, but they did not appear to know any fear. In their endeavour to place sticky bombs on the sides of the Tanks, they were either killed by the infantry or the Tanks managed to finish them off. They were being supported by 75mm and 105mm guns, which were being fired from their defensive positions up in the mountains not so far away. I was driving the Troop Leader's Tank, when it received a hit from a 75mm gun, and its right hand track was damaged, but it managed to leave the scene of battle and with the support of the Squadron's L.A.D. who brought a supply of new track blocks, this tank was quickly repaired, and returned to take a further part in the ongoing battle."

This account of Connolly's personal experience is significant in the annals of history. It provides an insight into the strategy adopted by the British during this Battle.

"Just after mid day, the order was given to completely evacuate 'Lion Box', to destroy as much as possible (a traditional scorched earth policy used by armies throughout history), nothing to be left that could be of any value to the Japanese. The trickle now leaving Lion Box was now becoming a hoard, in fact it bordered on panic a very diverse collection, many officers and N.C.O.'s amongst them, also many non-combatants, men who were employed in this large depot, all leaving as fast as their two legs could carry them. Many wheeled vehicles overloaded with personal possessions, packed in such a hurry, just ran off the road and crashed — the occupants as many as could hang on, all trying desperately to get away from the Japanese (Their haste to leave as also their fear of the Japanese was only natural in the circumstances). The squadron with their infantry withdrew to the outer perimeter of the Lion Box and at the stroke of 4pm the RAF flew over to bomb and strafe, inflicting many casualties upon the Japanese, also on some of the administration troops, who for some unknown reason, had been late in leaving. Our Tanks jumped up and down as these aircrafts flew low over us. I can well remember thinking, 'Thank goodness, they are on our side.' It was time for the Squadron to leave, for it was quite obvious that 'Lion Box' would not be held that night, so we returned back to our safe haven of Sengmai, but as we entered, the big Japanese guns heralded a welcome by throwing a few shells into our defensive box. Obviously, Sengmai was not the safe haven that the British envisaged. The tide of the battle can change in a moment.

The most important task that the tired and dirty crew had to do was to completely replenish the tanks ready for the following day, or whatever might be in store for us, then we would be fed. This was the first food since breakfast which seemed an eternity ago, at least twelve hours, we would then mount guard on our own perimeter. Everyone was so tired that they just wanted to lay down beside their tanks and go to sleep, but they would be wakened at various times of the night to take their turn on the Squadron defences. During the night the Japanese would lob a shell or two into the box, this just had a nuisance value, hoping to break up the few hours of rest that was available. This was the pattern of life for C Squadron for many weeks to come with the fighting centred on Kanglatongbi and returning to Sengmai. The object of the exercise being to stop the Japanese from taking their troops away from this area to use against 5^th^Indian Division, who were fighting hard in the hills to the East. Everyday, very early the Squadron would return to Lion Box to mix it with the Nips."

It must have been painful, distressing, disappointing for the weary British troops evacuating Lion Box and moving to the "safe" refuge of Sengmai, only to find it far from safe. And the soldiers had no respite, they could not cater to their hunger pangs nor their desperate need for rest for many hours, and even then they did not have the luxury of an undisturbed sleep. The occasional Japanese shell caused no physical damage but it is akin to swapping mosquitoes the whole night in order to get some rest.

"It was a daily ritual, going past the body of a dead Indian, one of those who had been killed by the RAF strike. He was a landmark and very well-known, not because of his deeds, but because of the stench he created, also he was the sign of imminent danger, and on passing this unfortunate Indian, the tanks would close down down and the guns cocked ready for immediate action."

A dead Indian being well-known for the stench he emanated and not for his deeds, is unfortunate; India was at that time under British rule, and the Britishers were using Indian soldiers to retain their hold over the country they had colonised. At the time the Freedom Movement of India was moving fast towards achieving its goal of Independent India — which came about in 1947, just three years after the Battle of Imphal. And using a dead Indian as a landmark is demeaning.

Connolly describes the travails of the opposing armies at the onset of the monsoons, "Everything was saturated, rations much shorter, low-lying ground was almost impossible. The pouring tropical rain beat down on the British/Indian forces who were exhausted, and riddled with dysentery, but in comparison with the Nips who were on the verge of starvation, were well supplied, and in spite of the appalling conditions the Carabinier tanks were always available."

The difficulties of fighting a battle over terrain which had "terrible ridges and peaks which sometimes were so steep that they (the Infantry) had to be winched up the slopes" in vile weather. The tanks also had gruelling trips to make up and down the hills. But all the British/Indian troops who had taken part in the engagement were rewarded for their war efforts, as probably a General in charge of 2ndBritish Division came over and congratulated them, and provided them with something they both greatly appreciated and relished — he sent them a lorry stocked with new uniforms, boots, rations, beer. For the British Indian troops the meal of bacon, eggs and bread was a veritable feast. Such foodstuffs are taken for granted in times of peace, but in a war, they are a "godsend". So also new uniforms and boots to replace the dirty, tattered ones they had been using, probably for an extended period of time.[30]

Richard Hill, a former Trooper of 3rdCarabiniers (Prince of Wales's Dragoon Guards), who did not take part in the Battle of Imphal, has written a short article titled: "Nungshigum? Where's that?"

It certainly would sound like Greek to someone not familiar with or having knowledge about Manipur. He writes:

"As a young soldier in the early 1960's, I stood on parade every April, and listened as an officer recited the story of Nungshigum. I can still hear him saying: 'On the 13thApril 1944 was fought one of the most crucial actions.' To me and my mates Nungshigum Day was an endless bout of drill parades and kit inspections. We had probably started off the day by drawing weapons from the armoury at 0730 hours, and had gone through various inspections before we marched on to the square at 1100 hours.

As I then refocused, I heard the finale: 'never again did Nungshigum fall into enemy hands.'

During the ranks dance in the Gym, our conversation was the usual squaddie banter about football, sex, politics and other mundane subjects, but the last war was definitely not one of them. Our knowledge of the War in the Far East was limited to the dog-eared Commando comics we passed around. In these, the Japanese soldier was always depicted as a little bloke wearing long puttees, and running around shouting 'Banzai'"[31]

This ignorance of the war in the Far East is echoed by a Manipuri lady, a member of the Royal British Legion, who was a Deputy Lieutenant of Greater Manchester in 2003 and an East Cheshire County Poppy Appeal Co-ordinator in 2013. Having grown up in Imphal, remembering VJ Day is particularly important to Khumi Tonsing Burton, and especially ensuring people remember those who served in the Far East in particular (Her uncle Pa Ralkapa fought in Burma under General Slim during the Second World War, and received the military cross for his actions and bravery). The 14th Army, which many feel is often overlooked or overshadowed by VE Day. In 2019, she organised VJ Day commemorations in Winslow with the support of our Remembrance Team, to honour those who fought in the Far East.

"One of the best things about the Royal British Legion is that they make people aware of the many sacrifices of the older generation who fought for our freedoms, which we enjoy today. I want to highlight that VJ Day is as important as VE Day, for those people who fought for their children, grand children and relatives, to know that they did not fight in vain.

"I am also very aware that there are many soldiers whose Regiments are not recognised who fought in the Far East, as what was happening nearer home had more attention from the public.

"The war in the Far East was too remote for the majority of the British public except for those families whose members fought there - they are the Forgotten Army.

"Whenever I go home to Imphal I visit Kohima and lay a wreath at the cenotaph, which stands proudly overlooking Kohima."

Having grown up in Imphal, Manipur in India, where some of the greatest battles of the Second World War took place, she has always been a "Champion of Remembrance", and has actively encouraged the community to get involved and support the Royal British Legion (She lives in Winslow, U.K.)[32]

"Many years have passed. Thanks to the rapid endowment of the media and in particular, the internet, our knowledge of WW2 and the Regiments part in it, has been vastly upgraded. With the work of WW2 Imphal Campaign Foundation (based in Imphal) we have now all seen colour photographs of Nungshigum, and have been amazed at just how steep it is. The narrowness of the tracks, the scrub where the enemy was lying in wait only yards away, the courage of the tank commanders who had to lean out of the turret guide their drivers with devastating consequences. We can only imagine the noise, the confusion, the sheer bloody terror of war. We salute the courage of such men as Trooper Smith who calmly dismounted to affix a tow rope when the starter motor on his tank jammed, and the Squadron Sergeant Major, Bill Craddock, who took command after all the officers were killed, and with his Indian counterpart from the Dogra Regiment, replanned the assault, and won the day.

We still commemorate Nungshigum every year with a dinner and the citation is still read out. The difference now is that we all now listen attentively and remember every word that is spoken, and, I think we all have a lot better understanding of what, and where, Nungshigum is, and how crucial the victory was.[33]

A wonderful Remembrance and an accolade to the British/Indian soldiers who fought in the Battle of Imphal.

Just as stated by Richard Hill and Khumi Tonsing Burton, Graham Summers, a defence writer states:

"South East Asia was seen as a backwater, as far as equipment went, in the early days of World War 2 for the RAF. Fighter squadrons were equipped in the main, with types that were cast offs from both the European and the Middle East regions such as the Curtiss Mohawk and the Brewster Buffalo. Similarly, the bomber forces were only just re-equipping with the Bristol Blenheim by 1941, with no medium bombers like the Wellington. The anti-shipping role was even worse off, using Vickers Vildebeest biplane torpedo bombers. Perhaps the war in South East Asia was not viewed from the same prism as the battles in the U.K. and Europe at the time. Yet, the transport role was vital in this region. One of the best known operations was the so called 'Flights over the Hump' which flew supplies between China and India. These flights, starting in the north-east corner of India, skirted the Himalayas.

By August 1944, all Japanese forces had retreated back across the Chindwin river, and soon the Army under

General Slim had begun to make its way to Burma. This, despite the awful conditions, wading through water-logged paddy fields."[34]

Jagan Pillarisette who co-authored two books on the IAF's (Indian Air Force) air wars, has provided an insight into the air war that raged over Imphal in 1944. He states:

No.1 Squadron, Indian Air Force had only arrived in the Imphal valley on 3rd February 1944 led by the dashing 25 year old Commanding Officer, Squadron Leader Arjan Singh (The Indian pilots like the Japanese pilots were very young). The Squadron at the time was operating the Hawker Hurricane Mk IIB aircraft. It was a capable aircraft, but by 1944, no match for the more nimble Japanese fighters. The IAF was vulnerable:

While the initial variants of the Hurricane were armed with eight 303 inch calibre Browning Machine Guns, the Mk IIB operated by No.1 was equipped with twelve Browning Machine guns – six in each wing. It could also carry two 250lb bombs, one under each wing, or an extra set of long range fuel tanks. Both the bombs or the tanks degraded the performance of the aircraft and they would be easy meat if they encountered aerial opposition.

The first of the fourteen Hurricane IIB fighters arrived at Imphal on 3rd February. The squadron flew more than 60 sorties on offensive, tactical, photographic and sector reconnaissance.

On 13 March, Imphal, Kohima and Dimapur were in peril from the Japanese assault. The Imphal valley saw the first air offensives by the Japanese air forces in mid-March. On March 16th, Tulihal airfield was attacked but a Beaufighter of 176 squadron shot down one of the raiders –

a Mitsubishi Sally bomber. On March 24th, Six Hurricanes from the squadron strafed Japanese gun positions east of Shangshak. On 29th March, when the Imphal-Dimapur road was cut at milestone 107, several offensive sorties were flown by the squadron throughout the day. Again at 1800 hours, all available Hurricanes were ordered to take off and head for the area North of Imphal to attack masses of Japanese troops. This was in the vicinity of Pukhao village, around 22 miles west of Shangshak.

In April, the Allied troops were fighting at Imphal with their back to the wall. The Japanese came so close that the Imphal airfield came within the range of Japanese artillery fire. Air operations were carried out to the maximum extent and the Squadron suffered casualties. But in May, even after the Monsoon had broken, (traditionally in India especially in the Ancient and Medieval periods, battles were not fought during the Monsoon period) and with greater violence than usual, although the hours of flying and making many sorties was cut down, No. 1 Squadron flew a total of 372 sorties of which 32 were by night. This was the first time the Squadron took part in night operations.

This last statement is significant, because even today there are no proper night landing facilities at Imphal Airport. The fact that Indian pilots gave a sterling performance was acknowledged by AOC, Air Marshal Sir John Baldwin on 18th May:

"For the first time in India's history, Squadrons of fighters and Dive bombers manned by Indian pilots have operated in strength against the enemy. As part of the third tactical air force, which I am proud to command, the air and ground crews of the IAF have made a significant contribution to our success. You and your pilots have won honour and glory. Squadron Leader Mehar Singh, who commands No. 6 squadron was awarded the DSO for his brilliant exploits, against the Japanese. He is the first of your fellow countrymen in the Indian Air Force to win this decoration.

You yourself have been awarded the Distinguished Flying Cross and one Indian Air Force Squadron which you command and which participated in distinction in the Burma campaign of 1942, is back again on operations."

One of the tasks of No. 1 Squadron was to assess the damage done by the bombs. Besides, the pilots dropped leaflets in various areas on several occasions. The monsoons created many difficulties for the pilots. The runways were often waterlogged, storms made flying hazardous, clouds and rain hampered visibility and returning pilots often found it difficult to locate their strips. Yet the pilots fought on with courage and determination, most of them young men. This was duly acknowledged when the Supreme Commander of Allied Forces in India and Burma, Louis Mountbatten, visited the Squadron, and personally pinned the DFC on Arjan Singh's lapel. It was a proud moment for the Squadron to witness its CO being decorated on the very battlefield that he earned the award.

By the end of the battle, the RAF had lost 119 aircraft between March and June. They had claimed 33 Japanese fighters and bombers destroyed as confirmed and another 22 as probables.[35]

At the Peace and Reconciliation Meet organised and managed by the 2nd World War Imphal Campaign Foundation in 2019 at Imphal were present interested and concerned nationals of the U.K., Japan and Manipur. The programme primarily comprised of four presentations, two from Japan, and two from the U.K. The British speakers were Terence O'Halloran and Christopher Johnson.

The first British speaker approached the subject of the meet by having recourse to the perspective of the Air Force: pushing supplies, directing weapons of war so precisely that no collateral damage ensues. He stated that a change has taken place in the views of the RAF with regard to Reconciliation. He spoke of an unarmed plane being sent to Imphal to bring back casualties of war but the unarmed plane could not fulfil its mission, as it was overrun by a Japanese aircraft. He narrated the story of a Japanese who cut a woman and child into half – that being the nature of war. A Britisher, Frank had to shoot this woman who had been knifed by the Japanese, as she was grievously injured, in terrible pain, with no hope of survival. This was an act of mercy on Frank's part but the memory and vision of that act of mercy could not be erased from his memory – he suffered from terrible nightmares for a period of sixty years – he died three months prior to this meet at Imphal at the age of 96. This in effect meant that Frank's life was forever changed by the Battle of Imphal – he was deprived of inner peace, without which life is meaningless. Most of his adult life was devoid of peace and contentment. But this change in Frank impacted his family, who must have been saddened by the change and witnessed his suffering day in and day out.

Just as the Japanese who participated in the Battle of Imphal were very young, so also were the British soldiers and pilots. Unlike the Japanese, there was no overriding reason for them to come to fight a war in a foreign land of which place they knew very little.

"From the little I know of young men who joined the Army in the First and Second World Wars, none of them were 'forced'. They all volunteered, as they were fighting for 'King and Country'."

Of this there can be no doubt as the British have always been, and are, loyal and extremely respectful of the Royal Family. The dignity of the Royal Family is sacrosanct.

"Some of them (the young men) cheated their age to join, as they were too young by a year or so. It was also an adventure for these young men."

This is evident from the action of the respondent's husband Richard. At the time of WWII, he was a year too young to join and go to war, when they (the British Army) were recruiting. He was in fact starting at Cambridge University then. But a year later, he joined the Duke of Wellington Regiment and then the Cheshire Regiment, by taking two years out of his university on a Short Service Commission.

As far as I can tell, the soldiers and their families had no regrets, as they felt it was the right thing to do for one's Country. (The vein of patriotism beat strong). I am sure that there are a lot of stories told privately about the Japanese soldiers, but openly, not a lot was said, except both sides fought for their countries.

I think the mentality was different too. The Japanese were invading, and wanted to expand (their reach), but the British/Allied Army were defending their territory. (Popular sayings about British colonisation not only in India but other parts of the world were: 'The sun never sets on the British Empire' and 'Britannia rules the waves'.) They were willing to protect India from the invading Japanese Army.

(The Japanese had the same intention — to free India from the white people).

As far as I know — no one talks about Imphal, except that it was a station where they could block the Japanese coming further into India.[36]

This last sentence about — no one talks about Imphal, is echoed by Mary Cole:

The one thing which was almost unique to those who fought in India and Burma was, that they rarely spoke of their experiences.

Often never, or not until their later years.

My father was typical of most servicemen and he only spoke in later years, and then only to other veterans or relatives who had seen active service during WW2. What I would say is, that what they experienced definitely affected their spouses and children. My father came home a 'changed' man, and as such did not like conflict. He left the discipline to my mother and, it was only on one occasion when I was a child, when he lost his temper with me, that I saw very briefly a side of him which was 'hidden'.

He went to hit me with a stick. I screamed and instantly his demeanour changed. He dropped the stick, picked me up and hugged me. His face changed back to his 'normal' and he never ever did this again, and I never again saw this side of the caring and loving father.

Many relatives I speak with tell of how their fathers drank, were violent or had terrible nightmares for years (as in Frank's case narrated by Terence O'Halloran) after their service, and many families were split up, or plagued by violence.[37]

In answer to the question about how the British felt during the Battle of Imphal, a place most of them had no knowledge of prior to the Battle, the answers varied greatly. One response was precise and to the point: It was War and it had to be done.[38]

I really cannot say what feelings they would have had, as thankfully I have never been in that position, and sincerely hope none of us ever will be. My Father never spoke about his time in South East Asia. He fought at the Arakan, Kohima which he described on the back of a photograph to my mother.

This is a sad picture today, we buried 128 of our battalion, 66 of which are buried at the Kohima War Cemetery, 11 of them also reinterred at Imphal War Cemetery. The rest re-buried in other cemeteries. This information was accessed after my Father's Death.[39]

Reticence was something common not just to British war veterans but to the Japanese veterans too. It must definitely have been too painful to describe the death and destruction that is part of any war, or the loss and grief one feels when their comrades/friends are gravely/fatally injured or gunned down. And these events occurred when minds were extremely impressionable, because of the young age of combatants. And burying a loved one far away from home, despite the fact that the Imphal and Kohima War Cemeteries are well maintained, and the dead souls are remembered and honored every year of the Anniversary of the Battle of Imphal, as also the painful process of reinterment or reburial, bring back alive the feelings of loss and grief to the families of the deceased — the wounds don't heal — one can forgive but it's not easy to forget. Akiko

Macdonald had stated at the Peace and Reconciliation Meet in Imphal in 2019 – Those who lived and fought in the war cannot 'forget' – her father's war diary was destroyed by his mother, because she said he should concentrate on getting food to eat on their table in Japan. But war memories cannot be obliterated, and reconciliation comes from within.

Another British respondent stated: I feel I have nothing other than supposition to offer here.[40]

As a relative of a veteran, it is very difficult to know what the thoughts of the British were at the time. I can only speak for my father (who served mainly at Kohima) who found the battles 'a terrifying experience'. He wrote about the noise and screaming, and how the Japanese would tie his mates to a tree with barbed wire and use them for bayonet practice. When he returned to the UK, he had 'changed' and walked around with his Bible for many months. It is my belief that he was suffering from PTSD (not really recognised in 1945). When he spoke of the local people of India and Burma, he always spoke of their great kindness.[41]

It would be only natural to be terrified of the horrors of war witnessed firsthand, as also the brutality dished out to the mates of the veteran by the opposing Japanese soldiers. PTSD now well recognised, especially after the Vietnam War, is a subject on which clients receiving treatment are not forthcoming; in many places in India and other countries of Asia, people are afraid to access treatment, as they are then stigmatised, as they are regarded as not being "normal". Possibly, in the UK too, people suffering from PTSD at the time would have been hesitant or apprehensive to approach a doctor or medical centre for help.

With reference to the average age of the British

combatants, a veteran's daughter stated that he was twenty-two years old, he did what he was told to do, he was an honest and gentle man – nothing about WW2 would have rested easy with him; he had no choice, the actions he was ordered to do had to be fulfilled.[42]

This is very similar to what the Japanese combatants also faced. Another veteran's relative wrote: My father was only just twenty-three during the battles, and I know from his character, that he would not have felt good about bombs being dropped on innocent people.[43]

Another veteran's family member wrote: My uncle was just turned twenty-one, when he was killed at Ukhrul. He would have been just twenty when he first saw action in the Arakan. I have no insights into his feelings about the local population.[44]

Such a young man coming all the way to Arakan and then Manipur, and being constantly engaged in military action, would have had no time to speak or write about how he felt towards the local people, and he died so early in the campaign. Most definitely his family and families of other British soldiers/pilots who took part in the Battle must have been torn apart with grief, losing a son at such a tender age. The war was at its fiercest in Manipur and Kohima.

"The average age of British combatants was about 22; the soldiers did not like the fact that the civilian population (indigenous/native population) were in the middle of the war but they felt they had no choice, if they were to drive the enemy out. They did give as much warning as they could."[45]

The last is certainly correct. The British taught the local people how to build trenches, when they should take shelter in the trenches, when they could come out safely, what the sirens meant, etc. They also provided fair warning to evacuate houses which would be destroyed, or requisitioned for use by the Allied Forces. The British forces engaged in the war did possess a sense of fair play as far as the local population was concerned.

Battles always cause loss, injury, grief and death. Many combatants must have known when they were fighting a losing battle, or when death was approaching. "I would think that (if death was imminent) they would have thoughts for their families. One of the Majors in my father's battalion when the Padre (priest/minister) reached him, just before he died of wounds said:

"Well done '2nd' Company".[46]

Even though the Major was dying his last thoughts were for his comrades who had fought valiantly, alongside of him.

"My father never discussed this but, I have heard stories and read books, where many men and women from both sides would call for their mother or family. Many asked for their death to be reported back to their families as a brave act.[47]

It would be only natural not to want to die alone; it's also natural to want your family to be around you. And the young soldiers did not want their families to worry about whether they were injured or had died, but wanted them to have closure by asking their colleagues to let their families know if they died in the battle, and also to assuage their grief by informing them that their deaths were not in vain, they died as they had lived by the military code of honor, and their final act was "an act of bravery". Their families even in their grief were proud of their father's, son's, husbands who took part in the Battle.

One respondent found it difficult to envisage what could have been the feelings of British combatants facing inevitable death. "Again, thankfully, I've never had to face this, and find it impossible to indulge in anything other than conjecture."[48]

But another stated: The last thought of the combatants would be 'of their home and loved ones, but also to support their fellow troops, and hold on as long as possible.[49]

The troops were all a fraternity, closely linked, each looking out for the other.

It must have been as difficult for British families as it was for Japanese families to lose one of their own in the Battle. Veterans and family members had however to come to terms with their loss.

"My father as mentioned never spoke of his war days, however, a couple of nosey Great Grandsons, wanted to know about his war service. So, they started to unlock the happenings in Myanmar (then known as Burma). They were horrified, shocked, saddened, by what they have now learned. Their Great Grandfather came home, but sadly died before they were born; as his daughter, I feel so much sorrow for the ones that did not make it home to loved ones. I suppose angry also too, at the way they were so badly treated."[50]

"I can only speak about the people I know, as my father came home, but many are sad that bodies of their loved ones have not been found, and others, are extremely proud to call themselves a relative of one of these very brave men and women. Many feel that we were fighting for the freedom of our own world. Any death in war is sad.[51]

It is an undoubtable fact that one cannot find closure

when the bodies of loved ones cannot be found. The task is practically insurmountable, in that this Battle occurred in 1944. But Rajeshwor was able to find the remains of Private Tod, he and his team of excavators put up a memorial plaque and a remembrance poppy cross at the spot where they believed Private Tod had died — the event was streamed live to his relative Sharon Gibson in Edinburgh.

"My grandmother was totally broken. She had lost her husband in a railway accident in 1926, her youngest daughter to tuberculosis in 1939, then the loss of Harry, her youngest in 1944. She died in 1947. My Dad and his surviving two brothers spoke little of Harry, because I feel it was too traumatic.[52]

The death of her youngest must have dealt a terrible blow, when she was already bereft of a husband and daughter who predeceased her.

"Many, (British families) if not all, did not learn until many months had passed, and of course they hoped that all was well, but in some ways it was a relief to know, one way or the other, but depended on the person or persons involved." [53]

Hope does spring eternal, but uncertainty causes stress which accelerates with time. And every family requires closure — the more it is delayed, the more stressful it becomes for the family members.

A descendant of a war veteran expressed "Total dismay" about the destruction, devastation and death, brought by the war: Total dismay that something as horrific and heart wrenching could go on for years unnoticed.[54]

"As a daughter of a veteran, I feel very sad that any country was ravaged by war, but I know that my father had no choice but to serve the King and politicians who made the choice to fight the Japanese."

With regard to the Japanese combatants: "I can never condone the brutality and cruelty of the Japanese during these battles, but I also believe that they were badly let down by their own seniors in not supplying them. More died on the retreat than in battle, and that seems to be a travesty. However, the Japanese waged war on the Pacific and South East Asia and should have been aware of the risks in not succeeding. I truly believe they were brainwashed by the military and the Code of Bushidō, who executed them to carry out impossible tasks. I bear no animosity towards present day Japanese people."[55]

These sentiments are in most part echoed by the Japanese respondents, and it certainly was a travesty that more of the Japanese combatants died on the long march home, rather than in the Battle itself.

"I am struck by the waste of so many lives on both sides, but revere their memory, as they had to endure these horrors by pure accident of the times in which they were born. As to the enemy, it is easy to demonise them as a coping mechanism but this was a meeting of very different cultures, at a time when understanding of other nations, their histories and ways of life was scant.

The family version of Harry's death was fueled by this attitude and was an amalgamation of factual events, but none of which had come together to cause Harry's death. He was in family tradition, in hospital (wounded) ill with malaria... (Depending on who was telling the tale.) When the hospital was attacked (bombed) shelled or by ground troops shooting and bayoneting (patients and medical staff) during which assault, Harry was killed.

Harry had a spell in hospital in late 1943 but emerged to go into action with his unit (2nd Batt. King's Own Scottish Borderers) in the Arakan. Here he fought at the "Admin Box", where there was an incident, where the Medical field station was overrun with ensuing War Crime Deaths, but he was not involved. There was another such Hospital attack when Singapore fell in February 1942. Doubtless there were others.[56]

These statements are indicative of the sense of justice and fair play on the part of veterans' families.

"My feelings are that war is wrong, and should be avoided if possible, no war is glamorous or desired, and the soldiers of both sides, especially so in SEAC regions, had a very hard time of it. I have no animosity towards the Japanese, worked for them many years ago."[57]

It is apparent that many members of veteran's families bear no ill will to the Japanese, because they understand the cruel nature of war, as also the reasons which made young men volunteer or enlist to fight in the war.

Many family members and friends of British veterans have visited the Battle sites in India, whereas others were not able to do so.

"No I have not travelled to Kohima. A friend took 66 crosses out with her from my Fathers G. Grandsons, and on behalf of their Grandad. They were laid on the 75th Anniversary of the Siege of Kohima, on Good Friday."[58]

This must have brought some peace and closure to all family members, and significantly, the Crosses were placed on Good Friday, a day of great significance in the Liturgical Calendar of all Christians.

"I have visited some of the battlefield sites, and found it most enlightening. I do not have a relative buried in any of these sites, but, I have laid over 200 tributes for other people who have been very emotional on seeing their tribute from 5,000 miles away."[59]

Most family members, friends and even visitors place tributes/memorials/wreaths/crosses on the graves of soldiers buried in the war cemeteries at Imphal and Kohima, (as Khumi Burton does on her visits), these actions are symbolic, significant and definitely emotional.

The WW2 Imphal Campaign Foundation had organised Peace and Reconciliation Meets between the British and the Japanese at Imphal. Some veterans' family members have attended these meets, some have followed its progress on the Internet. By and large, both sides are supportive of the Reconciliation.

A very poignant film on the Theme of Reconciliation was made in 2014, directed by a young Japanese filmmaker Junichi Kajioka entitled "Imphal 1944". It was screened here in Imphal by the WW2 Imphal Campaign Foundation Peace and Reconciliation 3rd Meet in 2019. It is difficult to ascertain how many Britishers have seen the film. But one veteran's relative stated: "I found it very moving." and another wrote: "I found it very informative and moving." and "I found it very emotional and informative."[60]

This is a 20 minute film and about how an individual Japanese veteran visits the UK to reconcile with a British veteran, who initially is extremely antagonistic and hostile, but is gradually won over by the Japanese veteran's sincerity of purpose, patience and desire for true reconciliation. The Japanese won the British veteran over, and over the course of a few years they became close friends. The Japanese veteran featured in the film was Masao Hirakubo who was awarded the distinction of MBE.

One of the veteran's relatives, although not possessing knowledge of the attitude of the Manipuris towards the British at the time of the Battle wrote that though he didn't have that knowledge, "I know from much reading and research, that very many (Manipuris) were loyal to the Allies, and still too till this day, tend to the graves of those killed in action at Imphal."[61]

Manipur was a part of British India after Manipur's defeat in the Anglo-Manipuri War of 1891, even though it remained a princely state. Most of the Manipuris remained neutral during the Battle, they showed favor to neither side. But certainly, the graves of all soldiers who have died and were buried in the Imphal War Cemeteries are meticulously cared for and the dead lie in a hallowed ground, in an environment of "Eternal Peace".

"I am not aware of the attitude of the Manipuri during the battles, but I know from reading and travelling, that many were very loyal to the Allies. I can only imagine that faced with a choice of 'defend the British' or 'help the Japanese', must have been a very difficult decision for many Manipuri people. I understand that many were forced or threatened if they did work for the Japanese." [62]

The last sentence is factually correct, but the Manipuris themselves had no reason to support either side. Their attitude "was mixed"[63], so it would be difficult to state with certainty whether the Manipuris wanted to support the Allies and how they felt towards the Allies. "I can't really answer this (the Manipuri attitude towards the Allied

Forces) in anything other than general terms. Manipur has in part, quite a strong Christian tradition, but we are talking of a time only three or four years ahead of Partition too."[64]

It is true that the tribals who mainly reside in the hills of Manipur were converted to Christianity, most converted before India became independent. But religion was not a factor that decided whether the tribals should support the Allied Forces, because only the British and Americans would have been Christians. And many of the Kukis who were already converted to Christianity, actively supported the Japanese.

However it was not all black or white as some section of the native population gave support, usually limited, to both the Allied Forces and the Japanese.

So the reason for this could have been: Expediency, I'd imagine. Co-operating with whoever holds the upper hand at the time in their area.[65]

Expediency would certainly be one of the factors.

"Some (Manipuris) wanted Independence and thought that the Japanese would help them achieve this. Others felt that the British were better".[66]

It is true that some Manipuris thought that the Japanese supported by Netaji's INA would help them to achieve Independence. (Manipur only lost its independence in 1891). At the same time, the British had been controlling the administration of Manipur for over fifty years, even though native rule was allowed to continue under a Maharaja.

"They were stuck in the middle of a Battle, and no doubt did what they felt best in order to protect their homes and families."[67]

This statement is undoubtedly true. This is reinforced in the words: "They must have been stuck between a rock and a hard place, to try and appease both."[68]

The British must have issued orders to destroy local houses for security reasons.[69]

The British did not want the Japanese to hide or shelter in local houses. In the same vein: "I can only assume that the British did not want the Japanese to use the resources found in local homes, or use the buildings as a shelter or ambush."[70]

This also included the rice stores kept in local homes, especially as the Japanese short of food provisions, were always on the lookout to source rice.

The British did not really issue orders to destroy local houses "they only tried to destroy properties that were being used by the Japanese, and there was no other way to get them out."[71]

This statement is also correct in the sense that the British did ask people to vacate their homes, but they also destroyed the homes. "I don't know. I do recall from the war diaries in the Arakan, instances of Headmen's houses being destroyed where they were believed to have gone above and beyond in assisting the Japanese."[72]

This too has a ring of truth.

The 2nd World War Imphal Campaign Foundation founded by Arambam Angamba Singh and Rajeshwor Y. came into existence in the year 2013 as a registered organisation. This Foundation has assisted many veteran's families, relatives and friends who have visited Imphal, and had queries to pose and battlefields to see, especially the battlefields where their loved ones fought and where many died. Some veteran families have requested the Foundation for help, usually to find out where their loved ones died, to bury their remains, and put up a plaque, cross or some kind of memorial in their honor, in the case of the British. For the Japanese veteran families they have carried out excavations as well.

"I did ask Raj (Rajeshwor) and his team to remember the 11 soldiers from the 2nd Durham Light Infantry, that are resting in Imphal Cemetery on the 75th Anniversary of VJ Day, and under the restraints of Covid-19, did a great job for me. Rajeshwor and the team, are such amazing people, they deserve medals themselves for all they do to help us when we are so far away. Nothing is too much trouble for them. A friend has found the resting place of her Great Grandfather thanks to the guys at ICF (Imphal Campaign Foundation) Thank you and God Bless all.[73]

WWII Imphal Foundation has not helped me personally, but I know of someone whose loved one was recently found, and a gravestone placed there. This was an amazing thing for Raj and his team, and I cannot thank them enough for what they are doing to find these lost souls. It brings closure, and some comfort to families both in England and Japan. I have written two articles for the Imphal Tourist Magazine, and have been sent copies to their 75th VJ Day Imphal magazine. Raj, Bobby (Arambam Angamba Singh), Yai, and numerous people from Manipur, have contributed to the WWII Burma Research Group, and brought a wealth of knowledge to the group."[74]

"One of the greatest ongoing tragedies is for those families with a lost loved one, with no known grave. I know that tremendous work is being done on the ground, to locate war dead and give then the appropriate burials and recognition. Kanglatongbi Ridge, where my uncle served a month or so, before he was killed, is a particular focus from the Allied side. There are still thousands of Japanese dead, unrecorded along the 'Road of Bones', and I would wish for as many as possible of these young men to be found and commemorated." At the end the respondent has written a touching sentence to her uncle: RIP Harry, A Seaham Lad, Always Remembered.[75]

An individual who has contributed in great measure to assisting the British and Japanese in their search for closure is the other founder of the ICF.

Arambam Angamba Singh, 48, gets up early to vacuum his room, and clean his collection of over 300 relics from a WWII battle fought 77 years ago in Manipur and Nagaland. (Like Rajeshwor, he has been extremely active in the excavations conducted by ICF to find the remains of fallen soldiers as also relics of the War.)

On the first floor of his home in Manipur's capital city in Imphal, most of the war collection – Japanese rifles, helmets, a water canteen, spent grenades, cigarette cases, even an old Japanese bicycle – came his way by chance, but they are, he says, found everywhere in his home state.

Arambam has the look of a body builder, but he treads cautiously on a construction site, strewn with war munitions. If he puts a foot wrong, chances are that he could damage or crush the old ammunition.

A former civil engineer, he has worked in the past in supervisory roles at construction sites. Since 2013, when he turned into a full-time history buff and tour guide, he has climbed up and down difficult terrain in the hills, where the British Army and the Japanese fought the devastating Battle of Imphal and Kohima in 1944. Over 50,000 Japanese died or went missing in the combat. The British Army that included Manipuris, suffered over 16,000 casualties. Pressing Arambam for exact numbers can, however, be a sore point. "The Battle wrecked local economies and lives. Bridges blasted, trees scorched, civilians massacred. But the number of Manipuris who died is still unclear. There is not much documentation about us," he says.

Sanitised History

The amount of detritus the war has left behind in the nooks and crannies of the state, however, acts as a reminder of the macabre conflict. Arambam and his team have devoted their time to salvage as many war remnants as possible. "I'd be at a site being dug for a house and a spent artillery shell would be hidden behind the rubble; a walk in the forest would yield a gun or a grenade lobbed by the British Army at the Japanese and vice versa. His eyes light up for a brief moment at the memory of these chance encounters.

The series of accidental discoveries got him thinking about a new career. For the past eight years, he has been arranging tours of the war sites of the Battle of Imphal and Kohima. He is now planning to expand this in a new direction: he is launching the Azad Hind or INA (Indian Nationalist Army) tour.

Arambam feels millions of Indians have grown up reading a sanitised version of history, in which the Battle of Imphal and Kohima are barely touched upon.

"Subhash Chandra Bose, the INA leader, and considered by many to be a political rival of Nehru, was in an alliance with Japan in WWII, an Axis power, which complicated the picture; British India was with the Allies", he says.

January 23 was the 125th birth anniversary of Bose, who besides being an INA hero, was also the contemporary of Jawaharlal Nehru, the Independent India's First Prime Minister. Arambam paid tribute and lavished praise on Facebook. His homage was in line with the Prime Minister Narendra Modi led government's initiative to revive Bose's standing in the Indian imagination. Bose's birthday was marked this year as 'Parakram Divas' on the Day of Valour.'

The Fallen Ancestors

Fifteen years ago, Arambam was a civil engineer, a job which he has grown disillusioned of. He would take his annual leave to explore the countryside, especially the hills on the outskirts of Imphal. His aim was to fill in the blanks of the war stories he had heard from his grandparents. He would ask the people in the hills, mainly the families of the survivors of the battles, to share their personal stories about the conflict.

After returning to work after one such annual leave, he found his desk piled with files and work. His mind suddenly drifted towards an old WWII Japanese gun, a gift he had received from a friend. At that moment, he decided to quit the job, and become a full-time collector of war relics.

I decided to make a career out of it. I wasn't taught about the Battle of Imphal and Kohima at school. There were many like me who didn't know, but it might seem important to them one day".

In 2013, the National Army Museum in Britain, picked

the Battle of Imphal and Kohima, over the more celebrated battle of D-day and Waterloo, as Britain's greatest battle.

In his own private museum, Arambam placed a platter of fresh flowers and incense sticks before framed mugs of the departed leader hanging from the walls. Next to it are Bose's black and white photos, taken during his time in Japan. He was captured in action, encouraging Indian soldiers in the battle to press forward – in the crucial battle of Imphal and Kohima, a team of the Indian National Army acted as the advance party, and also participated in active combat along with the Japanese against the British Army.

For the eight years, Singh and his team of volunteers, which includes tourism students and businessmen, have been taking small groups of tourists, mainly relatives of soldiers – British and Japanese – around the sites of the battle. Every month, Japanese tourists visit the combat sites in Manipur, to pay homage to their fallen ancestors who gallantly fought Britain and her Allies.

"War tourism is a concept travel motivated by a specific desire for an encounter with death, says Lina Moirangthem 27, a researcher who is associated with the WW 2 Campaign Foundation in Imphal. Sometimes, Arambam also has to deal with requests to find a missing relative. Finding a family relation 77 years after a war basically means mapping an area, and placing a plaque, but it's a job Arambam takes seriously. "This has to do with someone's sentiment, you can't play with that".

He works with the family documents, the maps or letters they provide of that time, or the address from where the soldiers sent his last letter home, matching it with the maps available in his area, does a recce, he is planning one soon

– talks to old - timers, looks up old birth and death records, and either plants a plaque on his own, or accompanies the families there to do that.[76]

Arambam Angamba Singh has made a substantial contribution to a little known facet of Indian History. Each relic carries a story, British or Japanese, and enriches the history of North East India, especially Imphal and Kohima and the Musuem he maintains in pristine condition – museology goes hand in hand with history. And his 'Battle Remembrance Tours' may be dubbed as 'War Tourism'. War Tourism as a concept and also as a livelihood, emerged first in Imphal.

In the Battle of Imphal – Kohima 1944, over 50,000 Japanese died or went missing, the British India Army that included Manipuris and soldiers from British African colonies suffered over 16,000 casualties. It is memorable also because had Imphal fallen, the British who had already lost Burma, might have lost much, if not all of India, to the Axis forces as well. 'I once found a family photograph of an unknown Japanese soldier. That kind of thing stays with you. I wonder from time to time, if he ever got back home'.

Last year Singh (Arambam Angamba) launched Battle Tours – 4 and 5, night trips to a range of sites, booked mainly by foreigners, who had family members fight in the war. He says he is happy to have made a career out of something he loves, and to be spreading his message of 'Peace' to all who visit.

Whenever, he and his team have found a relic like a photograph, diary, or other personal belongings, they put word out through 'war commissioners and foundations', to try and reach the families. Over the years, in this way, word has spread. Singh's dream is now to see a trickle of scholars turn into a stream. 'Manipuri civilians died in air raids. Families were devastated and displaced. You go for a walk in the forest, or dig at a site to build a house, and war relics, like a bullet or a gun, or a grenade, lobbed by the British Army or the Japanese, are everywhere. Keeping this history alive is important.'[77]

In conclusion, it can be said that the majority of the Manipuris did not actively engage in the Battle of Imphal. The V force which sided with the British was comprised of only a few thousands of tribals. A few Manipuris may have joined the British Indian Army, as evident from the story of Pu Lamkhothang, who however disillusioned with the British, left that army and joined Netaji. Maybe, the Manipuris stayed away, because of the nature of British administration in Manipur, and their system of taxation. But they did not display any animosity towards the British, with the exception of those Kukis who sided with Japan and the INA. (There were some Meiteis who also joined the INA).

It was both a spirit of adventurism and loyalty to King and Country, an emotion which runs deep in British psyche, that made many young Britishers to enlist in the army that won the Battle of Imphal. The young age of the British combatants is similar to the young age of the Japanese combatants. And loyalty to king and country was common to both nations.

However, even upto the present day, the British Royal Family is held in high honor, reverence and respect, and has a strong hold on the imagination of the people. This is evident from the huge following on social media of the British Royal Family. People across the world follow all events associated with them, especially now with the approach of the Platinum Jubilee of Queen Elizabeth the longest reigning monarch in history.

The testimonies, war memories of British veteran family members present a meaningful insight into the Impact of this Battle on the Veterans and their families. The testimonies are characterized by clarity, despite the emotional nature of the some of the responses, and add new and valuable information to the history of the Battle of Imphal.[78]

References

1 Lal Dena — British Policy Towards Manipur pp 1-4

2 Gangmumei Kamei cit. in Lal Dena's op. cit., p. 42

3 Lal Dena op. cit., p. 44

4 Ibid, p. 4

5 Ibid p. 75 Note - Pothang was of two kinds: Pothang bekari and Pothang senkai. According to the first, the people were under obligation to carry goods or baggage, or to make bridges, roads, new bungalows without payment, for the touring officials. According to the second, each household was to subscribe money, chicken, eggs, or other domestic animals to feed the touring officials, free of cost.

6 Sonthang Haokip, op. cit. p. 50

7 Ibid, pg. 183 cit. Sir Robert Reid pg. 88, History of Frontier Areas Bordering on Assam from 1873-1941, Guwahati, 1942.

8 Lal Dena op. cit. p. 5.

9 Ibid pp. 54-55

10 Ibid pp. 44-59

11 The London Gazette - Published by Authority, Tuesday, 4 December, 1917

12 Hemant Singh Katoch, op. cit. p. 31

13 Ibid, pg. 31-32 cit. H. Bhuban Singh - The Merger of Manipur pp. 53-55

14 Lal Dena op. cit. p. 69-73

15 Lal Dena, Colonialism and The Study of Christian Missions in North East India, Proceedings of the North East India History Association, p. 132

16 Salam Irene - Catholic Education in Manipur pg. 12-16, cit. G. Kabui - Social and Religious Reform Movements in Manipur in the 19th and 20th centuries pp. 15-16

17 Ibid, p. 17 cit. Sir James Johnstone - Manipur and the Naga Hills pp. 18, 43

18 18 Ibid p. 4 cit. G. Kabui, op. cit.

19 Lal Dena - Christian Missions and Colonialism p. 7, 19. cit. Sir James Johnstone op. cit. p. 43-44.

20 Lal Dena - British Policy Towards Manipur op. cit. p. 112

21 Christopher Johnson - The Box of Lions pg. 50 Souvenir 2014 op. cit.

22 Ibid - 2ndWorld War Imphal Campaign Foundation Meet, Imphal 2019

23 Ibid - Lion Box, Kanglatongbi pp. 19-23 cit. in Souvenir 2014, op. cit.

24 Note - Christopher Johnson participated in the Commemoration of the Battle of Kanglatongbi (Lion Box) on 7th April 2014, Manipur.

25 The Indian Express 2020 - The Manipur's Battlefield Diggers are unearthing stories from WWII

26 Tora Agarwala - F.B. on Aug. 30, 2020

27 Christopher Johnson - Lion Box op. cit. p. 23 Souvenir 2014.

28 The Indian Express 2020 op. cit.

29 Ibid

30 Malcolm L. Connolly - Memories of Kanglatongbi Lion Base, pp. 24-27, cit. in Souvenir 2014 op. cit.

Note - Connolly served with 'C' Squadron,3rdCarabiniers in India between 1942-1945, and was involved in The Battle of Imphal at the Lion Box.

31 Richard Hill - Nungshigum? Where's that pg. 28-29, cit. in Souvenir 2014 op. cit.

32 Khumi Tonsing Burton - Encouraging Community Support, 10th May, 2021, www.britishlegion.org.uk/stories

Note – Khumi Tonsing Burton has supported the Royal British Legion for over twenty years.

33 Richard Hill, op. cit.

34 Graham Summers, The RAF in South East Asia during WWII pp. 35-40, cit. in Souvenir 2014, op. cit.

35 Jagan Pillarisetti - No. 1 Squadron "Tigers" and the Imphal Siege pg. 41-46 cit. in Souvenir 2014 op. cit.

36 Khumi Tonsing Burton - Answer to Questionnaire, 30th April, 2021

37 Mary Cole - op. cit. October 2020

Note - She is the daughter of Pte Harry Hopton T282143 RASC, 2nd Infantry Division 1942-1945

38 Matt Stanyard - op. cit. October 2020

39 Paula McGuigan - op. cit. October 2020

40 Mick Balmer - op. cit. October 2020

41 Mary Cole - op. cit.

42 Paula McGuigan - op. cit. October 2020

43 Mary Cole - op. cit.

44 Mick Balmer - op. cit.

45 Matt Satnyard - op. cit.

46 Paula McGuigan - op. cit.

47 Mary Cole - op. cit.

48 Mick Balmer - op. cit.

49 Matt Satnyard - op. cit.

50 Paula McGuigan - op. cit.

51 Mary Cole - op. cit.

52 Mick Balmer - op. cit.

53 Matt Satnyard - op. cit.

54 Paula McGuigan - op. cit.

55 Mary Cole - op. cit.

56 Mick Balmer - op. cit.

57 Matt Satnyard - op. cit.

58 Paula McGuigan - op. cit.

59 Mary Cole - op. cit.

60 Mary Cole, Paula McGuigan, Mick Balmer - op. cit.

61 Paula McGuigan - op. cit.

62 Mary Cole - op. cit.

63 Matt Satnyard - op. cit.

64 Mick Balmer - op. cit.

65 Ibid

66 Matt Satnyard - op. cit.

67 Mary Cole - op. cit.

68 Paula McGuigan - op. cit.

69 Ibid

70 Mary Cole - op. cit.

71 Matt Satnyard - op. cit.

72 Mick Balmer - op. cit.

73 Paula McGuigan - op. cit.

74 Mary Cole - op. cit.

75 Mick Balmer - op. cit.

76 Paramita Ghosh 26 Jan. 2021 - A World War II Museum that shines light on lost Indian History.

Note – Arambam Angamba Singh on F.B. 26th Oct. 2020 - Am so honored with this task... meticulously picking out human bone fragments... remains from WW2 - ultimate patience.

77 Ibid - Hindustan Times - 7thNov. 2020

Note - Article on Arambam Angamba Singh

78 Note - All responses to Questionnaires to Respondents in the U.K. have been written verbatim.

5
Conclusion

The Battle of Imphal really came into public consciousness in Manipur, first when a young man from Delhi – Hemant Singh Katoch came to Manipur, became curious about this Battle, conducted meticulous research on the subject, culminating in the publication of a book titled " The Battlefields of Imphal" – The Second World War and North East India in 2016. He also wanted to inform the public not just of Manipur, but of other states of India, and people overseas, especially the British and Japanese of this canvas on which was transcribed the history of this Battle. To him goes the credit of initiating 'War Tourism' in Manipur. He began tours of the battlefields in and around Imphal and in fact the first tour he conducted was for the students and faculty of the department of History in Manipur University. This first tour took place on 26th June, 2013.Manipur has the distinction of being the first state in India to have initiated 'War Tourism' and besides its undoubted historical worth,it is an income generating activity as well.

But two locals of Manipur, not historians, also displayed an avid interest in learning about the Battle of Imphal. Till very recently, many of North East India's Contributions to

India's Freedom Movement were not known by people of other states of India. But unfortunately, as Angamba and Rajeshwor have expressed this historic event did not feature in the history books used in schools in Manipur. But this ignorance was not confined to Manipuri school children, even school children in Japan and Britain had little or no information about it.

So, the two young men Angamba and Rajeshwor decided to create an organization, known as the Second World War Imphal Campaign Foundation to remedy this gap in knowledge and information. ICF (Imphal Campaign Foundation) is a pioneer organization in the field of research, and preservation activities of WWII heritage in the country. It is located in the state of Manipur on the eastern most corner of the Indian sub-continent. It initially began about an odd twenty years ago as an individual pursuit of the two Co-Founders, Arambam Angamba and Rajeshwor Y. Early on, they felt the significance of the history and the importance in preserving the legacy of these twin battles that took place in Imphal and Kohima in 1944. Interestingly, this Battle is now widely acknowledged as Britain's Greatest Battle of all time. The greatest amongst various military campaigns, the Empire has taken part so far.

It was this treasure trove that was lying in our own backyard, uncared and unattended for a very long time that inspired. This was in serious need of a passionate and untiring effort. Moreover, this particular event made a great impact on the history of the erstwhile Kingdom of Manipur.

The need to seriously take up this task gave birth to the organization, 2nd WWICF, which was registered in the year 2013 with its head office at Tera Amudon Akham Leikai, Imphal West, Manipur. The organization was thus formed with an objective to keep the history of Manipur's connection with WW II alive. It now consists of 15 core members from various walks of life and professions, besides many volunteers.

The organization is now actively involved into various activities such as research of the history of the battle, conservation and preservation of the unique heritage of WWII, Commemoration of the Battles in the memory of those who laid down their lives in the battle, irrespective of country, colour, caste and creed, archiving, and most importantly, the Peace and Reconciliation efforts.

Some of the milestones of the organization, since the very inception are:

With support of the State Government, the annual event of the Commemoration has been successfully conducted since 2014.

The organization has signed an agreement with Japan Association of Recovery and Repatriation of War Casualties, a Japanese Government appointed organization for the mission: Leave No Man Behind, to search for Japanese soldiers' remains from WW2 in Manipur.

The organization is a managing partner of the Imphal Peace Museum which is being commissioned (it has been commissioned in 2019) with the support of Nippon Foundation, Japan. It now stands as an everlasting symbol of Peace and Reconciliation effort, from the People of Manipur.

The organization conducts an exhibition on the theme 'Know Your History' – "Battle of Imphal 1944", as a part of the Sangai International Tourism Festival each year, organized by the Government of Manipur. (The festival is usually held in the last part of the month of November)

The organization had also jointly commemorated the 'Battle of Imphal 1944' at various significant battle locations with the Assam Rifles (a para-military force)

Both the Co-Founders had been invited to Japan for intellectual dialogues on Peace Museum by Sasakawa Foundation. They are also the first in Asia to become members of the International Guild of Battlefield Guides, London.

An ongoing series "The Imphal Talks", on various topics on the war history, films, international peace efforts etc., is run successfully.

Promotion and training of Battle Tour Guides, another aspect of Tourism Promotion in the state.

It has also published and contributed many articles, on the Battle for Commemoration souvenirs, magazines, national newspapers and for various other media.[1]

Angamba has also spoken on 'Integration with India' 'Indians too, are getting interested in this lost history'. His most recent tour was in early March with a group from Kolkata just before India went into a national lockdown. 'People think WWII, and they think Europe. In 1944, a World War II battle was fought right here' says Sukti Sarkar, a retired bank official from Kolkata in Eastern India, who went on one of the tours. "Arambam knew exactly who fought who, who was up on which hill, who came down, who didn't". (The ideal manner to teach history today). The Sarkar family visited Tengnoupal, one of the five major war-sites of the battle in Imphal, the other four being Nungsigum, Kanglatombi, Shanshak and Bishenpur.

Manipur was the stage of a major theatre of war; Manipuris gave lives in the Battle of Imphal. Shouldn't someone have taken notice? (A poignant question) That hurts Arambam somewhere deep; this is a history he wants to piece together for the next generation.

Unlike us, who came of age in the 80's and 90's, young people today are asking questions. There was no mention of this battle in the history textbooks, the Azad Hind Fauj, which joined the Japanese Alliance against the British, finds mention, but very briefly. Manipuris took part on both sides but mainly in the British Army. The world once converged here, and we were the people in the middle.

This suppression of history rankles with Manipuris of all generations. So they did the next best thing – passed them on as stories or oral histories from one generation to the next. My grandfather, Lalmani Singh, was trained by the British in Kolkata as part of an air-raid protection team. He told me about how to construct camouflage shelters for aircrafts. War you see, was always with us. We are a martial race, we have fought with the Burmese, Nagas and the British. Manipur was an independent kingdom, till its Merger with India in 1949.

Integration with India is still a prickly subject with many Manipuris. I mean we don't think about it. And honestly, we are a little tired of everything being seen from either a for or against perspective. The Battle Tours are "a people's initiative", The Armed Forces (Special Powers) Act is still operational. It was imposed in 1980 when the state was a hot bed of militancy. The Act allows the army to use force to maintain law and order, enter and search any premise, and arrest without warrant.

The Battle of Imphal, which Manipuris call the 'Japanese War', thus is a neutral territory to build a new history of reconciliation with Manipuris of all political affiliations and mainland India (Mainland means all parts of India outside of North East India)

Arambam says with a laugh that he grew up knowing all about the Great Mughal Emperor Akhbar, and the Cholas and the Pandyas, the great kingdoms in the south of India, and 'next to nothing' about his own backyard. "We always had to look at the big picture, and look away from our own history".

Arambam is excited about the Indian Government's new initiative to revive Bose's legacy. It coincides with a new Indian National Army or Azad Hind tour, he has recently added to his itinerary.

Arambam has cast his eyes on an old museum in Moirang, which is 45 Kms away from Imphal, where the flag of Bose's Indian National Army (INA) was first unfurled on Indian soil. He wants to expands the map of his military tour and include Moirang.

"Bose is much larger than we think he is. And, Manipuris fought from his side as well"

Since Bose's contribution to India's nation building has been neglected for so long, he says the people of Manipur can see the reflection of their own story of alienation from the rest of India, just like Bose's historical contribution has been sidelined. All Arambam needs to do now is focus on building a 'solid tour itinerary'.[2]

The Co-Founder and Vice President of the 2ndWorld War Imphal Campaign Foundation, ArambamAngamba Singh stated that this foundation came into existence because: I was passionately involved in various activities connected with the Battle of Imphal 1944, in my own personal capacity for a long time. Eventually, things got bigger and more serious. Our activities also inspired many with similar interest. This led to the forming of the organization to carry forward the mission to keep the history alive.

I am involved in various levels of activities with the organization, right from planning to implementation. Some of the main ongoing activities are Research on the Battle, Collection and Preservation of relics and war remnants, Curating the Imphal War Museum, Search of Japanese soldiers' remains, and British as well, Promotion of War Tourism (this word was coined in Manipur), Archiving and Publication of Articles, and features of the Battle, and Commemoration of the Battle.

The Battle of Imphal is remembered as the 'Japan Lan' or the Japan war in the local memories. It is hard to ascertain how it originated, but probably, the anti-British sentiment was still very strong, and in this light, the Japanese could have been viewed as the 'liberators'. The racial similarity could be another reason.

With reference to the devastation brought to Manipur by the Battle of Imphal in 1944, the scale of devastation to Manipur caused by Seven Years Devastation by the Burmese in the early part of the nineteenth century was much greater, in terms of civilian casualties. Whereas, there were only 2000 households in Imphal after the Seven Years Devastation, in 1944, the population of Imphal was 5.13 lakhs.

With regard to the work of the Foundation in assisting combatants families and relatives who visit Imphal, to experience closure, when the foundation successfully accomplishes the task of finding the remains that had previously never been found, the Foundation members, experience a deep sense of accomplishment and the contentment that comes with helping someone's family in the search of their loved ones.

It is not an easy task to locate and carry out excavations. 'It's a long shot, taking into account the number of years that have lapsed, but so far, we have handed over the human remains of about three to four individuals. A few years ago, we had also discovered a mass grave, which is believed to be of Japanese origin, and yet to be investigated'.

In recent decades, many family members and friends of the veterans who fought in the Battle of Imphal have been visiting Manipur on a regular basis. Some come even more than once a year. The two main factors that can be attributed to this increase in footfall are

(1) The growing awareness amongst people and families of veterans, who were then part of the battle that took place 77 years ago, and a wish to retrace the 'trails' of their loved ones, (2) Drastic improvement in terms of law and order in the region, and the helpful government relaxation of travel regulations.[3]

Imphal, the capital of Manipur was chosen to be a World War 2 battlefield in India, and here the fiercest battle of World War 2 was fought, yet, Imphal was a place unknown to most Indians, and even more unknown to the Japanese and the British. Yet this Battle in local parlance, was known as 'Japan Lan'. Every battle brings death, devastation, trauma and disruption, and Manipur which had no stake in this battle, experienced all of the above. At the time when

Japanese invaded, many Manipuris were not even aware of why the Japanese had come. They looked so much like the Manipuris themselves.

Although the Maharaja of Manipur Churachand Singh, pledged support to the British, most of the local inhabitants remained aloof, and sided neither with the British or the Japanese. But as a result of the battle being fought in Manipur, the local inhabitants were exposed for the first time to people of various nationalities having different lifestyles, cultures, and religions. The result was that Manipuris was catapulted forward and embraced what can be termed as 'Modernity'. Even the demography of Imphal town was a kaleidoscope of soldiers of different nations, including Indians from outside of North-East India.

What stands out is that though the Japanese were the aggressors, the local population in Manipur displayed a strong empathy and liking for their Japanese, especially large section of the Kukis. There were certainly many similarities between the Manipuris and the Japanese, and they were both of Mongolian stock. So ethnicity could have determined the attitude of the Manipuris towards the Japanese. Some few Manipuris were attracted to the INA because of the charisma of Netaji Subhas Chandra Bose and because the INA were in alliance with the Japanese. As a result of this exposure to the people of different countries, the world-view of the Manipuris was greatly changed.

Most books written on the Battle of Imphal are military or war histories, and the Voice of the Manipuris is never heard. To correct this omission in the books on the Battle, the testimoniesof Manipuris, expressed in their own words, has been the focus of the second chapter. The true stories of the Tangkhuls, Kukis, MeitiePangal and the Meiteis, present a completely new and different perspective on the Battle of Imphal. From these stories and recollections it is once again evident that Manipuris found the Japanese to be a very friendly people and both the Kukis and Tangkhuls, but especially the former, propagated myths claiming that they were related by blood to the Japanese, both being descendants of two brothers. One Kuki Chief even opened a school at that time where Japanese language and script was taught.

All these recollections follow a pattern – how the villagers and town people were forced to evacuate their houses during the war, how they had not only to supply rice to the Japanese soldiers, but also pound the rice, how livestock was appropriated from the villages to feed the starving Japanese army. But the Japanese soldiers did not steal food provisions they paid the local communities in cash, but in Japanese currency which was worthless in Manipur. The soldiers of the Allied Forces often used young children to perform errands which they were happy to do, because they were rewarded for their services by receiving exotic, novel items of food, and sometimes even clothing – they specially liked the English biscuits, butter, condensed milk, etc. While adult Manipuris who assisted in setting up infrastructure for the Allied Forces, were allowed to buy at very cheap rates, articles from the British canteens, and they favored the British as also American cigarettes, liquor and canned meat. At the end of the war, the local people collected a lot of guns, ammunitions, vehicles etc. left by the Allied and Japanese forces. Many of the guns and ammunitions hold a place of pride in the homes of many local residents – however many of the guns collected had to be surrendered to the Government.

One unfortunate incident that impacted the local inhabitants was the bombing of 200 civilians who had gathered for a Gopi ChakKhangba feast in April 1943.

The majority of the soldiers of the Japanese Imperial Army and even the pilots were extremely young, and this was their first war mission. They fought in a foreign land against the Allied forces because they had been taught that no sacrifice, even of one's life, is too great, for the sake of the Emperor and the Japanese nation. There is no certainty of survival in any war, but while the young soldiers strictly abided by the famed 'Bushido Code', their families in Japan, although proud that they were parents of dashing,intrepid young soldiers, were simultaneously afraid that they may never see their sons, husbands, brothers, who made up part of the Japanese Army that fought in Imphal. But from fear, even when they received news of the death of their loved ones, they never grieved in public. It was taboo in Japan to talk about this war where about 60,000 Japanese soldiers lost their lives.

Many of these families' descendants continue to visit Manipur to look for the lost souls of the Japanese who died in the war. And the Japanese in the views expressed in the third chapter have been extremely apologetic to the Manipuris for the trauma and anguish caused to them during the Battle of Imphal. The Japanese Imperial Army tried to win over the local people by the use of propaganda – that they were in alliance with Netaji's INA and came to Manipur to give them liberation from the British.

The attitude of the local communities to the Britishwas very different, because after the defeat of the Manipuris in the Anglo-Manipuri War of 1891, a British Political

Agent was stationed in Manipur, and many administrative changes were effected, including the imposition of new taxes, which was certainly not acceptable to the people. As a result, many revolts and uprisings occurred during the period 1891 to 1947 when India became Independent. The most important was the Anglo Kuki War of 1917-1919, the Zeliangrong Revolt, the Two NupiLans, all fought against colonial oppression. Moreover, the British had followed a Divide and Rule policy, a policy deployed all over India. They asked the foreign Christian missionaries who came to Manipur to conduct their evangelizing activities only in the hills of Manipur, the home of 34 Scheduled tribes. The result of this policy was that the tribal converted almost en masse to Christianity before India attained Independence. This widened the divide between the tribals and the Meeteis who resided in the Imphal Valley, especially as the Meiteis themselves had only converted to Vaishnavism in the early eightteenth century in the reign of King Garib Niwaz. This conversion to a major religion so recently, made them disinterested in another major religion Christianity. Perhaps for this reason the V Force commanded by a British officer was manned by a few thousand tribal only.

The families and friends of British veterans of the Battle of Imphal visit Imphal frequently, more so, in the last two decades. The number of visitors has also increased. Like the Japanese veteran families, the British veteran's families come to Manipur to either pay homage to their soldiers buried in the Commonwealth Cemetery at Imphal, which is extremely well maintained, or they come to look for the remains of those soldiers who could not be buried and whose final resting place has to be excavated. They also take part in the Battle Remembrance Tours. These activities have provided closure to some veterans' families whose loved ones died in the Battle. They have also requested for help in the search for their loved ones' remains from the World War II, Imphal Campaign Foundation. The Annual Commemoration of the Battle of Imphal is attended by many Britishers in Manipur.

Unlike the Japanese, where talking about war was taboo, many veterans' families have written accounts of the Battle and how it impacted their families. Some of the accounts are very personal stories, the writers providing a clear glimpse into how British families impacted by this war, still experience that impact. This is illustrated in the extremely poignant accounts written by family members of British combatants, who when visiting these stories, once again relived the trauma and grief of an event that occurred in 1944.

The soldiers of the British Army were also very young, and they enlisted in the army, first because of their loyalty, reverence, and respect for the British Royal Family. This sentiment is easy to understand, as this sentiment is reflected today in the enormous following that the Royal Family commands, especially as they prepare for the Platinum Jubilee of the longest serving monarch in history. Secondly, they were motivated by a spirit of adventure. The realities of war however were brutal and harsh and made a lasting impact on those who survived the Battle, apparent from their personal testimonies. Some suffered from PTSD, especially those who witnessed death of friends and comrades in the cause of the war. Memories such as these, cannot be obliterated.

The Imphal Campaign Foundation of Manipur has facilitated and organized a series of Peace and Reconciliation

Meets at Imphal between former enemies – the British and the Japanese. Such meets were organized in Burma as well and in the UK and Japan. Although it is no easy matter to forgive, both the British and the Japanese believe in 'Peace', and present generations of both the British and the Japanese bear no animosity to each other. The relations established by the Manipuris with both the British and the Japanese can be a lodestar for relations between India and the UK, India and Japan. The stories and views expressed by the Manipuris, Japanese and the British, will not only provide a new insight into the Battle of Imphal, but will revive a forgotten chapter of Manipur's History.

References

1. ArambamAngamba Singh – 2nd WW Imphal Campaign Foundation
2. Paramita Ghosh *op. cit.* on video call with ArambamAngamba Singh
3. Interview with ArambamAngamba Singh, 15th May, 2021.

Index

U

V

W

Z